9
T
T
c

D1499286

life and

The Virgin Warrior

The Virgin Warrior

THE LIFE AND DEATH OF JOAN OF ARC

⚜

LARISSA JULIET TAYLOR

YALE UNIVERSITY PRESS
NEW HAVEN AND LONDON

For information about this and other Yale University Press publications, please contact:

U.S. Office: sales.press@yale.edu   www.yalebooks.com
Europe Office: sales@yaleup.co.uk   www.yalebooks.co.uk

Set in Adobe Caslon Regular by IDSUK (DataConnection) Ltd
Printed in Great Britain by TJ International Ltd, Padstow, Cornwall

Library of Congress Cataloging-in-Publication Data

Taylor, Larissa.
  Joan of Arc : the maid of Lorraine / Larissa Juliet Taylor.
    p. cm.
  Includes bibliographical references and index.
  ISBN 978-0-300-11458-4 (cloth : alk. paper)
    1. Joan, of Arc, Saint, 1412-1431. 2. Joan, of Arc, Saint,
1412–1431—Military leadership. 3. Christian women
saints—France—Biography. 4. Women soldiers—France—Biography.
5. France—History—Charles VII, 1422-1461. I. Title.
  DC103.T39 2009
  944'.026092
  [B]   2009007424

A catalogue record for this book is available from the British Library.

10 9 8 7 6 5 4 3 2 1

Biblical quotations from The New Revised Standard Version with Apocrypha, copyrighted © 1962, 1973, 1977 by Oxford University Press.

For
My best friend and muse, Kitikat

Contents

Illustrations

Maps

Acknowledgements

I CAME TO THE STUDY of Joan late, without the fascination or adoration so many authors mention. After seeing a spate of films based on her life in the late 1990s, I became interested in Joan as a historical figure. Prior to that she had seemed an anomaly, and I resisted studying one of the few "exceptional" women who had made their way into my college textbooks in the 1970s. Her accomplishments, which seem impossible even in a more egalitarian modern age, began to intrigue me, and in 2000 I started teaching a senior seminar on Joan. Thanks to my students, the course has provided extraordinary insights into the woman. On the first day, when asked to give their impressions of Joan, they give predictable responses: that she was anorexic, schizophrenic, or psychologically deluded. It does not take long for them to realize how simplistic – and just plain wrong – such assumptions are. Joan's physical and emotional strength, recovery from wounds and falls, and her plainspoken eloquence all give the lie to such categorizations. Reading first secondary and then primary sources, students begin to see the complexities in Joan that are too often masked by the desires of screenwriters and biographers to dramatize the story.

My first debt of gratitude is owed to those students whose work has inspired me. I would especially like to thank Adam (Sam) Boss, my brilliant, talented, and indefatigable research assistant for three years, whose study of the *Journal du siège d'Orléans* and other fifteenth-century chronicles and military works made my work much easier. Sam has been at my right hand almost since the project began and beyond his graduation from Colby. His insights and suggestions have provided me with fresh ideas and arguments. Thanks also go to Ben Davis, Melissa Murray,

Becky Anderson, Cynthia Anderson-Bauer, Meade Barlow, Lauren Baumgarten, David BurtonPerry, Camille Dugan Campanile, Shannon Corliss, Jenny Cox, Tim Cronin, Margo Derecktor, Meg Distinti, Sarah Eilers, Mike Feldman, Julia Gilstein, Rob Girvan, Juliana Green, Paige Hanzlik, Kirsten Isaksen, Kate Crocker Jordan, Annie Kearney, Sam Kennedy-Smith, Jess Laniewski, Lindsay Masters, David Mitchell, Kate Nevius, Katie Packard, Laura Perille, Kyle Ross, Sarah Ross-Benjamin, Neila Sage, Scarlett Slenker, Meg Smith, Jason St. Pierre, Eric Strome, Tara Sweeney, Sarah Thein, Cathy White, Ted Wright, and Mary Zito.

I would also like to thank the staff of the Colby College library, especially Eileen Fredette and Kathy Corridan, who procured hard-to-find books and medieval city maps, along with Peggy Menchen, Alisia Wygant, and Anna Graves for their research into flora and fauna in the Vosges region. The French Department at Colby, especially Marina Davies, Valérie Dionne, Jane Moss, Adrianna Paliyenko, and Jonathan Weiss, provided invaluable assistance in understanding the meaning of particularly difficult words or phrases. Members of the Maine Medievalist Association, especially my colleagues Elisa Narin van Court, Véronique Plesch, and Katharine Lualdi, all offered helpful suggestions. Many of my early ideas developed at conference presentations at the International Medieval Congress at Kalamazoo, the Sixteenth Century Studies Conference, and Renaissance Society of America. I would like to thank my colleagues in the International Joan of Arc Society, especially Gail Orgelfinger, Ann W. Astell, Kelly DeVries, Daniel Hobbins, Deborah Fraioli, Jane Marie Pinzino, Nadia Margolis, Bonnie Wheeler and many others. To all those who attended conference or invited presentations and offered helpful suggestions and comments, my debt is enormous. Any errors are mine alone.

As a historian, I had to "feel" Joan's places. Walking the path under the shaded trees that lead up to Notre Dame de Bermont, sitting under the beech trees in the *bois chenu*, looking from the remnant of Les Tourelles across the river to Orléans, sitting in the cathedral at Reims, or contemplating the spot where she was burned in the Old Market of Rouen, my goal was to follow Joan's travels from Domremy to Rouen. As far as my scholarly abilities and historical imagination would allow, I wanted to see the places through her eyes. Social Science Research Grants from Colby College provided funds for travel and research in France over a number of years. There I would like to thank the staff of the Bibliothèque Nationale as well as librarians, archivists, and museum directors in Orléans, Rouen,

Reims, and Domremy. I am deeply grateful to M. Alain Olivier, conservator of Notre Dame de Bermont, who gave me a guided tour of the chapel and hermitage.

Special thanks go to Leelee Sobieski, in my opinion and that of many others the best actress ever to portray Joan, for her insights into the challenges and difficulties in recreating the role at the same age as when Joan first set forth on her mission. Leelee helped me understand the challenges of armor, horsemanship, and especially the physical and emotional exhaustion that comes from acting the part of Joan.

I would particularly like to thank my editor Heather McCallum for believing in me and inspiring me with her infectious enthusiasm for the project. She has been not only an editor but also a friend and someone on whom I have been able to try out ideas. I am forever in her debt. Many thanks are also due to those at Yale University Press, London, who brought the book to fruition, including Candida Brazil, Elizabeth Bourgoin, and Lucy Isenberg.

The vast array of primary sources from the trial, the nullification proceedings, and journals and chronicles from French, Burgundian, and English perspectives have to be handled with great care because of bias and conflicting versions of events. For a discussion of how I have used the sources, see Appendix B.

All translations from French sources are my own. Rather than a literal, word-for-word translation, often clumsy because of medieval French punctuation and notarial language, I chose a freer style that I hope captures the intent and flavor of the original passages. Although Joan is almost always referred to in both English and French primary sources as "The Maid," "Jeanne," or "La Pucelle," I have most often chosen to refer to her simply as Joan.

Because the trial may be of greatest interest to the general reader who would like to learn more about the questions, responses, and decisions, I have used the most complete English translation, that of W. P. Barrett, *The Trial of Jeanne d'Arc, Translated into English from the Original Latin and French Documents* (New York: Gotham House, 1932). It is available online at http://www.fordham.edu/halsall/basis/joanofarc-trial.html. Besides the transcript, it also contains all the deliberations of the doctors and the letters that were inserted before, during, and after the trial. The translation is generally good, but there are some inaccuracies. In those instances, I have referred to the original French/Latin version of Pierre Tisset and Yvonne Lanhers, eds. and trans., *Procès de condamnation de Jeanne d'Arc*, 3 vols. (Paris: Klincksieck, 1960). I have also modernized the English and in some cases deleted the repetitious "asked if" questioning format.

Chronology

c. Mar. 1–21	Questioned by theologians and examined by matrons at Poitiers; no harm found in her
Mar. 27	Official presentation to court at Chinon
Apr. 2	Men sent to find sword at St. Catherine of Fierbois
Apr. 6–20	Joan at Tours where armor, banners, and standards are made; she meets her second confessor, Pasquerel
c. Apr. 24–27	From Blois Joan sends "Letter to the English" dictated at Poitiers
Apr. 29	Arrival at Orléans
May 1–3	Joan rides through city, reconnoiters surrounding areas
May 4	Attack on St-Loup
May 5	Ascension Day; sally against the fort of St-Jean-le-Blanc, already deserted by the English
May 6	Fall of the bastille of the Augustins
May 7	Fall of Les Tourelles; Joan wounded by arrow
May 8	English lift siege and head toward Janville
May 13	Meeting with the king at Tours/Loches
May 13–23	At Saint-Florent with the Duke of Alençon
May 23–24	Joan meets with the king
May 29–June 6	Selles-en-Berry
June 9	Return to Orléans
June 10–12	Successful attack on the English at Jargeau; Joan knocked off ladder
June 15	Bridge of Meung-sur-Loire secured by French troops
June 17	Joan meets with Arthur de Richemont; fall of Beaugency
June 18	Major French victory at Patay
June 29	Royal army with Joan heads for Reims
Early July	Auxerre opens gates to king and Maid
July 9	Troyes submits after three-day siege
July 17	Coronation of Charles VII
Aug. 27–Sep. 7	Joan at Saint-Denis; prepares to attack Paris
Sep. 8	Failed attack on Paris; Joan wounded in thigh
Sep. 21	Dissolution of French army
Nov. 4	Fall of St-Pierre-le-Moutier to Joan's forces
Nov.–early Dec.	Siege of La Charité-sur-Loire
Dec. 2	Siege lifted
Dec. 29	Joan and her family ennobled as "du Lys"
Jan.–Mar. 1430	Joan at Sully-sur-Loire

Late Mar.	Dictates letters
Apr.	Victory at Lagny-sur-Marne; "execution" of Franquet d'Arras
Apr. 16	Truce with Burgundy expires
Apr.–mid-May	Joan at Compiègne, Soissons, Crépy-en-Valois and Senlis
May 14	Banquet for Joan at Compiègne
May 23	Capture of Joan at Compiègne
May 24–Jul. 10	Captivity at Beaulieu-les-Fontaines; attempted escape
Jul. 11–early Nov.	Captivity at Beaurevoir; attempted escape
Dec. 24	Arrival at Rouen
Jan. 9, 1431	Trial procedures decided upon and officials appointed
Feb. 21–Mar. 17	Preliminary trial
Mar. 18–25	Passion to Palm Sunday; articles read to assessors
Mar. 26	Beginning of Ordinary Trial
Mar. 28	Articles read to Joan
Apr. 16	Joan becomes sick "after eating carp sent by Cauchon"
May 2	Public Admonition
May 9	Joan threatened with torture
May 15	Deliberations of assessors on torture
May 23	Explanation of charges to Joan
May 24	Abjuration at St.-Ouen
May 25–27	Joan resumes wearing men's clothing
May 28	Trial for relapse
May 29	Deliberations of assessors
May 30	Joan executed in Old Market of Rouen
1435	Treaty of Arras with Burgundy
1437	Charles VII retakes Paris
1449	French army captures Rouen; Bouillé begins looking into original trial
1450	French retake Normandy
1452	Inquest of Cardinal d'Estouteville into possible nullification of original trial
1453	End of Hundred Years War
1455	Pope Calixtus III authorizes opening of nullification proceedings
1456	Nullification inquiries; declaration of nullification and vindication of Joan and her family on July 7
1909	Beatification of Joan
1920	Canonization of Joan

Preface

"It is no wonder that truth is stranger than fiction. Fiction has to make sense."

Mark Twain

In spite of his assertion, when Mark Twain wrote his *Personal Recollections of Joan of Arc*, he produced a work of fiction based on original sources. Twain portrays Joan as a "wonderful child" with a "dear and bonny face." Among Americans, her name is probably the most recognized in medieval history; for Europeans she is the most famous woman of the Middle Ages. Yet few know more than what they have seen in films. Even fewer know that Joan was a real soldier and military leader, wounded several times in battle before her capture and execution at age nineteen. Joan, for all her commanding presence and military victories, remains for many "that wonderful child, that sublime personality."[1] In 1896, James Westfall Thompson complained that a "life as remarkable as Joan's did not need fictionalizing;" for him, Twain's book was "neither good history nor good literature."[2] Instead, although often called a biography, like almost all other works on Joan of Arc, it tells us more about the author than the subject.[3] Ann Astell writes:

> Making Joan's story their own, modern authors . . . contributed to the decay of the saint's aura through the multiple retellings, reproductions, and reenactments of her singular, mysterious history. . . . Every represen-tation somehow reduces Joan. . . . What distinguishes her various repre-sentations is the eye of the beholder as it contemplates her image, which

becomes, in turn, a mirror for those who marvel at her. The need to interpret Joan in order to reach some sort of conclusion about her makes her person . . . akin to a beautiful work of art.[4]

Too often the line between fiction and nonfiction has been blurred because of this problem. Joan is a "work of art," a "representation," and most of all "a mirror for those who marvel at her." While the agendas of many authors are often concealed within a seemingly straightforward text, others describe "their" Joan. Mary Gordon is typical: "My Joan, who is just as much a mirror of my own desires as anyone else's, is, above all, a young girl. . . . I do homage to her instability [as] . . . a saint [who stands for] . . . the single-minded triumph of the she – and it must be a she – who feared nothing, knew herself right and fully able and the chosen of the Lord."[5]

Joan has, in the nearly six centuries since her death, become everything to everyone – a Catholic, a proto-Protestant, a right or left wing partisan, anti-Semitic, nationalist, anti-colonialist, and even the face on cheese, chocolates, baked beans, and cosmetics. The reasons for Joan's broad appeal are obvious. Her time on the historical stage was short – only two years – yet it was "stranger than fiction," as her actions helped turn the tide of the Hundred Years War. Joan's dramatic departure from the family home to seek the dauphin,* her relief of Orléans and other towns, and the unlikely coronation of Charles VII are all the material of drama, especially considering that the protagonist was a teenage peasant girl. Yet however improbable, Joan's life and death were real historical events. But the historical figure of Joan of Arc has too often been lost in the fictions – literary or pious, well meaning or malicious – that have taken shape around her since her life ended so tragically. Joan became a legend within her lifetime, coming to believe in the legend herself, but the legends, mystique, and even her sainthood have often obscured the girl who accomplished marvels.

Tens of thousands of works of fiction, drama, satire, art, and scholarship depict the life, death, and afterlife of the teenage girl who helped to create a country called France. Yet as Daniel Hobbins noted, "there is no standard critical biography of Joan of Arc."[6] How can this be? There are more original sources – trial and nullification records, chronicles, letters,

---

* Since Joan always maintained that Charles had to be crowned to become the true king of France and not merely the "rightful heir," she usually referred to him as dauphin even though his courtiers called him king.

theological treatises, poems, and other documents – than exist for any other medieval figure. The trial record is of special importance because in it, despite layers of translation from French into Latin and editing by the notaries and judges, Joan's voice comes through loud and clear.

Part of the answer is Joan's elevation to sainthood in 1920. Many of her contemporaries saw her as holy, inspired, and deeply pious, but only a few spoke of her in the context of sainthood at a time when "living saints" abounded in Western Europe.[7] Viewing her through the lens of her canonization distorts the historical Joan as much as do the creative interpretations of writers.

My premise for this book is that there is no need to dramatize the story of Joan of Arc. In her case, the truth is more powerful than imagination, creativity, authorial intrusions or selections of the most dramatic, rather than the most factual, accounts from the sources. Unlike most books, *The Virgin Warrior: The Life and Death of Joan of Arc* will not consider what has often been called Joan's afterlife: it is about her life and death. The truth of her story may be stranger than fiction, but it is far more interesting.

The Hundred Years War

THE FIGHT FOR FRANCE served as the bitter backdrop for Joan of Arc's short but eventful life. Growing up in a border region in which raids and pillaging were commonplace, she knew firsthand the horrors of war. Children in her village fought with those of nearby villages whose allegiance was to the other side. It was in this atmosphere that an adolescent girl emerged who would change the course of history. What made Joan of Arc as a historical figure possible?

Although fighting between the two countries had gone on for centuries, in 1337, Edward III of England declared himself king of England and France by virtue of his descent through the female line, thus beginning what came to be known as the Hundred Years War. After he invaded France for the first time in 1340, England had the upper hand for decades.

Military innovations changed the face of warfare in the fourteenth century. Although the longbow had existed for some time, the English had become particularly skilled in its use, allowing them to gain the advantage in military encounters with the French in several key battles. Both sides began to experiment with gunpowder.[1] The great victories won by Edward's son, the Black Prince, at the Battles of Crécy and Poitiers in 1346 and 1356 and the capture of the French king, John the Good, demoralized the French armies in the first decades of the war. After the death of the Black Prince and the succession of his young son Richard II in 1377, English domestic affairs took precedence as the young king struggled to assert control over his powerful uncles and barons. Under the capable leadership of France's King Charles V (r. 1364–80) and his great knight Bernard de Guesclin (d. 1380), the tide began to turn in France's favor. Between 1376 and 1380, England even had to endure sea raids from France that resulted in the sacking of Rye, Plymouth, Dartmoor, and Exeter. The Scots helped with an attack in Anglesey.[2] In 1396, Richard II married Charles VI's six-year-old daughter Isabelle. Although it was a purely political alliance, it signified the king's lack of interest in pursuing the French war.

After Henry IV (r. 1399–1413) usurped the throne from Richard II, Isabelle returned to France and married Duke Charles of Orléans.[3] Facing continuous threats from within England as well as from the Welsh and Scots, Henry continued his predecessor's policy of non-involvement in continental matters.

At the same time, conditions in France deteriorated. A tangled web of family relationships and marriage alliances made peace impossible.[4] When Charles VI (1380–1422), began to suffer increasingly serious bouts of madness, the kingdom was left in the hands of his queen, Isabeau of Bavaria, and his brother Louis of Orléans. True or not, rumors swirled that the powerful and unpopular queen was having an affair with Louis.[5] John the Fearless, the king's cousin, duke of Burgundy since 1404, had himself named regent, setting him against his cousin Louis, who tried to regain power. The two agreed to a public reconciliation in 1407, but three days later John had Louis murdered in Paris. The head of those seeking revenge for this outrage was Bernard, count of Armagnac, whose family name was taken by the royalist side. Most of the principal military leaders in France had ties to both Burgundy and England, creating problems of layers of allegiance that plagued the French.

In 1410, the poet Christine de Pizan, who nineteen years later would celebrate Joan of Arc's deeds in a poem, wrote a "Lament on the Evils of Civil War":

For God's sake! For God's sake! High Princes, let these facts open your eyes and may you see as already accomplished what the preparations for taking arms will do in the end; thus you will see ruined cities, towns and castles destroyed, and fortresses razed to the ground. And where? In the very heart of France! . . . The noble knights and youth of France, all of one nature, one single soul and body, which used to defend the crown and the public good, are now gathered in a shameful battle one against another . . . covering the pitiful fields with blood, dead bodies, and limbs. . . . And what will follow, in God's name? Famine, because of the

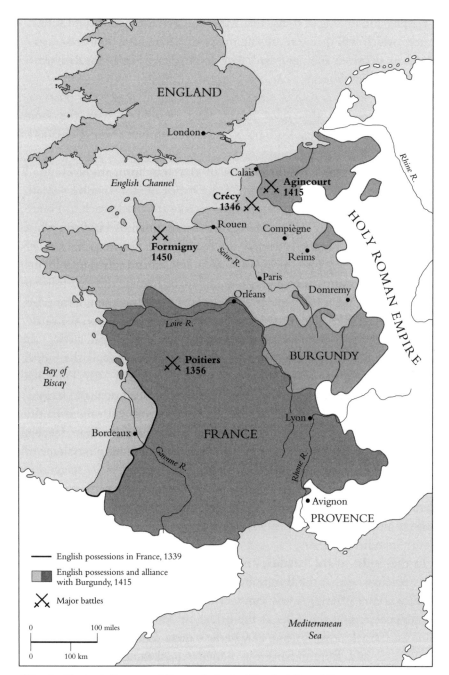

Map 1   England, France and Burgundy in the Hundred Years War.

wasting and ruining of things that will ensue, and the lack of cultivation, from which will spring revolts by the people who have been too often robbed, deprived and oppressed, their food taken away and stolen here and there by soldiers.[6]

Christine saw that this royal family feud, combined with the king's madness and inability to lead, posed a greater problem than England in these years.

All that changed a year after Joan of Arc was born, when Henry V ascended the throne of England in 1413. One of the great military strategists of all time, Henry was determined to take the battle back to France. Landing in summer 1415, he besieged the port town of Harfleur, which fell in October. Henry retreated toward Calais, planning to rest his soldiers and regroup for a spring campaign, but was surprised by a French army near Agincourt. Although the numbers of French versus English at the battle have been vastly overstated in most accounts, there were probably about 12,000 French pitted against some 9,000 English on the battlefield. Thanks to a combination of Henry's leadership and tactics, the superior English longbow, strategic formations, and deep mud, the French army was nearly annilihated. The tide of the Hundred Years' War had turned again. One battle had completely changed perceptions of Henry V. He had invaded France "as the son of a usurper and with his own title insecure. . . . He returned as God's chosen king and warrior. He had proved himself. Now no one could challenge his title or his obsession with France."[7] The slaughter of the French aristocracy was staggering, including three dukes, five counts, ninety barons, and the constable. Henry's renewed invasion in 1417 took full advantage of the French disarray and factional animosities, and after the city of Rouen fell in 1419, Henry marched on Paris.

In the midst of the English onslaught, the dauphin Charles chose to exact revenge against the Burgundians for the death of his uncle, Louis of Orléans. After offering a safe conduct to John the Fearless, Charles and his supporters met the duke at the bridge at Montereau in 1419, where John was struck down by one of Charles's men. The breach between the Armagnacs and Burgundians was complete, allowing John's successor, Philip the Good, eventually to ally himself with the English by marrying his sister Anne to Henry V's brother, John, duke of Bedford. Yet it was never an easy alliance, as their goals differed. Philip did not want an

English king of France, but the alliance suited his purposes by helping him retain and extend the lands he held in its northeastern corner.

Isabeau, left with few options, concluded the Treaty of Troyes with Henry V in 1420, disinheriting her son, the dauphin Charles, and giving her daughter, Catherine of Valois, to Henry in marriage. Edward III's original designs seemed to have paid off when a male heir was born in late 1421. But campaigning in northern France in 1422, Henry died of dysentery. His talented brother John, duke of Bedford, was named Regent for France, while the dauphin, penniless, dispirited, and with only a small retinue, retreated to his castles in the Loire Valley. France was in need of a savior. She would be found in the small village of Domremy.

CHAPTER I

Jehannette

— ⚜ —

In June of 1429, Perceval de Boulainvilliers, a counselor of the French king, Charles VII, wrote a letter to the duke of Milan that included a bit of gossip about a young girl who had appeared at the king's court two months earlier:

> She was born in a small village called Domremy . . . on the edges of the realm of France, along the river Meuse near Lorraine. . . . On the night of the Epiphany, when Christians joyfully commemorate the life of Christ, she first saw the light of this mortal world. It was a marvelous thing to behold the poor villagers seized by unbelievable joy. Not knowing of the girl's birth, they ran one to another, asking what had happened. . . . What can be added? The roosters, like heralds of this new joy, burst forth with songs that one would not expect from them. They beat their sides with their wings and for almost two hours one could hear them announcing the good news of this new arrival.
>
> The child was breastfed, grew up, and reached seven years. . . . Her family had her watch the sheep. Under her care not even the smallest animal was lost; not one suffered the bite of wild animals. As long as she was in her father's house, she protected them so that they lost nothing, either from evildoers, surprise attacks, or violence from brigands.[1]

So began the legend of Joan of Arc. The only person to provide a date for Joan's birth, Boulainvilliers named the feast of the Epiphany, the day on which the Roman Catholic Church commemorates Jesus' baptism as well as the coming of the Three Wise Men to Bethlehem. His Christlike depiction of Joan is almost unique among contemporary writings. No other documents corroborate Joan's date of birth, but during her trial that began on February 21, 1431, Joan said that she was about nineteen years old, which reinforces the probability of her birth in the winter of 1412.

Joan was born on the frontier of the realm. In the final stages of the Hundred Years War, few areas were so contested by rival loyalties as the region surrounding Domremy, a fact that would become critical in view of prophecies about a maid who would save "France." Although at her trial Joan repeatedly stated that she had to leave and go to France, her house on the north bank of the Meuse was in fact in French territory, as was the walled garrison of Vaucouleurs twelve miles to the north. The lands south of the river belonged to the lords of Bourlémont, subjects of the duke of Bar and the pro-Burgundian dukes of Lorraine. The ruins of the château de l'Île, owned by the Bourlémonts, stood on a small island in the center of the Meuse. In times of threat, Joan and others herded the village animals onto the island for protection. To the east of Domremy, the village of Maxey-sur-Meuse was subject to Burgundian control.

What did Joan mean by France? France as a nation did not yet exist, but French-Burgundian infighting, English claims to the French throne, and Joan of Arc's deeds would begin to make it a reality. At the age of seventeen, when she left Domremy for the final time, Joan and most of her contemporaries probably thought of France in dynastic terms, as the place where she would find the dauphin Charles, whom she believed to be the rightful heir to the French throne.

In the time of Joan of Arc, Domremy was not the isolated village it is today. The region of northeastern France/Burgundy had grown in importance in the second half of the fourteenth century after the marriage of the duke of Burgundy to the heiress of the count of Flanders. The village lay along a heavily traveled route that connected the northern and southern parts of Burgundy's holdings. Large horse-drawn carts and convoys carried fine wines from the vineyards surrounding Dijon to the towns of Flanders in return for Flemish cloth. The house in which Joan grew up was on one of the busiest roads in the eastern part of the realm.[2]

While not a rich village, Domremy had most of what it needed for subsistence. In the valley along the river and streams, wheat, rye, and oats were grown in small quantities, but livestock, especially pigs, cows, horses, and some sheep, along with waterfowl and birds, provided the economic backbone of the community.[3] The heavily forested hillside, with its gnarly

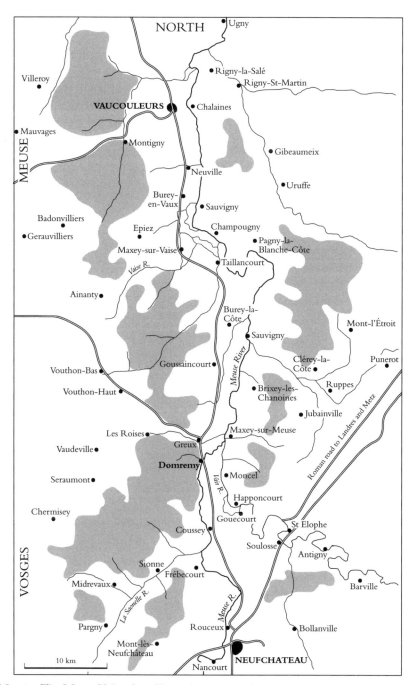

Map 2   The Meuse Valley from Vaucouleurs to Neufchâteau.

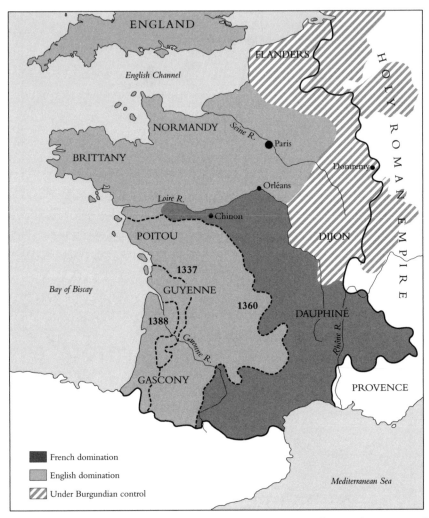

Map 3   Domremy's position on the border of France in the late fourteenth century and its strategic importance along the route from Flanders to Dijon.

beech and oak trees, supplied wood for heating and acorns to fatten up the pigs.[4] In good times the villagers lived on a diet of milk and cheese from the cattle, along with pork, poultry, and the wines grown on the hillside vineyards of Greux.

Domremy was adjacent to Greux, where the parish church of St. Remy and the cemetery were located, just north of Joan's house; a wall in the garden separated her house from the cemetery. After being burned down during the Thirty Years War, the church was rebuilt with an orientation opposite to that of the original. The modern choir replaces the west façade and entrance of Joan's time, which was nearest to the family garden. Despite its reconstruction, the church still contains Joan's baptismal font and a holy water basin. Several thatched huts surrounded Joan's house in the late Middle Ages.

When the philosopher and essayist Michel de Montaigne visited Domremy in 1580, he described "the front of the house painted all over with her deeds," although he commented that weather and time had seriously damaged the paintings.[5] In the ensuing centuries, more homes were built in front of and around the house, which was reduced to a stable. With the restoration of Louis XVIII (r. 1814–24), the situation changed as Joan began to serve as a symbol of French patriotism. Henri-Prosper Jollois, the head architect of the Vosges' Roads and Bridges division, was given the task of restoring the house. In addition to Joan's dwelling, his office bought all the buildings that stood around it, Jollois knocking them down to isolate and restore Joan's home.[6] Yet the house that still stands corresponds to the description of the building bought by Louise de Stainville in 1586, six years after Montaigne's visit. It was "a two-story house, with two lofts above the rooms, two small corridors in front of the house with a small chicken coop; together with right of usage on each side, and all that it contained . . . and people called this the home of the Maid."[7] The main room, which contained the hearth, probably served as a foyer and kitchen. The room Joan and her elder sister occupied, from which Joan might have been able to see the church through the tiny window, is at the back left of the house.

Although descendants of the d'Arc family have put together lengthy genealogies tracing their ancestry back to Joan's brothers, only a basic family tree is possible for Joan's immediate family (see Appendix A). Joan's father, Jacquot or Jacques Darc, Dars, Tart, or Day, was born at Ceffonds in Champagne between 1375 and 1380.[8] As dean he was a village leader in Domremy, responsible for the defense of the town and the local watch as well as collection of taxes and supervision of weights and measures. In 1423, he accompanied the mayors of Domremy and Greux and seven other "notable" inhabitants of the two villages to pay protection money to the lord of Commercy.[9] Four years later he was appointed to represent the village before Robert de Baudricourt, captain of the French stronghold of Vaucouleurs.[10] Jacques died in 1431, the same year as his daughter Joan, some said of grief after her execution.[11]

Joan's mother, Zabillet (Isabelle) Romée, came from Vouthon, about four miles west of Domremy. One of Isabelle's brothers, Henri de Vouthon, whom some sources identify as her uncle, encouraged his sister's religious devotions and pilgrimages and probably negotiated her marriage with Jacques.[12] He had left Vouthon to become prior of the eleventh-century Benedictine church at Sermaize. Henri convinced his brother, a roofer named Jean, to join him there. Later at Joan's request, Jean's son, Nicolas, a Cistercian at the abbey of Notre-Dame de Cheminon, would serve as her chaplain when she left to join the king's army.[13] Jean's grandson remembered Joan visiting his father's house in Sermaize frequently, even though it was quite a distance from Domremy, recalling that they had a good time, eating and drinking together. He also visited Domremy with his father, where they stayed in the d'Arc household. Joan was a nice young girl, he said, known by all to be very devout toward God and Church.[14] Isabelle's sister, Aveline, gave birth to a daughter, Jeanne, who married Durand Laxart of Burey-le-Petit, the man who would be instrumental in advancing Joan's mission.[15] Jeanne's pregnancy in 1429 would provide Joan with a pretext for leaving her immediate family.

Joan had three brothers, Jacquemin, Jean, and Pierre, and one sister, Catherine, married to Jean Colin of Greux, who died of unknown causes before Joan departed on her mission. Catherine is rarely mentioned in the surviving records, but according to Joan's niece Catherine Robert, Joan had asked that her niece be named after Joan's deceased sister.[16] Jacquemin married in 1419 and moved to land Isabelle had retained in Vouthon; he was still living there in 1427, but apparently returned to Domremy to help support his father and mother after his brothers left to fight alongside Joan. Jacquemin died some time between 1431 and 1455. Jean later became captain of Chartres before obtaining a post at Vaucouleurs that he held until 1468. Pierre was captured alongside Joan but, unlike her, he was ransomed. The duke of Orléans endowed him with the Île-aux-Boeufs and the domain of Bagneaux, where he lived with his wife. Knighted by Duke Charles, he was created a member of the Order of the Porcupine, which had been founded in 1394.[17] He died around 1467.

Most of Joan's life before she left Domremy must be reconstructed by comparing her testimony at trial in 1431 with the deposition of over a hundred witnesses at the nullification proceedings from 1450–56 that were intended to overturn the original verdict. Jehannette, as she was known in the village, was named after one of her godmothers, either Jeannette, wife of Thiesselin de Vittel, or Jeannette Roze Le Royer. Joan did not know her last name, or so she said on February 21 at her trial. Later Joan changed her story and "said that her surname was d'Arc or Rommée, and that in her part girls bore their mother's surname."[18]

Joan's family was "not rich," as several villagers testified at the nullification proceedings in 1456, but they were well off by the standards of their neighbors, a fact that is obvious from the size of the house. They owned nearly "50 acres, 25 in their own property, 10 contiguous, and 10 more in woods," including part of the oak forest (known as *le bois chenu*). In addition to their house and furniture, they had possessions and a reserve of 200–300 francs. Their worth by modern standards would have allowed them to give alms and hospitality to mendicants and other travelers in the region.[19] It also provided enough money for Joan to offer candles when she attended mass or went on pilgrimage.

Joan's trial testimony reveals a great deal about her youth before she began to hear her voices. She said she was baptized in the church of Domremy and that "one of her godmothers was named Agnes, another Jeanne, another Sibylle; of her godfathers, one was named Jean Lingué, another Jean Barrey; she had several other godmothers, she heard her mother say." The sheer number of godparents attests to the family's importance.

Joan said she was about nineteen in 1431. She was adamant that she had been taught the Pater Noster, Ave Maria and creed by her mother, and no one else.[20] By all accounts, Joan confessed and received communion more frequently than was usual. Annual confession and communion had been mandated for all Roman Catholics in 1215, but most men and women fulfilled the requirement only once a year, in preparation for Easter. When Joan could not confess to her local priest, she would ask his permission to confess to Franciscans in Coussey and Neufchâteau.

Joan's childhood occupations were typical of the rural peasantry; she bragged to her trial judges that "in sewing and spinning she feared no woman in Rouen."[21] Although she has often been portrayed as a shepherdess, there were relatively few sheep in the village and while she watched over animals when she was very young, that changed when she became a teenager. She still helped with the plowing but usually only herded the farm animals to the meadows or to the ruins of the castle on the island when danger threatened the village.[22]

Joan's answers to questions at trial about the villagers reflected the different jurisdictions in the immediate vicinity of Domremy. When she was asked:

> if at Maxey the people were Burgundians or enemies of the Burgundians, she answered they were Burgundians.
> Asked if the voice told her in her youth to hate Burgundians, she answered that since she had known that the voices were for the king of France, she did not like the Burgundians. . . .

Joan said she did not think she had ever taken part with children who, in play or earnest, fought for her party, but added that sometimes she saw children from Domremy, who had fought against those from Maxey, return wounded and bleeding.[23]

The judges then turned to a subject they hoped would produce evidence of sorcery, the famous tree in the *bois chenu* that could be seen from Joan's house. She told them:

> near Domremy, there was a certain tree called the Ladies' Tree, and others called it the Fairy Tree; and nearby is a fountain. And she has heard that people sick of the fever drink of this fountain and seek its water to restore their health; that, she has seen herself, but she does not know whether they are cured or not. She said she heard that the sick . . . go to the tree and walk about it. It is a big tree, a beech, from which they get the fair May, *le beau may*. It belongs, it is said, to Pierre de Bourlémont, knight. She said sometimes she would go playing with the other young girls, making garlands for Our Lady of Domremy there. Often she had heard the old folk say (not those of her family) that the fairies frequented it.

She added that her godmother Jeanne, the wife of the mayor of Domremy, said that she had seen the fairies, but Joan did not know whether or not it was true.[24]

Joan vehemently denied any involvement with sorcery. When her judges asked "what she had done with her mandrake," a plant in the nightshade family that was associated with sorcery, magic, love potions, alchemy, and pagan rituals, Joan denied that she had ever had one; although she claimed not to know what it was used for, she had heard that it was a dangerous and evil thing.[25] She added, however, that even though she had never seen it, she had heard that there was one near her village. Was her godmother, the one who had seen the fairies, a wise woman? The judges were trying to find out if she had been a healer or a cunning woman, someone who concocted ointments, helped find lost items, and sometimes made love potions. Joan denied it, saying that people knew her godmother was an honest woman, not a witch or sorceress.[26]

As Joan matured and began to hear voices (according to her testimony), her behavior began to change. She said that "since she learned that she must come to France, she had taken as little part as possible in games or dancing." Still, she admitted that on occasion she may well have frolicked around the tree with the other children, but insisted that she sang more than she danced.[27]

Despite her clever answers and disclaimers at trial, Joan's childhood was fairly normal. How did her testimony compare to what villagers and local notables at the nullification proceedings stated twenty-five years later?

The promotor of the proceedings, along with two assistants and a notary, began to interview witnesses in Domremy, Vaucouleurs, and Toul on January 28, 1456. Since Joan's mother and brothers had, with the aid of Pope Calixtus III and the Grand Inquisitor of France, initiated the process to overturn the results of the first trial, they were not allowed to testify. Thirty-four witnesses were interviewed between January 28 and February 11.* Most of the interviews were brief: two-thirds testified between January 28 and February 1. Everyone was expected to answer, to the best of their knowledge and ability, twelve questions that had been decided upon in Rouen the previous December. Considering the short space of time in which the interviews were conducted, witness contamination was certainly possible. Some probably repeated what others had said and yet subtle differences emerge that give us further glimpses into Joan's childhood and adolescence.

---

* See Appendix C for a list of the witnesses, their ages at the time of deposition, occupation, relationship with Joan and the date they were interviewed.

Especially important events from the past would be expected to trigger stronger memories, sometimes enhanced, in which some individuals claim to have played a more important role than they actually did. As a result of Joan's accomplishments and the royal tax exemption she had won for Domremy and Greux, it would therefore have been normal for witnesses to say good things about her or inflate their role in her story. Surprisingly, few did so. Some may have remembered answers they had given twenty-five years earlier, when the bishop of Beauvais had conducted a brief investigation in Lorraine. A lawyer from the region who had interviewed about a dozen people complained that the bishop had not paid him because he had failed to elicit any scandalous information about Joan, only things he would "have liked to have heard about his own sister."[28] Joan's close friend Michel Le Buin remembered where the lawyer and his assistants had stayed but did not think they had found out anything bad about Joan. Likewise, Beatrice d'Estellin recalled that some Franciscans had come to the village to make an inquiry, but claimed that she knew nothing more about it because they had never asked her anything.[29] The bishop of Beauvais' investigation in Joan's home region was perfunctory; he was only looking for evidence of a bad reputation, which he did not find.

The interrogators in early 1456 made all those interviewed swear on the gospels that they would tell the truth. Each individual was told that if he lied or did not tell the full truth, it "showed contempt for the Creator, deceived the judge, betrayed his neighbor, and . . . that he would go to hell for his infamy."[30] On the whole the villagers' accounts can be trusted, because oaths sworn on the gospels were taken very seriously in the Middle Ages; most of the witnesses would have responded in good faith, especially since they had not been accused of wrongdoing.

Twelve questions were posed to the villagers. Unlike the brief 1431 inquiry, these questions were framed in order to obtain information that would quash the earlier verdict.

ARTICLES FOR THE INQUIRY IN LORRAINE

1. Her place of birth and parish
2. Who were her parents and what was their status? Were they good Catholics of good reputation?

3. Who were her godparents?

4. Had she from a young age been properly raised in the faith and good morals, in particular as to that which her age and personal condition required?

5. What were her habits from the age of seven until her departure from her father's home?

6. Did she frequent church and holy places, and if so did she do so willingly and often?

7. What kinds of things did she do and how did she occupy her time during her youth?

8. During this period did she confess often and willingly?

9. What was the general opinion regarding the tree called the "Ladies' Tree," and was it normal for young girls to go there to dance? And as to the fountain next to this tree, did Joan go there often with other young girls and for what reason and/or on what occasions?

10. In what manner did she leave her village and set off [to Burey, Vaucouleurs, Chinon]?

11. In the region where she was born, was information sought by the judges after she was captured before the town of Compiègne and detained by the English?

12. Was Joan, when she fled her village to go to Neufchâteau because of [marauding] soldiers, always in the company of her father and mother?

Made at Rouen, December 20, 1455[31]

Village life cannot be reconstructed based on the responses. The questions revolve solely around Joan's behavior, her parents, and the "Ladies' Tree," which the judges hoped would establish that Joan had been a dutiful and pious girl who had exhibited no evidence of the heresy and sorcery of which she had been convicted. Reading the responses, one might assume that things were relatively peaceful in Domremy, Greux, and Maxey, aside from the inhabitants' flight to Neufchâteau to avoid outlaws in the area who burned part of the village. In reality, mercenaries, unpaid soldiers, and brigands regularly menaced the village; for France's inhabitants, the entire Hundred Years War must be viewed as "disturbed

space." Near continuous incursions and pillaging by outsiders of all
sorts – soldiers, rapacious lords, warring knights, and of course the English
and Burgundians – were what the Hundred Years War meant for most
villagers, not the great chivalric battles described by chroniclers. While
peasants were often the victims of such depredations, village solidarity
provided a way to fight back or at least maintain a semblance of stability.[32]

A closer look at the testimonies gives more insight into Joan's childhood. Joan's closest friends at that time, of those still alive to testify in
1456, seem to have been Hauviette, Mengette, and Michel. Her many
godparents and those who lived nearby, including Jean Morel, Jeannette
Roze le Royer, Beatrice d'Estellin, and Jeannette, widow of Thiesselin de
Vittel, all had close ties to the family. The "Burgundian" Joan mentioned
at trial, Gérardin d'Épinal and his wife Isabelle, were especially close to
Joan, and she confided in them more than most. Yet she had claimed that
in her home region "she only knew one Burgundian; and she would have
been quite willing for him to have his head cut off, that is, if it had pleased
God."[33] As with much of her testimony, this was a fabrication. Gérardin
and Isabelle had chosen the young Joan to be godmother to their son
before she left Domremy. Unfortunately, Durand Laxart, married to
Joan's cousin Jeanne, did not know her godparents' names since he had
never stayed long in Domremy.[34] Laxart, the man who would be pivotal
in helping her gain an audience in the fortified town of Vaucouleurs,
apparently knew little about Joan before she came to stay with him
in Burey.

Some answers to the second question are puzzling. While eighteen
witnesses said Joan's mother was named Isabelle or Isabet, others did not
know her name.[35] Those who did were villagers; the latter were notables or
priests from Vaucouleurs or Toul. Joan's family was well off by village standards, although the witnesses often described them as poor. Beatrice
claimed that they "were not very rich ... while Etienne de Syonne
described them as poor."[36] Joan's godmother Jeannette de Vittel, echoing
Beatrice, said that they "lived decently in their poverty ... and were not too
rich."[37] Most of the others simply said that Jacques and Isabelle were good
and honorable peasants. The differences in the answers may derive from
the status of the individuals involved and simple word choices. Both
Beatrice and Jeannette said they were not *very* or *too* rich – not so clear-cut
a designation as it appears. The villagers' conception of rich would have
meant the Bourlémont family or other local lords and ladies.

There is little evidence of collusion in the villagers' testimonies. When asked about Joan's godparents, some gave the maiden names of the godmothers, while others gave their married names. Some said they did not know. The sacristan of the church said that "she had those called godfathers and godmothers, whom he didn't know, except that . . . there were two women who were considered godmothers [le Royer and le Vittel]."[38] They confirmed Joan's statement that she had many godparents.

In most cases, the villagers or those recording their statements combined the responses for questions four to nine because they concerned Joan's behavior before she left Domremy. Here the witnesses knew more and probably offered general statements about Joan, which provided what the notaries needed as well as a question-by-question answer would have done. This extraordinary testimony of ordinary peasants, men and women, young and old, fills out the picture of the girl who would become the Maid. Many of their statements agree with what Joan said at trial. Beatrice and Jeannette le Royer said that she was well and sufficiently instructed in the Catholic faith like the other girls of her age; Joan's friend Mengette agreed that she was well instructed. Even allowing for legalistic language, the lack of embellishment suggests that Joan had been just like the other children in terms of her religious training.[39]

Many of Joan's acquaintances spontaneously mentioned the deceased village curate, Guillaume Fronté. Isabelle d'Épinal said that when she was young she had stayed with Joan's parents and that she often accompanied Joan to confession with Fr. Guillaume.[40] Colin *fils*, son of Jean Colin, recalled hearing Fronté say that he had never seen anyone better than Joan in his parish.[41] A priest from Neufchâteau, who had also heard Joan in confession, mentioned that Fronté had often told him that "Jehannette was a good and sincere girl, pious, of good morals, fearing God, so good that there had never been the like in the village. She confessed to him regularly and told him that if she had the money, she would give him alms to celebrate masses. He added that every day that he celebrated mass, she was there."[42] Joan never swore, though on occasion she would exclaim "*sans faute!*" (without fail!).

Joan loved bells. The church sacristan testified that "Joan frequently went to church for mass and compline [evening prayers] and when he did not sound the bells, she reproached him, saying it was not good." He added that "Joan had promised to bring him little cakes if he would be more diligent in sounding the bells."[43] With her house next door to the parish church, Joan would have heard them often, not only as a call to mass but to sound the alarm when danger threatened the community. Whenever she heard the ringing of the bells, she crossed herself and fell to her knees. One of her godfathers added that if bells sounded for mass when she was in the fields, she would stop and go to the church.[44] Although everyone remarked on Joan's piety, at times she came across to others – except priests, who applauded the behavior – as too devout.

An interesting difference in opinion emerges about Joan based on the age of the witness. According to Morel, seventy when interviewed, practically everyone in the village of Domremy loved her, while Albert d'Ourches, sixty, said that he would have liked to have had so perfect a daughter.[45] One lord who had only met her on a few occasions in Maxey summed up her character: she seemed to him a good, simple, and pious girl.[46]

By contrast, some of the children closer to her age mocked Joan's piety. Colin *fils* claimed that "she prayed to God and the Virgin a great deal, to the point that sometimes he and the other young people made fun of her."[47] Waterin agreed that when "Joan took herself aside and spoke to God, as it seemed to him, he and the others made fun of her."[48] Joan's lack of interest in dancing did not help; one of her godmothers mentioned that when the other young girls sang and danced, Joan would go to church.[49] Isabel d'Épinal added that the other young people complained that she did not dance.[50] According to her friend Hauviette, who often slept at the d'Arc house, Joan was embarrassed because people told her she was too devout in her churchgoing.[51] Joan's behavior was noticed and it was enough to single her out from others her age, for better or worse.

Many villagers described Joan's pilgrimages most Saturdays to the hermitage of Notre Dame de Bermont, which had originally been founded in the eleventh century as a Benedictine abbey dedicated to St. Thibaut and the Virgin. In 1263, the chapel and hermitage were joined to the hospice of St. Eloi at Gerbonvaux to attract pilgrims en route to Compostela. Statues of Christ, Saint John, and the Virgin Mary, dating from the thirteenth and fourteenth centuries, filled the small chapel.

The route from Domremy to Notre Dame de Bermont, about an hour's uphill walk, winds through Greux, over hills and through fields of chamomile, poppies, wild mustard, cornflowers, violets, and vetch until it reaches dark and meandering forest paths. Nearby was a spring whose waters are still believed by some to cure fevers. Sometimes Joan went to the chapel alone, at other times with friends or relatives. Michel recalled that she went almost every Saturday with her sister and that he often accompanied them.[52] Jeannette de Vittel mentioned that she sometimes went along when Joan traveled there with other young girls to pray to the Virgin Mary.[53] Several people commented on Joan's special devotion to the Virgin, saying that she took candles as offerings for the love of God.[54] Joan was not above using a bit of deception to follow her inclinations: "she sometimes went to the hermitage of Notre Dame de Bermont . . . when her parents thought she was in the fields at the plow or elsewhere."[55] While it would be hard to fault Joan for such little white lies, lying and omitting information to achieve her goals would form a pattern in her short life.

In popular depictions, too much has been made of Joan's other charitable activities. Musnier remembered that "she took care of the sick . . . because when he was young, he'd been ill and Joan had cheered him up."[56] Isabelle d'Épinal said that Joan gave alms frequently, and lodged the poor in her room: "She would spend the night in the kitchen so that poor people could sleep in her bed."[57] Yet these few instances, along with Joan's offering of candles at religious sites, hardly make Joan a Daughter of Charity.

The villagers agreed with what Joan said at trial about her activities before she left for Vaucouleurs. When it was her father's turn, she fed the animals and occasionally helped with the plowing. Joan prepared hemp and wool along with the other girls and women and sometimes sewed with Mengette while the two were watching the flock.[58] They agreed that in olden times people had believed in fairies, but personally they had never seen them. Gérardin d'Épinal, who was sixty at the time of his testimony, fondly remembered the springtime ritual, often held on *Laetare* (Fountains) Sunday, the fourth Sunday of Lent, when repentance turns to joy at the approach of Easter:

> He would see the feudal lords of Domremy and their wives in springtime, one or two times, carrying bread and wine and going to eat under the beech tree because it was beautiful like blooming lilies, and its leaves and branches reached close to the ground. The girls and young people of the village of Domremy had the habit on Fountains Sunday of going to the tree. With bread baked by their mothers, they would go to the tree "to do their fountains." There they sang, danced around in circles, and finally came back to the other fountain of Rains, where they ate bread

and drank the water. Joan went there with the other girls and did the same things they did.[59]

A local curate believed the children went and danced under the tree because it was so beautiful.[60] All provide reminiscences of childhood innocence, a time of joy at the advent of spring and approaching Easter when children sang and danced, played, and celebrated the season under the beautiful old beech tree. The villagers had never believed evil spirits were associated with the tree.[61]

Joan's testimony and those of the witnesses from Lorraine twenty-five years after her death are remarkably consistent, even though the latter had no access to the trial transcript. Based on the villagers' responses, biographer Régine Pernoud has argued that the key to Joan's childhood personality was the word "willingly." She writes that "no word recurs more frequently in these depositions, which reinforce one another and produce a portrait of a young girl taking joy in daily labor."[62] While Joan may indeed have undertaken her daily tasks willingly, Pernoud reads too much into the witnesses' responses. Most people used the word "willingly" because it was part of questions six and eight. As a result, most said Joan went to church and holy places willingly and often, and that she confessed willingly and often. The answers to question two, which asked if Joan's parents were "good Catholics of good reputation," demonstrate the problem in reading the answers too literally. Not surprisingly, most of those familiar with Joan's parents rephrased the question into a response, affirming that they were indeed "good Catholics of good reputation." Joan was simple and good, more than typically pious, yet her devotional behavior was not typical of the extreme mortifications or asceticism of late medieval female saints. Hers was a simple piety, based on the ringing of bells, going to church often, making Saturday pilgrimages, and sometimes leaving her chores to do so.

The larger picture that emerges from the villagers' testimonies is curiously flat. One would expect the girl who changed the course of French history to have been remembered more vividly, embellished more. Yet few recalled much that was out of the ordinary, at least until her departure. For all that the priests and many adults said what a good girl Joan was, some of the village children picked on her because she was "different." Joan was a little odd. Preferring devotions to play, she was teased by the other children to the point of embarrassment. While a couple of boys and girls seemed especially close to Joan – Michel, Mengette, and Hauviette – most were disappointed by, or laughed at, her overly serious demeanor. Her elders were more supportive, praising her pious ways and good behavior. She certainly did many of her tasks willingly. But she was also willful, as when she went to Notre Dame de Bermont instead of staying in the fields, or scolded the sacristan for failing to ring the bells.

The life of the peasantry in France in these years was difficult, especially in villages that were part of competing jurisdictions. There was a "serious lack of centralized control of military activity and a bewildering diversity of small-scale conflict. The Hundred Years War was as much a state of affairs, a condition of chronic instability, as the story of an Anglo-French power-struggle."[63] Yet nothing about life in Domremy or Joan's family and friends gave any indication that Jehannette would be anything more than a pious young girl, perhaps much like her mother, who may have earned the name Romée because of her pilgrimages. Although around the time Joan turned thirteen, the differences between her and other children became more striking, none of those who knew her in Domremy mentioned any of the events that she claimed changed her life in the summer of 1425.

CHAPTER 2

The Mission

T HE SIXTY YEARS BEFORE Joan was born were times of uncertainty and fear. Besides the war between England and France, the plague of 1348–50 and its recurrence every few years had undermined the social and economic structures of Europe. In the 1370s and 1380s, tens of thousands of laborers, peasants, and serfs rose up against the oppressive rule of lords, killing many, burning castles and palaces, and eventually forcing an end to serfdom in the west. The Church, too, which for over a thousand years had organized the rituals of life and death and tried to give meaning in the most desperate of times, was in crisis. Pope Boniface VIII, who attempted to revive the idea of papal monarchy at the beginning of the fourteenth century, had incurred the wrath of the king of France and his Italian allies who attacked and beat the pope at his palace at Anagni in 1303. Two years later the Frenchman Clement V moved to the papal enclave of Avignon, where the papacy remained until Gregory XI's return to Rome in 1377. A little over a year later he died and, after a disputed election, a group of French cardinals returned to Avignon and elected a rival pope. The Great Schism lasted until 1417, with three different men claiming to be pope at one point. At the same time, the Church was forced to confront two major new heresies, those of John Wyclif (1330–84) and his Lollard followers in England and of Jan Hus (1369–1415) of Bohemia, who challenged the hierarchy and argued for greater lay participation in matters of faith.

This context of crisis helped make the next stage of Joan's career possible, as the literature of prophecy helped shape historical reality.[1] Unlike most positions in the Church, prophecy was open to women as well as men, with ample support in both the Old and the New Testaments. In most biblical cases the prophecies were overtly political, calling Israel to reform or fight against oppression or occupation. The prophetess Deborah played a critical role in the success of the Israelites in defeating the army of the king of Canaan, summoning men to fight for the liberation of Israel. They fought with her at their side. Part of the Song of Deborah, to whom Joan would later be compared, celebrates the victory:

> Then Deborah and Barak son of
> Abinoam sang on that day, saying:
> "When locks are long in Israel,
> when the people offer
> themselves willingly—
> bless the LORD!
> Hear, O kings; give ear,
> O princes;
> to the LORD I will sing,
> I will make melody to the
> LORD, the God of Israel. . . .
> The peasantry prospered in Israel,
> they grew fat on plunder,
> because you arose, Deborah,
> arose as a mother in Israel.[2]

At this critical moment in the late fourteenth and fifteenth centuries, an unusual number of inspired women began to speak out in warning about the dire situation of Church and State.

In 1360, St. Bridget of Sweden claimed that the unhappy state of France resulted from its sins. Bridget had prophesied that if the French king "who is designated only as 'that king who now holds the kingdom' refuses to obey 'his life shall end in misery, his kingdom will be given over to tribulations, and his line held in such detestation that all shall be amazed. . . . When the French acquire true humility, the kingdom will devolve to the true heir and experience a good peace.' "[3] Colette of Corbie (1381–1447) had experienced visions that told her to reform the Franciscan order of Poor Clares. Although they never met, Colette traveled in Joan's region, using the emblem "Jesus Maria" in her letters. Jeanne-Marie de Maillé (1331–1414), a Franciscan of Tours, first prophesied about which gate of the city King Charles VI would enter, a seemingly trivial prognostication, but one that led to her introduction to the king by the duke of Orléans: "She had a 'secret and prolix' conversation with the king, to be repeated at greater length a few years later . . . in Paris. But what was said, alas, only God and the king knew."[4] Joan, too, would use the emblem Jesus Maria, and would have a secret conversation with her king, warning him of the need for action.

Marie Robine of Avignon was the most important prophetess of the time. She had experienced twelve visions from 1398–9, most of which dealt with the French king's role in the Great Schism. Marie met King Charles VI in February 1398. In her eleventh vision, God told Marie that "He ordered the king of France to repair the state of the Church Militant and yet he wants to do nothing for us. We will remove him from his position by the means of his subjects and there are others who will die in great rivers of blood. . . ."[5] A lawyer who met Joan in Poitiers in 1429 remembered that a professor of theology, who was also present, reported that he had spoken to Marie at the time she met with Charles VI.

> [Marie d'Avignon] told him that the realm of France would suffer greatly and sustain numerous calamities, adding that she had had many visions touching on the desolation of the realm. In particular she saw large plates of armor presented to her. She was terror-stricken, fearing she would be forced to wear armor herself but was told not to be afraid, that she would not carry weapons. But after her there would come a maiden who would be armed and deliver the realm of France from its enemies. And Érault firmly believed that Joan was the one about whom Marie d'Avignon had spoken.[6]

The combination of Robine's visions, which "told of a virgin who would bear arms, and the Merlin prophecies [see Chapter 3] placed the virgin, armed and on horseback, in the middle of the fray. Thus the prophecies lent respectability to the idea of the virgin who actually engages in combat."[7] Some men also figured in the prophecies that helped propel the mission of Joan of Arc. The hermit Jean de Gand received instructions from heaven in 1421–22 commanding him to find the dauphin of France, the future Charles VII. He promised Charles that if he truly desired peace, God would give him victory.[8]

Prophets came from all ranks of society, but the very large number of prophetesses in the late Middle Ages inspired skepticism among some theologians. Many argued for caution, since charlatans without divine inspiration posed a danger to the faithful. Nor did all voices come from God. The University of Paris theologian Jean Gerson (1363–1429), who wrote a treatise in support of Joan's mission, was open to, and believed in, prophecy but felt that in each case discernment was essential to determine whether visions were authentic.[9]

These women and their biblical prototypes provided both the context and the basis for Joan's acceptance and success. But a deteriorating military situation and conditions at her home propelled her forward. During the last half of 1424 and the first six months of 1425, the border regions experienced a series of attacks by mercenaries and brigands. Étiennes de Vignolles (known as La Hire), one of Joan's future comrades, was fighting in the region for the dauphin, conducting raids and making truces with Duke René of Anjou, some of which involved Joan's future judge, Pierre Cauchon, in his capacity as bishop of Beauvais. At Vitry-le-François, in the heart of Anglo-Burgundian Champagne, La Hire signed a treaty promising that neither he nor his company would destroy any houses or buildings and would desist from all acts of war, including capturing men, horses, livestock, goods or any other belongings.[10] Vitry was a considerable distance from Domremy, but such actions and ensuing truces were typical during these years. In late 1425 parts of the village, including the church, were probably set on fire and pillaged. After this a period of relative calm descended on the area because of discord between the regent John, duke of Bedford, who had returned to England, and Philip the Good of Burgundy.[11] All that would change again in early 1428, when the French villages on the right bank of the Meuse became the site of major skirmishes between Anglo-Burgundian forces and the captain of Vaucouleurs.

Nothing in the villagers' 1456 accounts allows us to date the flight to Neufchâteau after parts of Domremy were attacked and burned by Anglo-Burgundian soldiers. Although many believe this incident occurred in 1428 or 1429, it probably happened in 1425, the same year in which Joan said she began to hear voices.[12] The villagers mention only one occasion when most of the inhabitants of Domremy and Greux fled to Neufchâteau. Question twelve asked if Joan had always been in the company of her father and mother when she fled to Neufchâteau because of the bands of soldiers. Most witnesses answered that all the villagers from Domremy and Greux had fled with their livestock, and that Joan remained in Neufchâteau four or five days with her family at the house of an honest woman named La Rousse. While all of the villagers stated that the exodus had lasted only four to five days, Joan testified at trial that she had been there for two weeks. Since several of Joan's godparents lived in Neufchâteau, it is likely that she stayed there on more than one occasion. The time away from Domremy did not deter Joan from her devotions. She heard mass in the churches of Saint-Nicolas and Saint-Christophe. Once the villagers returned, Béatrice d'Estellin recalled that after Domremy was burned, Joan went every feast day to hear mass in Greux.[13]

When did Joan's pious behavior begin? Even before she heard voices she was unusually devout. Friends, neighbors, and priests would have remarked on a sudden change in behavior, especially in view of later events. Joan said she first heard a voice at age twelve or thirteen, the time when most young girls begin to undergo the transition to puberty. When Joan later adopted the title "La Pucelle," she was referring to a stage of life. While *pucelle* can simply mean a virgin or maid, such a translation fails to convey the significance of Joan's choice. Based on usage in medieval literature, it has:

> distinct shades connoting youth, innocence, and paradoxically, nobility. . . .
> It denotes a time of passage, not a permanent condition. It is a word that
> looks forward to a change in state. . . . [In its medieval context], the word
> implied no rank, and it was current at every level in society. This made it
> an inspired choice in Joan's case. It cancelled out her background, without
> denying it. . . . It expressed not only the incorruption of her body, but also
> the dangerous border into maturity or full womanhood that she had not
> crossed and would not cross.[14]

At her trial Joan claimed that it was in 1425, amidst these attacks and raids on the village, that she first heard voices. To the modern mind, hearing voices suggests psychiatric or medical illness,[15] but for medieval people, voices and mystical experiences, while not commonplace, were an accepted part of existence even though they were usually met with a healthy skepticism. No one from Domremy who was still alive to testify in 1456 said anything about Joan hearing voices. Since some recalled sewing with her and others spoke of her disdain for dancing, surely someone would have mentioned her saying she heard voices? Why would she have told no one, not even her closest friends? Joan may have feared being made fun of even more than she already had been – what would the other children have said if she not only went to church more than was necessary but also claimed to hear voices? It is also possible that some traumatic event involving the raid on the village in 1425 triggered dreams, hallucinations, or nightmares that Joan believed came from God. Finally, Joan may have made up the voices or elaborated on an unusual experience so that she could leave Domremy.

As with Joan's early life, all direct mention of her voices comes from Joan's testimony at trial in 1431, six years after she said she first heard them, and from 1456, when the majority of witnesses in the nullification proceedings gave their accounts. The only exceptions are some chroniclers who began to talk of "the Maid" after she arrived at Chinon in March 1429.

Joan told her judges that "she had a voice from God to help her and guide her. And the first time she was much afraid. And this voice came towards noon, in summer, in her father's garden and Joan . . . had [not] fasted on the preceding day.[16] She heard the voice on her right, in the direction of the church; and she seldom heard it without a light. This light came from the same side as the voice, and generally there was a great light." Joan's words derive from the prophetic tradition of which she was very aware by the time of her trial. Her statement that she was "much afraid" echoes the beginning of the gospel of Luke. When an angel appeared to Zechariah, father of John the Baptist, "he was terrified; and fear overwhelmed him" for he and his wife Elizabeth were old and had had no children. When the angel Gabriel came to the Virgin Mary "she was much perplexed by his words. . . . The angel said to her, 'Do not be afraid, Mary, for you have found favor with God.' "[17] So too in the gospel accounts of the Resurrection, Mary Magdalene and the women are described as terrified or afraid at the appearance of the angel at the tomb.

Joan's mention of her "father's garden" and the voice from God speaking to her around noon conjure up images that are symbolic and prophetic. Was it Jacques d'Arc's garden to which Joan referred? Or was it the Garden of Eden, a time of innocence for Adam and Eve before their expulsion? Did the first voice come around twelve o'clock in the afternoon? Anthropologists describe noon, especially in rural societies, as an example of "liminal time," a period of suspension betwixt and between the natural and the supernatural when magical or divine influences are heightened. Just as she had chosen the designation of *pucelle* or Maid to define herself as neither child nor woman, so she said her voices spoke to her in transitional time. Finally, Joan mentions light, a symbol of creation and illumination. In these few lines, Joan was describing herself to the English as God's Chosen One.[18]

When pressed to elaborate on how she could see the light about which she spoke, Joan's answers became more vague and she either did not reply or changed the subject. She said that if she was in a wood she easily heard the voice. "It seemed to her a worthy voice, and she believed it was sent from God; when she heard the voice a third time she knew that it was the voice of an angel. She said also that this voice always protected her." The voice told her to be a good girl and go to church often. It also told her that she must come to France.[19]

At the beginning then, when the voice or voices came to her around age thirteen in her father's garden, Joan saw a light, and she said the source was God or perhaps an angel. Her initial instructions were twofold: to behave well and to go into France. She added that later, those on her side "knew well that the voice was sent to Joan from God . . . [and] that there is not a day when she does not hear this voice; and she has much need of it." She said she never asked for any reward but the salvation of her soul.[20] Joan continued to talk about the voice, and when "asked whether this voice, which she says appears to her, comes as an angel, or directly from God, or whether it is the voice of one of the saints, she answered: 'This voice comes from God.' "[21]

Even as she expanded upon when and where the voices came to her, Joan did not identify them by any other name than God. Indeed, her special devotion to God and the Virgin Mary is evident from the villagers' accounts as well as those who came to know her later. Contrary to the sinister meaning the trial judges gave to the Fairy Tree, Joan said that she and the other girls made wreaths in honor of the Virgin. A priest who had been a member of the choir in the chapel of Notre Dame at the time of Joan's stay at Vaucouleurs said he "often saw Joan the Maid come to church very devoutly; she heard mass there in the morning and stayed to pray. He also had seen her in the crypt of the church on her knees before Our Lady, sometimes with her face lowered and sometimes raised."[22] As her mission progressed, Joan's banners and pennons bore the inscription JHESUS MARIA, as did a ring she treasured. In her famous "Letter to the English," dictated in March and sent from Blois in late April of 1429, Joan began with +JHESUS MARIA+. Midway through the letter of admonition she says that if the English obey her, she will have mercy on them. But if not, "you will not hold the realm of France from God, the King of Heaven, son of Holy Mary, for it will be held by King Charles, the true heir, because God, the King of Heaven wants it to be so, and this has been revealed by the Maid."

What Joan did not say is revealing. Only at the fourth trial session, on February 27, 1431, did she name saints. Increasingly, her answers became more specific and elaborate, in response to leading questions. Compared to her earlier assertions, when the judges pressed her about whether the voice was "that of an angel or of a saint, male or female, or straight from God, she answered that the voice was the voice of Saint Catherine and of Saint Margaret. And their heads were crowned in a rich and precious fashion with beautiful crowns. . . ." How did she know who they were? Sometimes she said simply that she knew who they were by the greeting they gave her, while other times she claimed they told her their names. She added, contrary to what she had stated earlier, that it had been seven years since they had first undertaken to guide her.

As Joan began to confuse her answers, she played for time to formulate her responses when the judges asked for specific information about the saints. In all likelihood, she was making up her answers as she went along. She varied her responses, sometimes saying she would say no more, at other times that "she had not leave to tell them." But when they asked who had appeared first, she initially said: "I knew well enough once, but I have forgotten. If I had leave, I would gladly tell you. It is written down in the register at Poitiers."[23] Then she went on to say that Saint Michael came first.[24]

The exchange must be read on several levels. At trial, Joan was answering these questions two years *after* she had acquired the sword of St. Catherine, *after* she knew of the steadfast and singular loyalty of Le Mont St-Michel, the only site in Normandy that never fell to the English, and *after* events that made her life seem comparable to the legends of St. Catherine of Alexandria and St. Margaret of Antioch. By doing so, Joan situated herself in the context of divine and political history.

Both Catherine and Margaret were virgin martyrs of the early Church. According to legend, Margaret of Antioch, who had a difficult relationship with her father, was guarding her sheep at age fifteen – much as Joan would be described – when a traveling official expressed his desire to marry her. When she refused she was imprisoned and her many torments included being burned.[25] Saint Catherine, having refused an earthly spouse, had a vision of Jesus asking her to become his bride. Famed for her eloquence, she stood up to a Roman emperor who was persecuting Christians. The emperor decided to put her to the test by gathering the fifty most renowned rhetoricians and grammarians of the land; they were not amused, some being described as trembling with indignation at being summoned to respond to a mere girl. But Catherine was up to the task, although she protested, asking, "Is it fair for you to array fifty orators against one girl, promising the orators rich returns for winning, and forcing me to fight without any hope of reward? Yet my reward will be Jesus Christ." The virgin went on to contradict the orators with great skill, refuting them with such clear reasoning that they were dumbfounded and reduced to silence.[26] In the late fourteenth century, and particularly after 1418, St. Catherine and St. Michael became intertwined in legends that portrayed them as patron saints of both prisoners and soldiers.

> The military cast to the legend was due in particular to similarities between Catherine and Saint Michael, the Prince of Knights. Both appeared adorned with sword and crown; both were virgins who fended off heresy and evil; both served as protectors of youth – Michael of young men, Catherine of young women – who often became intermediaries in divine revelations; both were intercessors on whom people called for help in times of danger or death.[27]

In response to the increasing specificity of the questions, Joan fit her story to those saints who most closely corresponded to her actions and behaviors as well as to the current situation in France. She had much earlier established, at least to her satisfaction, that God had singled her out for a special role in the salvation of France.

There are, too, more concrete reasons to explain the choice of saints. Closer to home, Joan's sister and niece had been named Catherine, and there was a statue of St. Margaret in her church of St. Remy. Both saints and the archangel Michael were widely venerated in the region. One would expect the villagers interviewed in 1456 to mention special devotion by Joan to these saints, yet not one of them did so. In the popular religion of the Middle Ages, saints were vital, sometimes appearing to eclipse God the Father and Jesus. Is it conceivable that Joan specially revered Saints Catherine and Margaret and the archangel Michael without someone from her village speaking about this? Was she silent because her "voices" told her not to speak of them? Perhaps, but open veneration of the saints was far more common than speaking directly with God. The 28-year-old Jean de Metz,[28] one of Baudricourt's soldiers who accompanied Joan in the early stages of her career, said she told him that "for four or five years her brothers in paradise, and her Lord, that is to say, God, had told her that it was necessary for her to go to war to recover the realm of France. . . ."[29] If in fact she said that to him in early 1429, Joan's mission had changed radically. Originally she had said that her voices had told her simply to go to France; now she claimed she had to fight to end the English occupation.

When Joan spoke to her military comrades, she did not talk of Michael, Catherine, or Margaret. To the Bastard of Orléans, she said, "I bring you the best help that could ever be given to a soldier or a city, and that is the help of the king of Heaven. It does not, however, come from me myself: it comes from God, at the request of Saint Louis and Saint Charlemagne."[30] The traditional patrons of France had been Saint Louis and Charlemagne, but the sites most closely associated with them were in the control of the English or Burgundians. As a result, in 1418, the dauphin Charles had named Saint Michael as his patron saint. Joan's mention of Saint Louis and Charlemagne to the Bastard, and her later use of Michael at the trial, underscore the political and military nature of her mission. For the French, Michael had become the Archangel of Resistance.[31] For Joan at trial, the same could be said.

Almost no one who knew of Joan prior to 1431 spoke of devotion to Catherine, Margaret, and Michael, instead referring to her love of God and the Virgin. Joan's voices changed over time, elements in her accounts differing when, on the one hand, she spoke about hearing the voice of God and, on the other, the saints she began to speak of in session four. Even the amount of information she volunteered and the way she deflected some questions changed depending on whether she was referring to God or the saints.[32] But at the fourth session, when she first named the saints, Joan seemed uncomfortable. Asked whether much time had passed since she first heard the voice of Saint Michael, she answered: "I do not speak of St. Michael's voice, but of his great comfort."[33] Her initial "reluctance to identify her voices disappears and is replaced by an apparent eagerness and spontaneity. . . . It is as if once Joan had been compelled to identify her voices with these three saints, she began to perceive them to be the individuals with whom she had identified them."[34] If that is what happened, Joan had a wealth of knowledge to fall back on. Itinerant Franciscan and Dominican friars regularly preached in her region, and their sermons abounded with stories about the saints, often relying on Jacobus da Voragine's thirteenth-century *Golden Legend*. Joan often visited the Franciscan friary in nearby Coussey, on the road to Neufchâteau. Because of the itinerant nature of the Franciscans, they often spread word of prophecies as well as political events.[35]

Later remembered for joking with her men in order to keep up their spirits during battles and sieges, Joan displayed a similar flippancy at the trial when pushed to describe "her" saints. It is almost impossible to read the transcripts of the trial without realizing that Joan was toying with those she knew to be her enemies. On February 27 and March 1, when she was asked if the saints who appeared to her had hair, she answered: "It is well to know that they have." Was their hair long and did it hang down? She answered: "I do not know." But they spoke beautifully and she said she understood them very well. Did they have arms and legs? Joan responded: "I leave that to God. She said the voice was gentle, soft and low, and spoke in French," which caught her judges by surprise. Didn't St. Margaret speak English? Joan retorted, "Why should she speak in English when she is not on the English side?"[36]

At times, Joan openly mocked the judges in her descriptions. When asked to provide more details about the archangel Michael's appearance, she stated that "she did not see his crown, and she knows nothing of his apparel." Was he naked? She retorted: "Do you think God has not wherewithal to clothe him?" Asked if he had any hair, she answered: " 'Why should it be cut off?'. . . . She does not often see him, or know, whether he has any hair."[37]

With Joan's increasing desire to speak more about "her" saints, it is possible that in the process she had convinced herself of their existence.[38] But there is another possibility. At trial, Joan knew that her questioners were "not of her party." As she was pushed to identify her voice(s), she may have allowed herself to elaborate, to have fun at the expense of the judges who persecuted her for hours in the morning and afternoon. Her answer about St. Michael suggests a mocking nonchalance. At the beginning of her trial, Joan's unwillingness to take an oath (although she eventually did so) and the reasons she gave show that she did not necessarily intend to tell the truth. The trial judges asked Joan to speak the simple and absolute truth.

Joan answered: "Give me leave to speak" and then said: "By my faith, you could ask things such as I would not answer." She added: "Perhaps I shall not answer you truly in many things that you ask me, concerning the revelations; for perhaps you would constrain me to tell you things I have sworn not to utter, and so I should be perjured, and you would not want that. . . . There is a saying among little children, 'Men are sometimes hanged for telling the truth.' "[39]

Whether the particular voices were created as a result of the persistent and directed questioning of the judges or whether Joan was engaged in purposeful deception because she believed she was acting for the greater good, there is little evidence to suggest that before the trial Joan believed her voices came from anyone but God or perhaps an angel. Joan may have venerated Catherine and Margaret, as many in her region did, but it is doubtful that theirs were the "voices" she had described earlier; the saints she named beginning at the fourth session simply fit her personality and her mission too conveniently.

Once Joan "named names" at trial, she sometimes added "Saint Gabriel," usually in connection with the archangel Michael. By doing so Joan associated herself more directly with the Annunciation scene in Luke: "In the sixth month the angel Gabriel was sent by God to a town in Galilee called Nazareth, to a virgin engaged to a man whose name was Joseph, of the house of David. The virgin's name was Mary. And he came to her and said, 'Greetings, favored one! The Lord is with you.' "[40] That Jesus was born poor in lowly Nazareth (rather than Jerusalem) to a carpenter was a common theme in late medieval sermons, with preachers stressing that those of poor and humble condition were specially chosen by God.[41] Who better to exemplify that message than a teenage peasant girl?

On March 3, when her judges "asked if she believed that St. Michael and St. Gabriel have natural heads, she answered: 'I saw them with my own two eyes.' "[42] Here Joan extended her earlier comment about Michael's hair, which suggests again that either her voices *were* taking on more concrete form as she was forced to describe them in ever greater detail or that she was fabricating some of her answers. On May 9, when threatened with torture, Joan declared more ambiguously that on September 14, 1430,[43] the Feast of the Holy Cross, "she received comfort from St. Gabriel: she firmly believes it was St. Gabriel, she knew by her voices it was he."[44] Joan, by then fatigued and confused, seemed to separate Gabriel from her other voices, again pointing to their fragile construction.

What did Joan experience in the three years between 1425, when she said she first heard the voice of God, and 1428 when she first left her family? Very little is known of these years. It is likely that her married sister Catherine died, possibly in pregnancy or from other natural causes, since neither Joan nor any of the villagers mentioned any deaths as a result of the raids. Jacques d'Arc was sent in 1427 to Robert de Baudricourt, the French captain of the town of Vaucouleurs to the north, probably because of escalating tensions between the warring factions. In July 1428, Domremy was attacked and most of the inhabitants once again sought refuge in Neufchâteau.

But between the last two events, in May 1428, Joan sought an audience with Baudricourt to tell him she had heard the voice of God and that he must send her to the dauphin Charles at Chinon. Her second cousin Laxart testified that he had gone to Joan's house to bring her to his home in Burey, about two-thirds of the way to Vaucouleurs. She told him of her wish to go into France to have the dauphin crowned.[45] At this point Joan's voices became more insistent – or conditions at home had grown increasingly difficult. At her trial, she said that now the voice told her once or twice a week to depart for France. But her father knew nothing of her leaving. She said that the voice told her "she could no longer stay where she was; and the voice told her again that she should raise the siege of the city of Orléans. She said moreover that the voice told her that she, Joan, should go to Robert de Baudricourt, in the town of Vaucouleurs of which he was captain, and he would provide an escort for her." Perhaps to convince her judges of her honesty, Joan continued, saying "she was a poor maid, knowing nothing of riding or fighting. She said she went to an uncle of hers,[46] and told him she wanted to stay with him for some time; and she stayed there about eight days. And she told her uncle she must go to the said town of Vaucouleurs, and so her uncle took her."[47]

Although he was interviewed in 1456, Laxart never explained why he believed Joan's seemingly outrageous claims and took her to Baudricourt. Even though he knew Joan's father, the captain was not about to risk his reputation by sending a teenage girl to the dauphin. The first visit failed and Joan was sent home. Laxart recalled that Baudricourt told him to take Joan back to her father and have him slap her around a bit.[48] But in late 1428, Joan tried again. Mengette recalled that Joan asked Durand Laxart to lie for her.[49] Isabel d'Épinal elaborated: Joan "asked him to tell her parents that she was going to help his wife who was in childbirth so that he could take her to Sir Robert."[50] Hauviette said that she had not known of Joan's departure but afterwards she cried a lot because she had loved Joan and they were good friends.[51] Several people recalled Joan leaving with Laxart, with a few remembering her saying "*Adieu!*" before she left.[52] The situation struck most of the villagers who remembered it for its oddity.

During the two months after she left Domremy with Laxart in late December 1428, Joan returned to Vaucouleurs, where she spent a few weeks with Catherine and Henri Le Royer. Again, her behavior was unremarkable. Le Royer said that when Joan first came to his house, she seemed a good girl and sewed with his wife. Joan told him "it was necessary for her to go to the noble dauphin, because her Lord, the King of Heaven, wanted her to go . . . and that if she had to she would go there on her knees. When Joan came to his house she was wearing a red dress."[53] Later, as she answered her judges, Joan reinvented her life based on what had happened since she left home.

Between the first and second trips to Vaucouleurs, Jacques and Isabelle had become thoroughly alarmed at Joan's strange behavior and arranged a marriage for her. Although she does not seem to have told anyone directly about her visions, did she behave in ways that made her family suspicious? Her piety, even if greater than average, would not have alarmed most parents. However, if she had told them about the vow of virginity she later claimed to have made at age thirteen, it might have thwarted their attempts to make a good marriage alliance.

Had Joan shown an unusual interest in the fighting between the children of Maxey and those of Domremy and Greux even though she denied direct involvement? Had she tried to run away before the first trips to Burey and Vaucouleurs? Her mother's grandnephew Perrinet admitted that he had told her brothers that she had gone to Vaucouleurs after the first visit of May 13 to try to get approval for her mission. They in turn told Jacques, who was "very unhappy . . . saying that it was a great folly and would bring dishonor and shame on their family."[54] In his 1456 testimony, a priest at Vaucouleurs testified that "he saw her father and mother when they came to Vaucouleurs."[55] Presumably, they had hoped to take Joan home.

Jacques d'Arc was sufficiently worried that his daughter might leave Domremy and become a camp follower[56] that he hastily arranged a marriage, possibly to her childhood friend Michel Le Buin or to Jean

Waterin, both close to her in age.[57] At sixteen, Joan would have been younger than the age at which most peasant girls wed in northern Europe, but not exceptionally so. Joan provided a bit more information at her trial when her judges asked about her appearance at the ecclesiastical court in Toul to respond to accusations of a breach of marriage contract. Although the records of the lawsuit no longer exist, it happened in January or early February of 1429 after Joan had left a second time to "help" her cousin Jeanne, Laxart's wife. Joan said that her mother told her that Jacques had:

> dreamed that Joan his daughter would go off with men-at-arms; and her father and mother took great care to keep her safely, and held her in great subjection: and she was obedient to them in all things except in the incident at Toul, the action for marriage. She said she had heard her mother tell how her father said to her brothers: "In truth, if I thought this thing would happen which I have dreamed about my daughter, I would want you to drown her; and if you would not, I would drown her myself." And her father and mother almost lost their senses when she left to go to Vaucouleurs.

Joan added that her father had begun having these dreams more than two years after she had started to hear the voices, that is, in mid to late 1427.[58]

When her judges asked her what had prompted her to summon the man for breach of contract, Joan retorted that it was he who had summoned her and that she had made no promise to him. She once again stated that the first time she heard the voice she had vowed her virginity, but when they asked if she had spoken of the visions to any priest, she said no, for she feared that the Burgundians would try to hinder her journey. But "in particular she feared that her father would stop it. Asked if she believed it was right to leave her father and mother without permission, when she should honor her father and mother, she answered that in all other things she was obedient to them, except in this journey; but afterwards she wrote to them, and they forgave her." Once again Joan's willfulness came through when she was asked if she had committed a sin by not telling her mother and father the truth. She said her duty to God came first and even:

> if she had had a hundred parents, or had been the king's daughter, she would have gone nevertheless.

Asked whether she asked her voices if she should tell her father and mother of her going, she answered that as for her father and mother, the voices were well pleased that she should tell them, but for the difficulty they would have raised if she had done so; and as for herself she would not have told them for anything.[59]

Joan acknowledged that this was her decision alone, since she feared her parents would use any means available to try to stop her from leaving.

The picture that emerges from the trial and the villagers' accounts of 1456 is of a headstrong girl determined to leave Domremy and go to the king, whatever the emotional cost to her family. Life in the d'Arc household had become intolerable for Joan. Gérardin d'Épinal, perhaps having gotten wind of something to do with a marriage, testified that she said to him before leaving the second time: "'Compère,[60] if you were not a Burgundian, I would tell you something.' He thought that it was about a boyfriend that she wanted to marry." He added that "she left her father's house, because it was painful for her, as she said, to remain there."[61] Whether it was because she really heard voices or because she wanted to seek adventures, Joan's situation in Domremy had become oppressive as her parents tried to constrain her every action.

In his first encounter with Joan, Jean de Metz recalled a girl who was confident, self-assured and surprisingly knowledgeable about politics:

When Joan the Maid came to the city of Vaucouleurs, in the diocese of Toul, he saw her dressed in poor women's clothing, red in color, and she was staying in the house of Henri Le Royer. Addressing himself to her he asked: "My friend, what are you doing here? Would it be better for the king to be chased from the realm and we become English?" The Maid responded, "I have come here ... to speak to Robert de Baudricourt, so that he will lead me or have me led to the king. He doesn't need to worry about me, or what I tell him; however, before Lent I will be with the king, if I have to lose my legs up to the knees. No one in the world, neither kings, nor dukes, nor the daughter of the King of the Scots[62] nor anyone else can recover the realm of France. His only hope comes through me. I would rather sew with my mother, that poor woman, because this is not my condition in life, but it is necessary that I go because my Lord requires it of me.[63]

Here Joan was disingenuous, since she had no intention of going home to sew with her mother. But phrasing it as she did placed her firmly in the biblical and prophetic tradition. Joan presented her mission not as a result of personal choice but of humbly doing the Lord's work, as the Virgin and others had done before her. Yet everything else in her statement to de Metz belies the humility uttered at the end. Only Joan could save France.

Her other main companion to Chinon, Bertrand de Poulengy, a noble serving as part of Baudricourt's entourage, seconded de Metz's testimony, adding that he heard Joan say that in spite of his enemies, the dauphin would become king and that she would lead him to be crowned. When Baudricourt had asked her to name her lord, she responded: "The King of Heaven."[64] Joan was impatient to set off but the captain was not yet ready to sponsor her. Her mission really began after Duke Charles of Lorraine requested her presence.

Jean de Metz accompanied Joan as far as Toul. He recalled that before they left, he asked her if she wanted to wear something other than her dress. When she agreed, he gave her clothing and shoes from his servants.[65] En route to Nancy to meet with the duke, Joan and Jean de Metz stopped in Toul to allow Joan to appear before the church court. The trip gave him the opportunity to report the results – and Joan's behavior – to Baudricourt. Escorted by Baudricourt's soldier and under safe conduct from the duke, she would not have had to contend with her father.[66] As she testified, Joan won her suit based on the fact that she had made no promise to the man: canon law stated that no marriage existed if a free exchange of promises had not taken place. While parents in the Middle Ages sometimes resorted to physical violence or other strategies to try to force an unwilling child to marry, a girl or boy who continued to refuse was protected by church law. Although we know nothing other than the outcome, Joan's first appearance before judges was a success.

From Toul, Joan was probably escorted to Nancy by nineteen-year-old René of Anjou (1409–80), heir to the duchy of Bar. René was son of the dauphin's mother-in-law, Yolande of Aragon, and son-in-law of the duke of Lorraine, so he had close connections to both the French and Burgundian factions. Neither titles nor authority impressed Joan, a trait that helped forward her mission but eventually led to her downfall. Joan told the duke she wished to go to France. However, having already heard of some of her deeds, the duke apparently thought she was a healer. When he asked her to cure him, she said she knew nothing about that. She also spoke little about the journey she intended to take, evidently not trusting him because of his relationship with the duke of Burgundy. The fanciful *Chronique de Lorraine* adds further details about the short trip, suggesting the duke needed to be convinced of her ability to carry out what little he knew of her enterprise:

> "How? You have never carried arms, nor ridden a horse." She responded that if she had armor and a horse, "I will mount it, and then you will see that I can guide it." The duke then gave her armor and a horse. . . . She was light. . . . In the presence of all, without putting her foot in the stirrup, she got into the saddle. . . . She was given a lance; she went to the courtyard of the castle and there she rode around. Never did a man of arms better race a horse. The nobles were astounded. . . . The duke wrote to Baudricourt: "Yes, take her there. God will help her accomplish her goals."[67]

Joan asked the duke to send his son-in-law René and others to escort her to France; she said in return she would pray for his health.[68] Before taking her leave and heading back to Vaucouleurs, Joan warned Duke Charles to get rid of his mistress: "She told him that he conducted himself badly and that he would not be cured unless he changed his ways. He had to take back his true wife."[69]

Although the duke declined Joan's request that René accompany her to the dauphin, he gave her four francs and a black horse and sent her back to Vaucouleurs. The behind-the-scenes role of Yolande of Aragon,[70] whose mother had been born in the duchy of Bar, was crucial in setting the stage for the Maid. Opposed to what she saw as the pro-Burgundian policies of Charles VII's counselors, Archbishop Regnault de Chartres, Georges de La Trémoïlle, and Raoul de Gaucourt, which would have affected her son's holdings, Yolande may well have promoted the "idea" of Joan at court. She may also, through René and the duke, have provided Joan with current information about political and military events that would have allowed Joan to "predict" events. Yet Yolande could have had no idea of the kind of force she was unleashing. Joan took orders from no one. According to Henri Le Royer, "it was pointed out to her that she should not go because soldiers were everywhere. She answered that she did not fear soldiers because her way was clear. If soldiers were around, she had God, her lord, who opened the route for her to go to the dauphin, and she was born to accomplish this."[71]

The interview convinced Baudricourt to act. Once back in Vaucouleurs, Joan still had to be outfitted for the trip. The people of the town provided her with a tunic and men's clothing, spurs, gaiters, a sword, and other items necessary for war.[72] By this time Joan had attracted enough curiosity that a priest approached her holding his ecclesiastical stole and began to exorcise her before Baudricourt, saying:

> that if she was a bad creature, she would back away from them, whereas if she were a good creature, she would come toward them. Joan then approached the priest and bent down on her knees. She said he did not act properly in doing so, because he had heard her confession. When she saw that Robert did not want to send her forth . . . to the dauphin, Joan said: "Have you not heard the prophecy that having been destroyed by a woman [Queen Isabeau of Bavaria, who had disinherited her son in the Treaty of Troyes], France will be saved by a maiden from the marches of Lorraine?"[73]

Was the exorcism necessary fully to convince Baudricourt or was it staged to showcase the Maid's mission at its outset? Several sources state that Joan quoted prophecies before she left. A vague notion of mission now became more concrete to her. The mistress of the house in which Joan was staying emphasized that she was so impatient to be off she was like a pregnant woman awaiting the onset of labor.

Joan's life before she left Domremy and Vaucouleurs was not the story of a simple shepherdess. Like the other children, Joan was confronted with the constant reality of war and turmoil. As the daughter of a well-to-do peasant who helped defend a border town, she would have learned more than her share about skirmishes, brigandage, and perhaps even regional politics. Wandering Franciscans as well as travelers along the routes of Champagne and Lorraine would have told of events happening in "France." Joan was clever and quickly learned whatever she set her mind to. However frustrating the delays had been, Joan had absorbed vital information and skills at Vaucouleurs, Nancy, and Toul that would make her a legendary figure during the next two years.

So much of Joan's story has been seen through the lens of her sainthood that it is important to emphasize that she did not fit the pattern of an adolescent saint of the late Middle Ages. Most future saints engaged in intense mortification of the flesh, often whipping themselves till they bled:

"They welcomed illness as a punishment and a test of faith. . . . Guilt-ridden piety began to appear in much more dramatic and personal forms."[74] Joan exhibited no such behavior during her life in Domremy or later. Her religious activities, while notable, were not extreme. By contrast, her military, political and legal adventures were characterized by boldness, pride, and impetuosity. When things became too emotionally difficult at home, she left. Perhaps she was guided by voices from God, but more likely she seized the opportunity to follow a course that had been described in prophecies. As she said "*Adieu!*" to the villagers of Domremy, did she do so with a twinkle in her eyes at the double entendre?[75] For centuries, religion had provided women of great talent with some of the few opportunities to receive an education, record mystical visions, write letters to popes and kings, and to prophesy.[76] For a woman who did not wish to marry, the religious life provided the best alternative. Joan left her village in the name of God, and spoke of religion frequently, but she followed a very different path from women in religious orders in the Middle Ages.

Joan approached life actively. She may have done household duties "willingly," but when it came to her life after 1428, she was anything but submissive. Her mission began to evolve after she first left for Vaucouleurs in May 1428 and during the later trip to Chinon. The siege of Orléans only began in October of 1428, a couple of months before her second trip to Vaucouleurs. When Joan first went to see the captain of Vaucouleurs, she had only a vague sense of mission. Her parents and, up to a point, Baudricourt, tried to impede her efforts. But the natural talent, strong will, and assurance that would help her succeed in war where others had failed could not be thwarted so easily.

CHAPTER 3

The Making of the Maid

❧

As she prepared to leave Vaucouleurs, Baudricourt gave Joan her first sword, saying: "Go, go, and come what may."[1] Joan says little in her trial testimony about the journey, because the judges did not focus on it. Accompanied by Jean de Metz, Bertrand de Poulengy, and four others, Joan left Vaucouleurs on February 12 or 13 1429.[2] Passing through Burgundian territory, they rode for eleven days, mostly at night to avoid enemy soldiers. Poulengy said that they experienced many anxieties along the way but Joan always told them not to be afraid.[3] De Metz asked Joan if she would do what she had promised when they reached Chinon. She told him not to worry, for she had a mission that she would accomplish. At night, he and Bertrand slept on either side of her, but Joan remained fully clothed, with her doublet tied and her shoes laced. Although later she would be dressed and armed by her squire or page, at this stage Joan was careful not to sexually arouse the six men who accompanied her. One of the women who later came to know Joan well remembered that in the beginning men lusted after her, but when they were about to act on their impulses "they felt so much shame that they did not dare do or say anything."[4] In a comment echoed by many others, de Metz claimed that "he feared her such that he never would have dared approach her and felt neither desire nor any physical response toward her."[5] Although statements made after the events of 1429 to 1431 call for caution, Joan *did* inspire an awe that kept men at a distance. Her stridency and self-confidence astounded military men who were used to camp followers. At the same time, Joan recognized that enemy soldiers might take them by surprise at any moment, so she had to be prepared. Remaining clothed at night served a dual purpose.

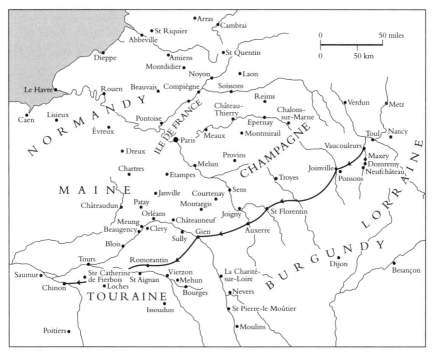

Map 4   From Vaucouleurs to Chinon.

During the journey Joan expressed her desire to hear mass regularly and urged her companions to do so whenever they could. They stopped at the cathedral when they stopped at Auxerre, probably on February 16 and 17, but for the most part they tried to attract as little attention as possible. By February 21 they had reached the pilgrimage town of St. Catherine of Fierbois, where Joan attended mass twice. From there she dictated a letter to the king to tell him of her impending arrival. The seventeen-year-old girl who left Vaucouleurs for the last time on February 13, 1429, had already been changed by her experiences. Her travels to Burey, Vaucouleurs, Toul, and Nancy had introduced her to a world much greater than the village she had left behind. She had come to know soldiers and nobles, men who informed her about the situation in France. The next major challenge awaited her.

On February 23, Joan and her small troop arrived in the lower town of Chinon, whose impressive castle and vineyards dominated the heights. Who was the girl who had won the grudging support of the captain and her traveling companions? She was charismatic, headstrong, stubborn, and determined to succeed against almost insurmountable odds. Yet for all that we can glean about Joan's personality and behavior, we know almost nothing of her appearance. At trial, when "asked if she had seen or had made any images of pictures of herself or in her likeness, she answered that at Arras she saw a painting in the hands of a Scot; and she was shown in full armor, presenting letters to her king, with one knee on the ground. She said she had never seen or had made any other image or picture in her likeness."[6] Clément de Fauquembergue, notary of the Paris *parlement*, sketched her in his record books although he had not seen her. A later fifteenth-century wall painting of two women, one of whom may represent Joan, adorns the wall of Notre Dame de Bermont. Even though the painter may have had some personal knowledge of Joan, the outlines suggest little in the way of physical features. The notary of La Rochelle, unusually well informed because of the close ties between his city and Orléans, wrote that Joan had black hair,[7] while two knights described her voice as feminine.[8]

The sight of a teenage girl dressed as a boy must have astounded those at court. Describing her appearance when she reached Chinon, one of Charles' magistrates wrote that "she had short hair and a wool cap on her head and wore men's garb, including hose, but of a very simple sort."[9] All of the sources agreed that Joan's hair had been cut around in a bowl shape, shaved at the base of the neck and cut above the ears, a style fashionable among men at the time.[10] The one physical feature consistently remarked upon by her military comrades were her breasts. The duke of Alençon later said that he saw Joan get dressed for battle and sometimes he saw her breasts, which were beautiful.[11] Her squire Jean d'Aulon described her as "a young girl, pretty and well built. Several times, while helping her to arm, he saw her breasts, and sometimes her legs completely nude, when he dressed her wounds."[12] She was of medium height and build for a girl her age. Considering the arduous journey and the battles and tribulations to come, Joan's good health and physical strength are indisputable.

So many legends and conflicting accounts surround Joan's first meeting with the king on February 23 that it is important to separate fact from fiction. Joan's soon-to-be squire, the 25-year-old Aulon, provided the simplest and most plausible description of the event. After being presented to Charles VII, Joan spoke with the king in secret. Charles then consulted his counselors, informing them that Joan claimed she was sent by God to recover his realm. They advised the king to have her interrogated.[13] The most important factor in Aulon's account is the element of secrecy in the first meeting between the king and only a few of his most trusted counselors.

Simon Charles, president of the king's household, embellished the story, changing the details and conflating two separate meetings with the king. Some parts of his account are accurate; others are fabricated. He wrote that the skeptical counselors deliberated as to whether or not the king should receive Joan, demanding to know her business with Charles. After some resistance, she told them that she had two orders from God: to lift the English siege of Orléans, which had begun six months earlier, and to lead the king to Reims for his coronation and anointing. Some of the counselors advised the king to ignore her and send her away. Others believed that he ought to listen because she declared that God had sent her. The king decided that first she would be examined by clergy and churchmen, which was done. Finally, with some reluctance, Charles agreed to meet Joan. Although his mother-in-law Yolande had facilitated the meeting, many of his closest counselors were adamantly opposed to an audience.

> At the time she entered the castle of Chinon, the king hesitated again about whether he should speak with her, following the advice of the great men of his court. But then he was told that Robert de Baudricourt had sent a message to him about this woman. She had passed through the territories of the king's enemies, crossing many fords and rivers in a manner that seemed almost miraculous to get to the king. . . . Once he knew she was coming, he took himself aside, separating himself from the others, but Joan recognized him easily and bowed before him. She spoke with him for a long time. After having heard her, the king appeared joyous. Finally the king, not wanting to do anything without the advice of churchmen, sent Joan to Poitiers to be examined by clergy.[14]

Part of the account is true but it suggests only one meeting, combining the first interview of February 23 with the formal introduction to the court that took place a month later. Joan's version contains elements of both Aulon's and Simon Charles' account. At trial, she recalled that she arrived toward noon and lodged at an inn. After her meal she climbed the zigzagging cobblestone road to the castle. She claimed that when she entered the king's room she recognized him among many others by the counsel of her voice, which revealed him to her.[15] Joan had used almost the same words to describe her first meeting with the captain at Vaucouleurs, when she said that "she easily recognized Robert de Baudricourt although she had never seen him before."[16] Either Joan remembered the second presentation to the court more vividly than the first or, more likely, she purposefully made use of the more spectacular version to convince her judges that the voice of God had led her to the king.

Picking out the disguised king in the midst of three hundred courtiers has often been portrayed as one of Joan's first miracles. It did not happen, at least not on February 23. The first interview with the king took place on the evening of Joan's arrival, probably in the presence of his closest counselors Georges de La Trémoïlle, the Grand Chamberlain of France, Regnault de Chartres, Archbishop of Reims, and a few others especially close to Charles. It was a secret and relatively short interview that culminated in her being sent to Poitiers for a lengthy theological examination. The official introduction was staged for maximum dramatic effect by the king and his mother-in-law Yolande once Joan had been tested.[17] Every step of Joan's journey revealed signs of organization, including access to "friends in high places, support at opportune moments, people who were well placed to forward her, all at exactly the right time."[18] Although in these years the king has often been portrayed as hapless and weak, he was not stupid. Whatever went on behind the scenes before Joan arrived, he had to be sure she could pass muster before he presented her to his court. By arranging it so that most believed the second meeting was the first, he was able to showcase the apparently miraculous foresight of a boyish peasant girl.

Contrary to most popular accounts, Charles was skeptical of Joan, and even ridiculed her. One of Queen Marie's ladies-in-waiting, Marguerite de La Tourolde, had "heard from those who took her to the king say that at first sight they thought she was mad and they thought to shut her away."[19] One of his counselors, Archbishop Jacques Gélu, who would later become a staunch defender of Joan, initially urged Charles not to meet with her. He stated in a letter to one of the royal counselors that the king should be wary of being taken in too easily by the words of the Maid, "especially since she was a peasant. . . . The king should take care that he not seem ridiculous in the eyes of foreign lands since the French already had the reputation of being easily taken in."[20] He urged the king to keep Joan waiting, in a state of uncertainty.[21] A Venetian noble wrote home that

Charles made fun of her, saying she was crazy, possessed by a demon and guilty of effrontery.[22] Skepticism was wise, since theologians warned that "one must be suspicious, especially of the young and women 'whose enthusiasm is extravagant, eager, changeable, uninhibited and therefore not to be considered trustworthy'."[23] Although he had little to lose, the dauphin needed to be convinced of Joan's physical purity and religious orthodoxy before he sent a seventeen-year-old girl to relieve the siege of Orléans. After the initial meeting, Charles decided Joan must undergo a process of "theological validation" to prove that she was a prophet: "unheard of wonders are greeted by ridicule until an initial sign . . . provides the intimation of legitimacy which leads to an ecclesiastical investigation."[24] Although Joan chafed at the constant questioning and delays, the measures Charles took to present her to the world helped her mission greatly.

After passing the first test, Charles sent Joan to Poitiers, almost fifty miles away, to be examined more fully. Arriving there on March 1, Joan was lodged at the Maison de la Rose, close to the church of Notre Dame and the palace of the dukes of Aquitaine. Several prominent women were assigned to observe her actions and behavior and then report back to the council. Yolande knew that even as a figurehead Joan would require moral stature and a solid reputation. First and foremost, Joan's virginity had to be established. Three upper-class matrons performed a physical examination, finding her to be of "perfect physical integrity."[25] They also reported that she was honest and respectable in her comportment. In eating and drinking she exhibited great moderation, fasting regularly. The page later assigned to her, Louis de Coutes, echoed what many others said: "frequently she would only eat a morsel of bread the whole day; it was astonishing how little she ate. When she was in her lodgings, she only ate two meals a day."[26] There was another reason Joan's purity of body and mind mattered, but that would become evident only after she returned to court.

While theological validation was necessary if Joan's mission was to proceed, it was equally important for the king to find out if Joan could withstand scrutiny and command respect. Gathered at Poitiers was the remnant of loyal doctors of theology who had fled from the University of Paris when the city fell to the English. Since Charles needed to be convinced, he and Regnault de Chartres traveled to Poitiers to keep an eye on how the examination progressed. The archbishop Regnault de Chartres presided over the sessions with the secretary, Jean Érault, who copied down Joan's first dictated letter to the English.[27] The interviews took place from March 1 to 21, without great formality at the Maison de la Rose, with Joan seated at the end of a bench.

Eighteen churchmen interrogated Joan. A squire of the king's stables who was present during the sessions remembered that at one point she clapped him on the shoulder, saying that she would like to have more men of his character at her side. When the leading churchman, Pierre de Versailles, explained that the king had sent her there to be examined, she responded: "I know well that you are here to interrogate me," but added disingenuously, "I don't know my A's or B's." She then informed them that God had sent her to lift the siege of Orléans and to conduct the king to Reims to be anointed and crowned.[28] Despite the difficulty of the questions posed to Joan, many commented that she responded with "such wisdom as if she had been a good cleric, to the point that they admired her responses and believed that divine inspiration guided her in view of her life and conduct."[29] One asked: "You have declared that the voice told you that the will of God is to deliver the people of France from the distress in which they find themselves. If He wanted to deliver them, it would not be necessary to have soldiers." Joan responded: "In the name of God, the soldiers will fight and God will give them victory." Her response satisfied him.[30]

Joan's answer carried theological weight. Why, after all, should God favor the French rather than the English? Theologians had debated this point and concluded that France, for all its failings, had been reduced to such a state of desolation that only divine aid could save the realm. The king could help neither himself nor his subjects.[31] They invoked scripture: for example, Paul in II Corinthians 12: 9: "My grace is sufficient for you, for power is made perfect in weakness. So I will boast all the more gladly of my weaknesses, so that the power of Christ may dwell in me." France had been brought so low that God would take mercy on it. Who was better suited to carry out such a divine plan than a humble peasant girl? Jacques Gélu wrote:

> The King of kings, the Lord of lords, has come to the aid of the king through a young girl . . . whom nothing had prepared for such a mission. . . . Dressed in men's clothing, she was presented to the king, saying that she was sent from heaven to lead his armies, put down rebels,

expel the enemies and regain possession of his lands, something marvelous in itself, since nothing had prepared her to lead such a mission. It should not, however, be astonishing, if one considers the power of God. If God so desires, He can conquer and vanquish by the means of a woman; doing so confounds human presumption, the pride of those who put their confidence in themselves is brought down, and He chooses the weak to confound the strong.[32]

Although France had committed many sins, Gélu pointed to the distant past when only France had been exempt from the horrors of heresy. "The sins of the king, the people, of all together, had been responsible for such a terrible scourge. But they were for our amendment and not the destruction of the royal house."[33] Some, however, expressed their discomfort that Joan wore men's clothing, since doing so was contrary to biblical injunctions against cross-dressing. But Gélu stressed that Joan *had to* wear men's clothing to carry out her mission since she was obliged to live among warriors and had to accommodate herself to their condition.[34]

Only the conclusions from the Poitiers inquiry have survived. In all likelihood, those around Charles ordered the records destroyed at some point between Joan's execution and the beginning of the nullification proceedings in order not "to preserve any damning evidence that would show that there had once been a time when the king had found 'no evil' in this relapsed heretic."[35] But the nullification testimony of a theologian who took part in the proceedings, the Dominican Guillaume Seguin,[36] offers a glimpse of Joan's demeanor. Confirming that Charles wanted to make sure that Joan would measure up to the challenges ahead, he indicated that Joan already displayed the sharp wit and self-confidence with which she would later confound her judges at Rouen. Asked about the language in which the voices spoke to her, Joan said " 'it was a better language than his, as he spoke the Limousin dialect.'[37] He then posed another question, as to whether she believed in God. She responded 'yes, better than he did.' " Seguin admonished Joan that God would not want them to believe in her without some sign and that they could not recommend that the king give her soldiers and put men in danger based solely on her assertions. She answered: "In the name of God, I have not come to Poitiers to give signs. Take me to Orléans and I will show you signs proving why I was sent."[38] She guaranteed results if the king gave her even a small number of troops.[39]

Then Joan asked if they had paper and ink – Joan had learned to sign her name, but otherwise could not read or write. She instructed Érault: "Write down what I say to you: You, Suffolk, Glasdale and La Pole, I summon you on the part of the King of Heaven, that you leave for England."[40] The letter, which would not be sent until later, demonstrated Joan's determination and her increasing knowledge of the political and military situation.

Finally the clergymen concluded that there seemed to be nothing bad in Joan or anything that was contrary to the Catholic faith. According to Seguin, the king and his subjects no longer had any hope: "It was completely the opposite, with all of them believing in defeat."[41] In such dire straits, they decided that Charles could send Joan forth to see if she could fulfill her promises. They concluded:

> Given the necessity facing the king and his realm, and considering the prayers of his poor people to God and all those who love peace and justice, he should not turn away the Maid, who claims she is sent by God. . . . Since her arrival, the king has had her life, birth, morals, and intentions investigated, presenting her to all sorts of people, including clergymen, pious people, soldiers, women, widows, and others. She has spoken privately and publicly with everyone. No evil has been found in her, only goodness, humility, virginity, devotion, honesty, and simplicity. . . . The king has asked for a sign, to which she says that she will produce it at Orléans and nowhere else, because that is what her voice commands of her. . . . The king must not prevent her from going there with her soldiers, but should have her taken there in good faith, placing hope in God.[42]

Hardly a ringing endorsement, this was rather a carefully phrased statement that left it up to Joan to prove her authenticity as a divine messenger by relieving the siege.[43] If she failed, it was not their fault.

Joan's religious and physical integrity having been established, she left for Chinon. Around March 27, the famous scene took place in which Joan was introduced to the whole court. It is entirely possible that the descriptions are accurate, even if the events were strategically planned, for only a few had seen Joan during the original interview in February. Many more first became acquainted with the strange girl wearing men's clothing in late March. The notary of La Rochelle describes what he had heard about the famous, almost comical, scene: "they showed her my Lord Charles of

Bourbon, pretending that he was the king, but she said right away that he was not the king, and that she would know him if she saw him, even though she had not seen him before. After that they had a squire come to pretend that he was the king."[44] Joan, who already knew Charles, played her part well, astounding the onlookers. Then:

> the count of Vendôme led Joan to the king and into the royal chamber. When he saw her, the king asked Joan her name. She responded: "Gentle dauphin, I am named Joan the Maid; and the King of Heaven commands you through me that you will be anointed and crowned in the city of Reims, and then you will be the lieutenant of the King of Heaven, the king of France." After the king asked several questions, Joan said again: "I say this to you, on the part of the Lord, that you are the true heir of France and son of the king and He sent me to you to lead you to Reims, where you will be crowned and anointed, if you are willing." Having heard that, the king declared to those in attendance that Joan had told him certain secrets that no one knew or could know except God. He also said he had great confidence in her.

Joan's performance at Poitiers had dispelled Charles' doubts, although he intended her to be a figurehead. But all the questions had tested Joan's patience. She confided to her confessor that she was not happy with so many interrogations, which kept her from accomplishing the task that had been given to her. It was time to go to work.[45]

Preparations now began in earnest, not only to equip Joan for her mission at Orléans, but to announce Joan to the world. Several theological treatises were produced about the Maid, including *De quadam puella* (About a Certain Maid),[46] a carefully argued discussion about Joan, gender, prophecy, and France. Although it was only circulated among theologians, it compared Joan to Amos, a shepherd-prophet who came from a simple background, and identified the French as the people of God.[47] Others linked Joan with Deborah, Judith, Esther, and the prophetic sybils of antiquity.

The court now began to spread new or elaborated prophecies that specifically fitted Joan. Some made her into "an armed feminine Mars, designed for the French soldiery as a challenge for them to match, and for the English (should the poem come into their hands) a formidable mythological figure."[48] The twelfth-century writer Geoffrey of Monmouth had composed two pseudo-historical works, *The History of the Kings of Britain* and *The Prophecies of Merlin*, which were well known in the late Middle Ages. The court now mined them for phrases that could be applied to Joan. One part of the Merlin prophecies was now translated and enhanced to say "out of this [oakwood] would come a maid who should work miracles,"[49] while another version maintained that "from the *bois chenu* will come a maiden who will cure our wounds. . . . Rivers of tears will flow from her eyes, and she will fill the island [England] with a horrible clamor."[50] One of Geoffrey's mysterious phrases claimed that "a virgin ascends the backs of the archers/and hides the flower of her virginity."[51] Based on this verse, a member of Charles's court now composed a new prophecy that appeared in Latin, French and German:

> The virgin, her maidenly limbs clothed in male attire, at God's prompting, hurries to raise up the fallen lily-bearer and king, [and] to destroy the abominable enemies, especially those who are now at Orléans, outside the city, and beset it with a siege. And if men have a mind to commit themselves to war, and to follow her arms, which the kindly [Maid] now prepares, she believes that the deceitful English will also succumb to death, when the French overthrow them with maidenly war; and then there will be an end to fighting.[52]

To be accepted by the army, and even more by the English, Joan had to become a figure of legend, one who had been predicted in precise terms. Did Joan know what was happening? Probably not, or at least not fully. Those promoting her at court wanted her to reach her own conclusions even as others began to refer to her as the Maid. Yet according to both Durand Laxart and Catherine Le Royer, with whom she stayed in Vaucouleurs, Joan had asked: "Have you not heard the prophecy that France, destroyed by a woman, would be saved by a maiden from the marches of Lorraine?"[53] Since neither had any connection with the court, it is possible that Joan had known at least some prophecies before she left home. Either way, she would come to believe they were true.

As her image was being constructed and reconstructed, what was the impatient girl from Domremy doing? Joan cared about the present and future rather than the past: her goal was to counter the immediate threat facing the realm. By the time she arrived at Chinon she had learned a good deal about the conflict between France and England, yet even now her knowledge of the history of the war was probably rudimentary. But she would learn much more in the coming weeks about the battles of the past ninety years that had brought her to the king's court.

Joan spent a good deal of time with the man who would become her favorite companion, Jean, duke of Alençon. Although he said he met her when she first arrived at Chinon after the journey from Domremy, it is much more likely that it was upon her return from Poitiers, based on his description and the secrecy of the first meeting with the king. While he was hunting quail, he learned of her arrival and rode to Chinon. When she met him, Joan declared: "You are very welcome here! Those of the royal blood of France will be stronger together, and that will be good." He was greatly impressed with her skills at holding and running with a lance, and gave her a horse on which to practice.[54] These meetings with and connections to some of the leading figures at Charles's court were essential to Joan's success.

Without making it public, Charles's military leaders were probably educating Joan in the art of war: if she was to be a convincing figurehead she needed to learn how to lead and fight. Although her horsemanship had undoubtedly improved en route to Chinon and she may have exhibited some skill with a lance to the duke of Lorraine, it was in everyone's best interest that Joan look and act like the armed virgin of the legends and prophecies. Secrecy was essential. What those around Charles VII almost certainly did *not* expect was that Joan would prove herself so adept in the role. Jousting, fencing, and riding were all pursuits of the court even in times of peace. Now they became a matter of utmost seriousness so that Joan could succeed. Many gaps in the calendar from March to early May provided opportunities for Joan's military training – and the efforts worked, as almost all chroniclers and witnesses acknowledged. Alençon, who would be at her side during many of the battles to come, recalled that in "war she was very talented, as much in wielding a sword as in assembling the army, organizing combat and preparing the artillery. All were full of admiration that she could comport herself so skillfully and prudently in military activities, as if she had been a war captain for twenty or thirty years, and above all in the preparation of artillery, in which she excelled."[55] A nobleman who met her at Orléans echoed Alençon's testimony, saying that "aside from deeds of war she was simple and innocent, but in the conduct and disposition of her troops, in deeds of war and in the organization of combat and the encouragement of troops, she comported herself as if she were the most adept captain in the world, trained for years in warfare."[56] The humanist Aeneas Sylvius Piccolomini, the future Pope Pius II, like so many others across Europe, would soon be enthralled with the stories that reached him from France. "They entrusted the matter of Orléans to the Maid. A woman was put in command of the war. Arms were brought, horses led up. The girl mounted the most spirited steed; then in her gleaming armour, brandishing her spear like Camilla in the tale she made him leap, run, and curvet. When the nobles saw this, none of them scorned to be commanded by a woman."[57] The plans devised at Charles's court in these months worked perfectly.

Although many of Joan's abilities only became apparent after the victories in the Loire Valley, it strains credibility that she would have *naturally* exhibited the talents of a great captain. The sources from Charles' court are silent about many of Joan's activities after her return from Poitiers; only a few nobles, such as Alençon, mention giving her a horse and watching her wield her lance. Yet Joan must have been trained and prepared for war. Even though most of those who met her believed she was divinely inspired, the skills she learned were concrete, the result of an intensive course of military education that was necessary for the battles to come. What *is* astonishing is how quickly she learned and her obvious aptitude for warfare. Along with the theological validation Charles had received from the churchmen at Poitiers, he and others at court began a campaign to publish treatises and prophecies that would pave the way for Joan's mission. While they almost certainly intended Joan to act the role of a figurehead, a virgin on horseback in shining armor at the front of troops, she had to be convincing. With her purity, theological correctness, and personality tested, she now had to be outfitted for her new role with the armor, standards, and weapons that she would need to fight the good fight, come what might.

CHAPTER 4

The Siege of Orléans

⚜

BEFORE LEAVING FOR ORLÉANS, Joan had to be equipped as a soldier. On April 5 1429, she left for Tours in the company of her squire Jean d'Aulon and page Louis de Coutes. While there she lodged with Éléonore de Paul, a member of Yolande of Aragon's inner circle of advisors and a former lady-in-waiting to Queen Marie. As a result, Joan had access to inside information about the court and politics. Although the king wanted to present her with a sword, she asked instead for a sword that she said would be found behind the altar in the church of St. Catherine of Fierbois. After the local clergy agreed that she should have the sword, an armorer from Tours went to retrieve it. "Asked how she knew that it was there, she answered that the sword was in the ground, rusted over, and upon it were five crosses; and she knew it was there through her voices." But she added that as soon as the sword was found the priests rubbed it and the rust came off effortlessly. The priests of St. Catherine gave her a scabbard, as did those of Tours. They made "two in all, one of crimson velvet . . . and the other of cloth of gold. She herself had another made of very strong leather."[1] Even in this matter, Joan showed herself a pragmatist.

How did Joan know of the sword's existence? Perhaps it was a miracle, as she claimed, but since Joan had spent two days hearing mass in the church at St. Catherine, it is also possible that she learned of its existence or even saw it there. After the battle of Agincourt, soldiers often left their armor and other offerings at St. Catherine as *ex votos*, gifts to saints in fulfillment of a vow.[2] A hospice for pilgrims en route to Saint James of Compostela had recently been founded at Fierbois, and the church had been endowed with numerous relics. The king was "marvelously astonished" at the discovery, asking Joan "if she had ever seen it before, to which she responded no."[3] Yet Joan's possession of the sword was far more important than how she acquired it, for "swords identify, authorize, and authenticate medieval warriors in fact and in legend" – whether Charlemagne's sword Joyeuse or King Arthur's Excalibur.[4] A special sword identified Joan as God's warrior. Although Joan later denied killing anyone, she used this and other swords frequently. She described one sword she had captured as "a good weapon for fighting, excellent for giving hard clouts and buffets."[5]

Joan also had to be fitted for a suit of armor and mail. Charles's treasurer in charge of war expenses authorized:

200 *livres tournois*[6] to Jean de Metz, for the Maid's expenditures
100 *l.t.* to the master armorer for a complete suit of armor for the Maid
125 *l.t.* to Jean de Metz and his companion to help them with armor and
    clothing while in the company of the Maid
25 *l.t.* to Haulves Poulnoir, painter living at Tours, to pay for fabric and
    paint a large and small standard for the Maid.[7]

Joan's full coat of "white" or plate armor included a cuirass that protected the torso, a neckplate, armor to cover her shoulders, forearms, hips, thighs, and calves, along with gauntlets and footwear. A typical suit of armor weighed 45 to 55 pounds. She also had different types of helmets, including a sallet, which fully covered the head with a crest and visor, a shallow cap known as a bassinet, and a capeline, a brimmed steel helmet normally used to protect the head when scaling ladders. The number and type of her helmets leave little doubt that Joan was more than a figurehead. Although one author suggests that Joan's armor could not have been much more than a collection of "ready to wear" pieces for this price, the duke of Orléans' armor for the battle of Agincourt in 1415 had cost less – 84 *livres tournois*.[8] Parts of Joan's armor must have been specially made to fit a young woman's contours.

Joan's standard also identified her as a soldier in the army of God. Her confessor described it: "On it was painted an image of Our Lord, sitting in Judgment in the heavens. There was also a painted angel, holding in its hands a fleur-de-lys, which blessed the image of the Savior."[9] This is more specific than Joan's description at trial, even though she said she "much preferred her standard to her sword:"[10] "She had a banner, with a field sown with lilies; the world was depicted on it, and two angels, one at each side; it was white, of white linen or boucassin,[11] and on it were written, *she thought*, these names, JHESUS MARIA; and it was fringed with silk ..." (emphasis mine). Joan's illiteracy may account for her vagueness in describing the words on her banner, as she might have seen the painted letters pictorially. Of her pennons she said they were made of white satin, and some were painted with a fleur-de-lys, the symbol of French kings. Her companions had pennons like hers so that they would be able to distinguish their men from others. When Joan was asked at trial whether she had sometimes said that the pennons made like hers brought better fortune, she answered "that she did sometimes say to her followers: 'Go boldly among the English,' and she herself would go."[12] The response was typical of her verbal sparring, yet she clearly understood the importance of such symbols of power. A typical large standard would have been atop a pole approximately 18 feet high, with the fabric about 11.5 feet long and 2.6 feet wide. Joan claimed she usually carried the standard herself but on numerous occasions it was borne in front of her by her squire or pages. The pennon was triangular, on a pole about 10 feet high with fabric about 4 to 5 feet long. Joan's pennon was painted with a scene of the Annunciation to the Virgin Mary.[13]

In Tours Joan met Jean Pasquerel, who joined her cousin Nicolas as her chaplain and confessor. He had first learned of her from Jean de Metz and others when he was in the pilgrimage town of Puy-Notre-Dame, about twenty-five miles from Chinon.[14] A lector in the Augustinian convent of Tours, Pasquerel came to greet her in her lodgings. She told him "that she was happy to see him, since she had already heard of him and wanted to confess to him. The next day, he heard her confession and sung mass in her presence."[15] How had she heard of him? Yolande of Aragon, who stood to gain from obtaining inside information about how Joan fared, probably orchestrated the introduction. Pasquerel would stay with Joan until she was captured at Compiègne. While at Tours she was also given a second page, named Raymond. Finally, preparations were complete. The king visited and saw Joan fully armed.[16]

On April 21, Joan left for Blois to join the soldiers who were rallying to the cause, Louis de Coutes recalling that once Joan was riding among them "the company had great confidence in her."[17] Between April 24 and 27, Joan sent the letter to the English that she had dictated at Poitiers:

+IHESUS MARIA+

King of England, and you, Duke of Bedford, who call yourself regent of France; you, William de la Pole, count of Suffolk; John, Lord Talbot; and you, Thomas, Lord of Scales, who call yourself lieutenant of Bedford, do right by the King of Heaven. Hand over to the Maid, who was sent here by God, the King of Heaven, the keys of the good cities that you have taken and ruined in France. . . . She is ready to make peace, if you set things right in France and pay for what you have taken. And among you, archers, gentlemen and others who are before the good city of Orléans, go in peace, by God. If you do not do so, wait for news of the Maid, who will come to you shortly, to your great harm. King of England, if you do not do as I have said, I am captain of war, and in whatever place I find your people in France, I will make them leave whether they want to or not. And if they do not obey, I will have them all killed. If they obey, I will show mercy. I am sent here by God, the King of Heaven, to kick you out of all of France, body for body,[18] against all those who want to carry out treason, deception, or harm in France. Do not be stubborn, because under no circumstances will you hold the realm of France from God, the King of Heaven, son of holy Mary. It will be held by King Charles, the rightful heir, because God, the King of Heaven, wants it so, and this was revealed by him to the Maid. He will enter Paris in a great company. If you do not want to believe the news sent by God from the Maid, in whatever place that we find you, we will make a greater uproar than has been heard in France in a thousand years, if you do not do what is right. Believe firmly that the King of Heaven will send more force to the Maid and to her good soldiers so that you will not know how to lead any attacks on her or her soldiers. Then you will see who has the better right. . . . Duke of Bedford, the Maid demands that you cause no more destruction. If you do what is right, then you can join her [in an effort] in which the French will accomplish the most wonderful feat that has ever been done in Christendom. Give your response in the city of Orléans if you want to make peace. But if you do not do so, you will very soon suffer great harm.[19]

By sending the first of several provocative letters, Joan threw down a gauntlet to the English. At trial she insisted that none of the lords dictated these letters, that it was she herself who did so, but she did acknowledge that she had permitted members of her party to see them before they were sent.[20] Although we do not know of the English response to this particular letter, they probably laughed or discarded it. But they kept the herald who delivered it.

The context of the letter has usually been ignored. Joan dictated it in Poitiers before the last week of March but it was taken to the English at Orléans a full month later. The content of the letter is basic, a demand for the English to get out of France soon or they would be driven out by God working through the Maid. Conversely, they could join Joan in a great undertaking. A crusade? Was this Joan's idea? The tone of the letter is strident and challenging, even emasculating. Her goals had been limited – to save France and, as her mission grew, to lift the siege of Orléans and to have the king crowned. Eventually it would come to encompass the release of the duke of Orléans from captivity in England and the recovery of Paris. Why was it not sent earlier? The delay in sending the letter coincides with the period when Joan was probably learning *how* to be the Maid. Had she failed the tests given to her at Chinon and Poitiers, would the letter have been sent? Would Joan have ever become more than a strangely dressed peasant girl? History would have forgotten her.

Joan complained repeatedly to Pasquerel and others that she was tired of so many interrogations and impatient to begin her quest to save France. If, as suggested, she was being trained militarily during the hiatus at Chinon, Tours, and Blois, that would not have weighed heavily on her, for it furthered her goals. But the endless questioning, the need for everything to be just so, greatly irritated Joan. She believed the voice of God was telling her to *act*, and everyone around her was preventing her from doing so. Yet if Charles could not have succeeded without Joan, it is equally true that the preparations made by the king and his mother-in-law Yolande's advisors – training, outfitting her as a knight, giving her background knowledge of politics and the military situation, and spreading prophecies – were essential to her successes in 1429. They had set the stage for a virgin warrior to confront the English. Could she do it? While it must have seemed unbelievable to many at the time, Joan had already done far more than anyone had expected. Despite family opposition and a potential marriage alliance, she had left her village and persisted until she finally persuaded the captain of Vaucouleurs to provide her with an escort to Chinon and a letter of introduction. She had stood up to men at court who called her crazy and wanted to send her away. She had endured physical examinations and had answered her erudite questioners at Poitiers with wit, intelligence, and sometimes sarcasm. On several occasions Joan had astounded those around her with her ability to handle a horse and a lance with great skill. Rebuking her men when they swore and reassuring them when they expressed fear, she began to demonstrate the qualities of a leader.

Provisioning began. Grain was loaded into wagons and carts and onto horses and steers. Pigs, cows, and sheep were herded together to follow the convoy. According to Pasquerel, during their three-day stay at Blois, Joan asked him to gather together the priests in the morning and evening. In the company of Joan, they sang chants and hymns to the Virgin. Joan ordered the soldiers to confess and put themselves in a state of grace with God. If they wanted to be part of her army, they had to give up the camp followers who accompanied them. Joan had no tolerance for "loose" women and would often threaten them and brandish her sword to chase them away. A squire who was only slightly older than Joan at the time recalled that "she never wanted to see women of evil life ride in the army with the troops and none of them had better find themselves near her. Whenever she encountered [camp followers] Joan ordered them to leave, unless the soldiers agreed to marry them."[21] While the men-at-arms may not have been pleased, the discipline Joan imposed focused them and kept order in an army that increased daily in size as interest in the Maid spread. Fighting for God and country revived the spirit of those who had seen little reason to fight for a weak and penniless dauphin.

Finally Joan was ready to set off for Orléans. Sieges had proven more efficient than pitched battles for both invading and occupying forces in capturing territory. Advances in the use of cannon had fundamentally changed the nature of warfare in the late fourteenth century. In the place of immobile and unwieldy large cannon, lighter, wheeled cannon, which could be packed with gunpowder, proved to be excellent offensive and defensive weapons. The besieging army could aim their artillery at the massive, thick walls, sometimes doing enough damage to allow combatants to enter a city; those inside could aim their cannon fire at the enemy in the field. By contrast, if an army lost a battle, entire swaths of land were left unprotected because of depleted forces. Successful sieges in Rouen and elsewhere had encouraged the English to pursue such a strategy.

Orléans, a city of about twenty thousand inhabitants on the Loire, appeared as the gateway to the south, which included English Gascony. How serious was the situation in the city that had been under siege since early October of 1428? Some suggest that the English siege was rather half-hearted. The people of Orléans remained provisioned, even as the English built *bastilles*, or bulwarks, surrounding the town. As early as

1417, fearing attack from the English, the Orléanais had begun to replace some of the gates and build boulevards, earthworks constructed around an elevated platform that was then covered with stones and held together by iron bars. On the north side of the river, walls about 7 feet wide and about 30 feet high protected the city, but on the Loire side the walls were lower since the river provided a natural defense.[22] Defensive towers were spaced out along the walls, and trenches had been dug outside the city. Between 1415 and 1427 the people of Orléans spent a significant part of their time repairing fortifications, digging ditches, assembling a formidable arsenal of defensive artillery weapons, and making other preparations. As the English expanded their control of areas to the north and east of Orléans, the city frequently paid spies, including women and clergymen, to collect information on the plans and movements of enemy armies.[23] They were as well prepared as a city could be.

Orléans should not have been besieged, since its duke, Charles, was imprisoned in England. Thomas Montague, earl of Salisbury, had earlier promised him that his city would not be attacked. In spite of this violation of the standards of knightly conduct, not surprising in view of Henry V's slaughter of prisoners and common soldiers after the French defeat at Agincourt, the siege of Orléans began in October 1428.[24] From their base in Janville, the English under Salisbury marched toward the city, hoping that if Orléans fell, Charles' hold on central France would be seriously jeopardized. They captured Meung-sur-Loire and Beaugency in late September. In early October the earl of Suffolk took the nearby towns of Jargeau and Châteauneuf, leaving Orléans and its inhabitants alone to defend themselves. The shelling of the city began about ten days later when Suffolk was joined by Salisbury. Enguerrand de Monstrelet describes the reception the people of Orléans had prepared for their attackers:

> The inhabitants of Orléans had destroyed and demolished good buildings in all their suburbs, including twelve churches and four mendicant houses. Besides the churches, many luxurious houses owned by merchants and lawyers were razed. They carried out their destruction to such an extent that it was possible to see all the suburbs and surrounding area unhindered and to discharge cannon and other war engines as if in the field. . . . Those within defended themselves vigorously with all their might, making several sorties, firing cannon, culverins [hand held

guns], and other artillery that killed and injured some of the English. Nevertheless, the English pushed back so valiantly and promptly that they were able to approach the ramparts several times, amazing the people of Orléans with their audacity and courage.[25]

During the fight the women of Orléans provided assistance, carrying to the defenders necessary items such as water, oil, boiling fat, lime, ashes, and *chaussetrappes*, spiked iron objects that were strewn on the ground for the purpose of causing lameness or other injuries.[26] Women were not merely support personnel but also engaged more actively, sometimes even pushing Englishmen from the walls.[27] The Orléanais also had a not-so-secret weapon, Jean de Lorraine, considered the master of his craft because he was so accurate and deadly when he aimed his culverin at the enemy. He also used trickery to confuse and demoralize the besieging soldiers. On one occasion he killed and wounded large numbers of Englishmen. "To mock them, he fell to the ground, pretending to be dead or wounded. He had himself taken into the city. But he returned immediately to the fight, and did so much [damage] that the English knew he was alive, to their great detriment."[28] Such ruses were a regular part of medieval warfare.

Finally, on October 23, the French abandoned the fortress of Les Tourelles at the end of the bridge and the ruins of the convent of the Augustins to its south. As they retreated into the city, they purposely broke part of the bridge to prevent the English from crossing to attack Orléans. In the meantime, Salisbury stationed a large number of his men in Les Tourelles. He lodged in the ruins of the suburbs while the English dug covered trenches in the ground for shelter.[29] Fortunately for the city's defenders, Salisbury, who was considered one of England's greatest military leaders, met with a bizarre and untimely death. Three days after his arrival outside Orléans he ascended to the third floor of Les Tourelles. As he stood in front of a window looking toward the city, trying to determine how best to take it, "a cannon salvo cut through the air and struck the window. . . . [He] drew back but was grievously wounded by the shards from the glass, and he had a large part of his face torn off. A gentlemen beside him fell to the floor, stiff in death. This caused great sadness. . . . [for] they believed him to be the most capable leader, with the greatest expertise and good fortune of all the princes and captains of the realm of England.[30]

With Salisbury's death eight days later, William de la Pole, count of Suffolk, assumed the English command, supported by Lords Scales, Talbot, and Glasdale. At any one time during the siege they had between 3,000 and 4,000 men attempting to force the city into submission. The English started building boulevards or bastilles in front of the main gates to the city, clockwise from the southeast side of the city to the north, manned by archers and gunners. Most were concentrated in the northwest suburbs, the areas most vulnerable to attack or provisioning from Charles's territories downstream. They also built fortifications on islands in the Loire to obstruct river traffic. The main English weakness lay to the northeast, a forested area that was England's route to and from their headquarters at Janville.

By October 25, the Bastard of Orléans, illegitimate half-brother of the captive duke, had brought reinforcements to the city in the areas that were least protected, beginning what would be a six-month standoff. Regular skirmishes and small-scale engagements, as well as short breaks in the fighting, were common but the English had settled in for a long siege and were not always vigilant. The inhabitants still received food and supplies from the king and the Bastard. For example, on January 3, "954 big, fat pigs and 400 sheep were brought through the port of Saint-Loup on the southern shore of the river before being herded in through the Burgundy gate at the east end of the city."[31] The city chronicles and treasury records regularly record such entries, but they also mention that on that day, the "people were overjoyed because they were in need."[32]

Although the city was surrounded on three of four sides, the people were able to survive without great difficulty until the disastrous Battle of the Herrings on February 12, 1429. Near the town of Rouvray, French forces, including the Bastard and his Scottish allies, attacked an English supply convoy led by Sir John Fastolf that was bringing herrings and other goods to the English for Lent. Although the allied French and Scottish forces of about 3,500 to 4,000 outnumbered the English by almost two to one, miscommunication between La Hire and the count of Clermont led to disaster. The former wanted to attack right away, but Clermont, who had brought a significant number of troops from Blois to prepare for the attack, was hesitant and wanted to wait for a greater numerical advantage. Even though La Hire had a strategic advantage when he first saw the English approach in single file, Clermont asked him to delay. By doing so they gave the English time to create a defensive fortification using their carts. The constable of Scotland, John Stewart of Darnley, grew impatient and most of the Scottish forces, who were more accustomed to fighting on foot, dismounted. They were overwhelmed before they could retreat; the Scottish contingent was virtually wiped out by the time Clermont finally engaged in battle. During the fight the Bastard was wounded in the foot by an arrow. With difficulty two of his archers pulled him from the field, helping him back onto his horse and thus saving his life.[33]

The defeat cost the French and Scots 400 dead. More importantly, it shattered morale. On February 18 the count of Clermont abandoned Orléans and retreated with all of his 2,000 men, taking himself and his troops out of the campaign. Other leaders, including La Hire, fell back to Chinon. At court Charles VII was said to be so demoralized seeing things go from bad to worse that he considered the advice of some members of his council that he withdraw to southeastern France or even abandon France altogether.[34] The account probably exaggerates Charles's sense of defeat, although the Bastard argued against further sorties. In all likelihood, however, it was the defeat at the Battle of the Herrings – which got its name from the herrings strewn over the field of battle, to the delight of the people of Rouvray – that made Joan's mission possible.

For the Orléanais, the battle was a major setback. With their hopes of relief diminished and the power of the English increasing daily, the leaders of the city turned to Philip the Good of Burgundy, asking him to put Orléans under his protection.[35] Philip broached the subject with John, duke of Bedford, regent of France, who met with some of his leading advisers in Paris. They dismissed the idea, giving as the reason their heavy expenditures and loss of troops during the siege. They added bluntly that considering Orléans was almost theirs, it was unreasonable to expect them to hand over "one of the most advantageous cities in France for he who held it."[36] Philip was not happy. He sent ambassadors to tell all his soldiers present at the siege to depart without doing any harm to the people of the city.[37] About 1,500 troops departed for Flanders, creating serious tension between England and Burgundy. Ironically, English hubris and the belief that the city would soon fall gave the Orléanais the chance to fight another day.

Moreover, despite the disaster of the Battle of the Herrings, food and military supplies continued to flow into Orléans through the late winter and spring. Supply wagons brought in herrings, cheese, and butter during

Lent, and after Easter more pigs and cows were sent, especially from the Bastard's castle of Châteaudun. The people of the city made regular sallies outside the gates, sometimes surprising the English. On April 3 they managed to intercept a convoy carrying nine tuns[38] of wine and livestock destined for the English but "instead the men and women of Orléans drank the wine and ate the pork and venison."[39] In the meantime, news of a Maid, a girl dressed in men's clothing, her hair cut around in a bowl shape, began to reach Orléans.

Joan and her company left Blois on April 26. She was anxious for the encounter. Her page, Louis de Coutes, remembered that Joan was bruised by the time she arrived in Orléans because the night before leaving Blois she had slept fully armed.[40] Was she concerned that they might leave without her? Joan, holding aloft her banner painted with a scene of the Crucifixion, brought together all the priests in the company to lead a procession of men-at-arms. They rode and marched through the forested region known as the Sologne singing *Veni creator spiritus* (Come Holy Spirit) and other hymns. The first night they camped in the fields. On the third day they approached Orléans, getting so close that both sides could see each other.[41] The staging of Joan's journey is important, for it turned the march from Blois into a virtual religious procession. Joan assumed a spiritual and martial role that many "soldiers of Christ" had adopted before her, taking as a cue Isaiah 59:17–18:

> He put on righteousness like a breastplate,
> and a helmet of salvation on his head;
> he put on garments of vengeance for clothing,
> and wrapped himself in fury as in a mantle.
> According to their deeds, so will he repay;
> wrath to his adversaries, requital to his enemies.[42]

Joan, and quite possibly the king and his mother-in-law Yolande, were determined to match the verbal threats conveyed in her letter to the English with corresponding visual imagery.

Entry into the city should have been difficult because the English held the towns of Beaugency and Meung between Blois and Orléans, as well as the fortifications around the city. The French forces, led by Joan, La Hire, Orléans' governor, Raoul de Gaucourt, and others, passed through the Sologne to the south, crossing the Loire near Chécy. They caught the

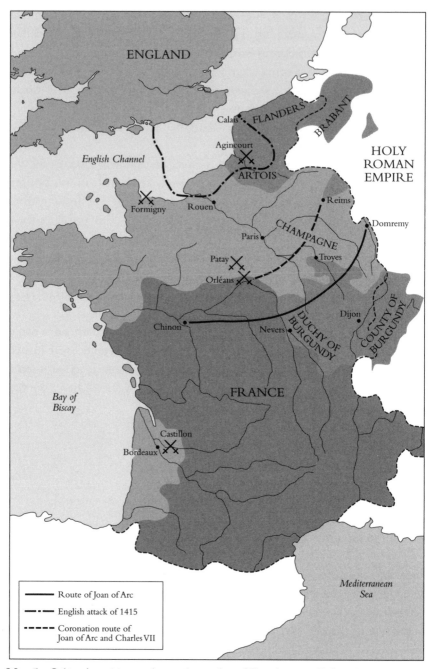

Map 5   Orléans's position at the northern edge of French-controlled territory.

English offguard at their weakest point to the northeast. It was at Chécy that Joan first met the Bastard, son of the assassinated Louis of Orléans, half brother of the captive duke Charles, and future count of Dunois.[43] He informed Joan that the royal troops were insufficient to get their men and provisions into the city and pointed out to her that the wind was adverse. Joan was indignant, fearing that they would draw back and leave the siege.[44] She asked: "Are you the Bastard of Orléans?" He responded: "Yes, I am him, and I rejoice at your arrival." She said: "Are you the one who gave the advice to bring me here, on this side of the river, and not to go directly where Talbot and the English are?" The Bastard admitted that he, and others even wiser, believed this was the best course of action. Joan disagreed:

> In the name of God, the counsels of God, my Lord, are more certain and wise than yours. You thought to mislead me, but you are the one who has been misled more, because I bring you the best help that could ever be given to a soldier or a city, and that is the help of the King of Heaven. It does not, however, come from me. It comes from God who, at the request of Saint Louis and Saint Charlemagne, felt pity for the city of Orléans, and could no longer suffer that enemies held the lord of Orléans [Charles in captivity] and his city.

Joan's invocation of two French kings, rather than "her saints" is significant. Despite the religious framework, her goal from the beginning was to save France from its English and Burgundian occupiers. Getting provisions from Blois to Orléans was no easy task, as the wind and current, which flows away from Blois, were against this happening. Under the conditions described by the Bastard, it would have been very difficult to get rafts and barges across the river. Yet he was astounded when "the wind that was contrary for leading the boats filled the sails."

On April 29 a few troops crossed on small barges and passed the bastille of Saint-Loup, at which point the Bastard pressed Joan to enter the city, since the people were asking for her. She refused, saying she did not want to wait any longer but was going to summon the English to lift the siege or make an assault on them. Nor did she want it to appear that she was abandoning her soldiers. Eventually, Joan acquiesced. The captains agreed to have their soldiers return to Blois, the closest passage where large numbers of men could cross the Loire and head back toward

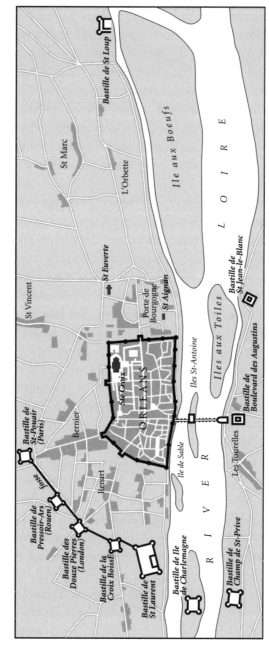

Map 6   The city of Orléans at the time of the siege. The shaded area is the walled city. The fortified positions surrounding the city mark the English boulevards and bastilles.

Orléans. Then Joan left with the Bastard and La Hire and entered the city through the Burgundy Gate.[45]

The Bastard's words and actions are significant. He had been prepared for a girl who would sit on a horse and follow his orders. Instead she spoke out against his strategy, claiming that hers was better because it was God's plan. The king's chronicler claimed that once she had arrived in Orléans, "she came to a contrary conclusion on everything, against all the opinions of the military leaders who were present. But they always took it well."[46] But as importantly, Joan had begun to win the personal loyalty of her men, whom the Bastard had to convince to accept his decision that the best route for success was to allow Joan to enter the city and to rally the townspeople while they returned to Blois to get supplies. While he and other experienced military leaders were used to making the decisions, they were now forced to reckon with Joan, who was determined to take part in tactical and strategic planning.

Why had they not been stopped? It is possible that the dense forest of the Sologne and trees on the islands of the Loire may have partially blocked view of their progress. The English had begun building another boulevard at Saint-Loup to the northeast, but it was not yet finished in the last days of April as Joan and the French troops approached. Perhaps even more importantly, the people of Orléans played a significant role in facilitating Joan's safe entry into their city. Learning that Joan, growing numbers of French troops,[47] and weaponry were heading for the city by way of the Sologne reinvigorated them. As Joan regularly said, "God helps those who help themselves." The soldiers and people of Orléans did everything in their power to aid the French troops, distracting English soldiers who had often become complacent:

> The same day there was a big skirmish because the French wanted to set a time and place for the goods to be brought into the city. To distract the English, the Orléanais sallied forth in great numbers and fought in front of the Boulevard of Saint-Loup. In the process, many were killed, wounded and taken prisoner on both sides and the French managed to capture one of the English standards, which they took into the city.[48]

This mini-battle provided the cover needed for Joan to advance.

The Bastard's first concern was for Joan's safe entry so they decided to wait until nightfall to avoid the expected pandemonium in the city.[49] Joan rode unchallenged into Orléans through the Burgundy Gate with about 200 soldiers. According to her squire, "the Maid and her men entered from the east of the enemies into the city of Orléans and did so in spite of the great power and number of enemy soldiers."[50] Bedford was paying about 3,800 troops at the time, but the number at Orléans was considerably lower since many were stationed at other positions along the Loire.

For the people of Orléans and the soldiers, Joan promised deliverance. The scene that followed must have astonished the seventeen-year-old girl, even in view of all that she had undergone up to this point. She rode through the streets with her standard carried before her and the Bastard at her side, followed by nobles, squires, captains, and ordinary soldiers. Men and women ran from their houses "carrying a great number of torches, and showing such joy that it was if they had seen God descend among them. . . . There was such a great press to touch her and her horse, that one of those carrying a torch approached so close that her pennon caught fire. She struck her horse with her spurs, turning it so ably that the fire was extinguished."[51] Finally she arrived at the house of Jacques Boucher, where she stayed throughout the siege.

The Bastard again encountered Joan's impatience and irritation at the slow pace that followed. He testified that she dictated another letter to the English in her native tongue, in very simple terms, the substance of which was that they must lift the siege and leave for England. If they did not, she would make a great assault and they would be forced to leave.[52] On Saturday evening, Joan sent two heralds to the English, demanding that they return the messenger who had delivered her first letter from Blois. The Bastard added his warning that if they failed to do so, all the English prisoners in Orléans would be killed. The heralds were returned but with a message from the English for Joan "that they would burn her for she was nothing but a whore and that she should return to tending cows." Enraged, she went out to the Boulevard of the Belle Croix on the bridge, from which she shouted at the English leaders in Les Tourelles. They taunted her, again calling her a cowherd, "yelling even louder that they would have burned as soon as they got hold of her."[53]

Members of Joan's entourage remembered some of the English insults. "They asked her why they should turn themselves over to a woman, and called her companions miscreant pimps."[54] Pasquerel recalled that after they received her letter, the English shouted: "Here is news of the whore of the Armagnacs!"[55] What worse epithet for a girl who despised camp followers and prostitutes? Joan's impatience and even belligerence became increasingly apparent as she waited for the return of the soldiers. The account also shows that Joan and the Bastard were working together, in spite of the tensions apparent at their initial meeting.

To the people of Orléans Joan was the prophesied Maid. While she was anxious to fight, she realized the psychological impact of her presence and had to give the citizens what they wanted. On Sunday, May 1, Joan rode throughout the city accompanied by several knights and squires after the people almost broke down the door of her lodging.

> So many great people of the city wanted to see her that as she rode through the streets, everyone pressed so close to her that it was very hard to pass through. It seemed to everyone to be such a great marvel to see her able to hold herself so nobly on a horse. In truth, she maintained herself so well in all respects that it seemed as if she had learned how to be a soldier, fighting wars since her childhood.[56]

One bourgeois of the city said that "she was received with so much joy and cheering by all the men and women that it was as if she were an angel of God. Joan exhorted them to pray to God."[57]

Although fiercely determined to boot the English out of Orléans and all of France, Joan showed another side of herself not only to the people of the city but also to her soldiers. Her charisma and belief in her mission were by now so great that those who had almost given up hope began to believe that they could win. She spoke of war like the other captains, and when there was a cry to arms or shout of alarm, "she rushed either on foot or on horseback . . . giving heart and boldness to all the men of the company, urging them to keep a good lookout."[58] On occasion she showed her lighter side. The Bastard recalled that Joan made jokes about feats of arms in order to urge on her soldiers, or talked about many things to do with war that probably never happened.[59] Gaucourt and other captains said that she was very knowledgeable in matters of arms, and everyone admired her skill.[60] Ordinary people and soldiers alike were impressed by her honest manner, wisdom, and piety. Joan reproached all who swore or who made hollow promises, no matter their status or position. One day a great lord, walking down the street, "swore villainously and denied God. Joan grew very upset, immediately going up to him and grabbing him by the scruff of the neck, she said: 'Ah! Master! You dare to deny Our Lord and Master! In the name of God, you will renounce what you've said before I leave here.' "[61] Some informally confessed their misdeeds to her apparently hoping for absolution, which they did not receive. A Scotsman enraged Joan when he told her he had stolen some veal, so much so that she said she wanted to hit him.[62]

On Monday, May 2, Joan mounted her horse and went to the fields to survey the English strongholds, attracting crowds wherever she went. At midweek, reinforcements arrived from Blois. On May 4, hoping to distract the English from the troops and supplies he was funneling into the city, the Bastard began an attack on the boulevard of Saint-Loup. Although there are some discrepancies in the accounts of her squire and her page, they indicate that Joan grew angry that she had not been informed. Her page recalled that after Joan had gone to her room, he thought she had fallen asleep. But she came down and said to him: "Wretched boy, you did not tell me that the blood of France has been spilled!" While she ordered him to prepare her horse, the mistress of the house armed her. Seizing her standard, Joan rushed to the Burgundy Gate to observe the skirmish at the bastille of Saint-Loup, which was taken by the French almost immediately after her arrival. As she rode up, she witnessed the horrors of war. Aulon said that the first time she saw a wounded Frenchman, Joan was so horrified that she never again saw the blood of the French spilled without her hair standing on end.[63] She also displayed compassion for the casualties on the English side. On one occasion a Frenchmen who was leading English prisoners away struck one of them on the head so hard that it left him almost dead. When Joan saw this, she dismounted and held the Englishman's head, consoling him as best she could.[64] She also would not allow any harm to come to priests and monks who had been captured. Yet at the same time, Joan's later denial that she ever shed blood has to be considered within the context of the fighting. Even if she did not personally kill anyone, Joan's strategic decisions and actions resulted in numerous casualties on both sides. In this attack alone, 140 English were killed and many others taken prisoner. All the assaults leading up to the raising of the siege were hard and violently fought, and Joan continually pushed for aggressive action. But that evening when Joan dined in her lodgings she was described as very restrained.[65]

In 1429 the Feast of the Ascension, the occasion when Christ was believed to have ascended to heaven, fell on May 5. Joan and her company, happy at the previous day's victory, decided to attack the boulevard of

Saint-Jean-le-Blanc, on the south side of the river. They crossed on barges to the Île-aux-Toiles in the center of the Loire and from there to the south shore. Finding that the English had already deserted Saint-Jean, they rode toward the boulevard that had been built around the ruins of the Augustinian convent. Since they did not have enough troops with them to take the Augustins, they left a small force behind and crossed back to the city. Much has been made of the fact that Joan supposedly did not fight on May 5 because of the holiness of the day, but only Pasquerel said that she refused to fight and ordered others not to do so.[66] However, at trial, Joan never said that she would not have fought that day, and it is clear that she and her men had prepared for skirmishes, if not an outright assault, against the English. On May 6 Joan took the initiative, against the advice of the French leaders, ordering the Burgundy Gate and a small door situated near the Great Tower to be opened so that the soldiers could go on the attack.[67] Joan encountered opposition from Gaucourt, the governor, who had been sent to guard the gates and prevent sorties. But Joan pressed forward, enlisting the support of soldiers and townsmen. She called Gaucourt "a bad man, adding: 'Whether you want it or not, the soldiers will come, and they will win as they have won elsewhere.' The soldiers poured through the gate against the will of Gaucourt . . . who believed he was in great danger."[68] The governor exhibited the same caution that had hindered French efforts in the past, most recently at the Battle of the Herrings. By forcing the issue, Joan assumed the offensive and caught the English offguard.

Joan, La Hire, and their men headed for the boulevard of the Augustins, where they clashed immediately with the English. One powerful Englishman stood in the trench, trying to prevent anyone from passing. But he was pointed out to the great gunner Master Jean who aimed his culverin and shot him dead. The French rushed to the bastille and "with ferocity and swiftness" attacked from all sides and in a short time French troops had taken the boulevard. Many English soldiers were killed, while the greater part of them retreated to Les Tourelles.[69] At some point Joan suffered her first wound of the siege, stepping on one of the spiky traps that the English had scattered on the ground.

The taking of the Augustins, immediately to the south of Les Tourelles, was important but the French leaders wanted to give their troops time to rest and regroup. They felt they had too few soldiers compared to the English, and preferred to wait for reinforcements from the king before attacking the fortress. Joan would have none of it. She told her confessor: "Get up early in the morning, earlier than today and stay close to me, for tomorrow I have much to do, things much more important than I have ever done before. Tomorrow the blood will flow above my breast."[70] Her confessor, some of her comrades, and even some people of Orléans recalled her predicting the significance of the day and the wound she would receive. When Joan was questioned at trial, she said that earlier she had told the king that she would be wounded in the course of fighting, but that she would not give up the work she had to do on that account. The likelihood of injury was always present in battle, but was it more than that? Could Joan and her men have planned the kind of ruse that was common and even recommended in military manuals of the time?

Joan's decisiveness and perseverance paved the way for victory at Les Tourelles the next day. On May 7, Joan, the captains, and their men attacked in a battle that would last from sunrise to sunset. Late in the day, when everyone on the French side was worn out, they were ready to call for a retreat. Joan's squire had been holding her standard but out of fatigue handed it to a man he called the "Basque," believing him to be a courageous fighter. As he and the Basque headed toward the ditch they became separated. When Joan saw her standard in the hands of someone other than her squire she thought it was lost. She rode forward, crying out "Ha! My standard! My standard!" and grabbed it by the end. The French troops mistakenly thought she was signaling for them to advance. They rallied and in a short space of time took Les Tourelles. The victorious French entered the city by the bridge. Her squire added simply that once they were inside Orléans he dressed the arrow wound Joan had received during the assault.[71]

The wound has frequently been portrayed as a turning point, the time when all around her came to believe Joan truly was God's messenger – or a witch – depending on which side they were on. So many conflicting accounts make it difficult to know what really happened. The city's chronicler said that "among those wounded that day was the Maid, who had been struck by an arrow between the shoulder and the throat *as it passed by her.*"[72] Her confessor said that after she had been struck some of the soldiers wanted to use charms or incantations, but she refused, declaring, "I would prefer to die rather than do something I know to be a sin." But she did allow them to apply olive oil and lard.[73] The Bastard's version strains credulity: he claimed that Joan was wounded by an arrow that "penetrated her skin between the neck and the shoulder by a half foot," adding that she did not want any remedy for her wound. He said she asked him to wait a bit and not call off the assault while she retreated to a vineyard to pray for about fifteen minutes. When she returned, "she immediately took her standard and placed it on the bank of the ditch. At that instant when she appeared, the English trembled and took fright and the soldiers of the king felt their courage rekindled and began to go forward, delivering an assault on the boulevard without encountering any resistance."[74]

Joan and her military colleagues once again had help from the people of the city. Those inside Orléans went on the offensive, some sallying out of the city by the bridge. And because several arches were broken, they brought a carpenter along and carried ladders and other materials they needed and made planks. Since these were not long enough to connect the two ends of the broken bridge, they joined a piece of wood to one of the largest troughs. As soon as they had begun, the English lost the will to resist and tried to get back into Les Tourelles. Joan yelled "Glasdale! Glasdale! Give yourself up to the King of Heaven. You have called me a whore, but I have great pity on your soul and those of your men."[75] But as they fled, some four to five hundred combatants were killed or drowned, including Glasdale, who fell into the river when the bridge gave way.[76] After taking Les Tourelles, the Bastard, Joan, and their men returned to the city, where they were received with rejoicing. Joan was taken to her lodgings so that her wound could be tended and after that "she ate four or five slices of toast along with wine mixed with water."[77]

Although her impatience to attack made no sense to the seasoned French commanders, the speed with which the boulevard and bastille were taken show the force of Joan's leadership along with the importance of morale and chance happenings. Even ruses could change the course of events. The Bastard's account reads like a morality play. If the arrow had penetrated 6 inches between the plates of her armor, Joan's wound would have been fatal. There is no way she could have continued on horseback, discussed strategy, or made a conscious decision to retire to the vineyard to pray, let alone raise her standard. The usual explanation is divine intervention. At her trial, Joan said only that she had been wounded in the neck by a crossbolt when she first planted her standard against the fortress, but that she had fully recovered within two weeks.[78]

All the accounts mention Joan's arrow wound, although the versions vary considerably, with most of them not making a great deal of it. Aimed from above, the arrow glanced off the area between her shoulder and neck, which was not covered by armor. It was a flesh wound, not a puncture from an arrow, but such wounds often bleed profusely. Surrounded at all times by her men, is it so unlikely that some around her would make it out to be more serious than it was? War tricks and mind games were common in late medieval warfare. Master Jean had played dead for that very purpose and lived to kill many more Englishmen. Would Joan have objected to having it appear that her wound was more serious than it actually was if it helped her attain her goals? Is it far-fetched to think that she recognized the strategic value that could be gained by making the English think she had been fatally wounded and the French that she had miraculously recovered? Joan was well enough to eat and drink that night. And the goal had been achieved. The English were terrified of her, and in the ensuing fight her worst enemy, Glasdale, was killed along with so many of his countrymen.

Raising the siege was not in itself the decisive military engagement to turn the tide in the Hundred Years War, but for morale, recruitment, and a change in French outlook it was a critical new beginning. Although at this stage Joan may not have done much of the actual fighting, she was instrumental in raising the siege. Being the first to plant the ladder to scale the walls, if true, had been a symbolic gesture, but in future engagements Joan would play an ever more active role.

Joan's strategic leadership was pivotal. Almost every day the war council tried to delay action, and it was only Joan's perseverance and insistence to "go boldly" that led to the defeat of the English. She inspired the townspeople and the ordinary soldiers and participated in the front lines of the assault. When "wiser" counsel was offered she rejected it. Unlike most of the French commanders, Joan exhibited an "overwhelming sense of urgency. . . . She especially honored the principles of maintenance of morale, objective, offensive, speed, maneuver, mass, and economy of force. . . . Every single battle Joan fought was an attack of some kind."[79] While Joan's policy of direct engagement was costly in terms of men and materiel, it was more effective than any other method in stalling the English momentum.[80] Along with the battles to come, it began to demoralize and dishearten the enemy. John, duke of Bedford, thinking back on the situation at Orléans in June 1434, told King Henry that:

> All things there [in France] prospered for you till the time of the siege of Orléans taken in hand by God knows what advice. At the which time after

the misadventure that befell the person of my cousin of Salisbury . . . who fell by the hand of God, as it seemed a great stroke came upon your people, assembled there in great numbers, caused in large part, as I believe because of lack of confidence and doubt that they had of a disciple and limb of the fiend, called the Maid, who used false enchantments and sorcery, by which stroke and discomfiture lessened in great part the number of your people there, and also withdrew the courage of the remnant in marvelous wise.[81]

Indeed, after the English were chased from Orléans, the duke of Bedford faced increasing problems with desertions and recruiting, as well as raising more money from England for his French enterprise. Bedford recognized the significance of Orléans and blamed it on Joan the Maid.

CHAPTER 5

"She Would Only Last a Year"[1]

❧

T HE NIGHT LES TOURELLES was taken, the people of Orléans celebrated joyously, devoutly chanting *Te Deum laudamus* (We Praise You,
God), ringing all the bells in the city, and humbly thanking their Lord and
the saints for the glorious victory.[2] The next day several of the French
commanders wanted to continue the fight. But Joan's leadership was now
tacitly acknowledged. The Bastard recalled that early the next morning, the
English left their tents and ranged themselves in battle order, prepared for
combat. But when Joan got out of bed, she dressed in chain mail and gazed
out at the field. She made the decision that no one would attack them: "Let
the English leave, don't kill them. They'll go. Their retreat is enough for
me." When they did so, the siege was lifted.[3] The English abandoned all
their other bastilles, setting fire to some of them. When they saw the
French were not going to attack, they retreated in two groups: Lords Talbot
and Scales left to take command of the forces at Meung-sur-Loire, while
Suffolk and his men headed to Jargeau. Some soldiers and Orléanais made
sallies against the departing English troops, forcing them to leave behind
their great bombards, cannon, arrows, arbalests, and other artillery, but the
majority of the English made their way, "greatly confused and discom-
fited"[4] but without mishap, to Meung. At the same time, Sir John Fastolf
began to gather reinforcements in Paris so that his army could meet up
with Talbot and Scales and fortify those sites in June.

The Orléanais continued to celebrate with jousts and processions to all
the churches in the city, thanking God and their patron saints Aignan and
Euverte for their deliverance. They also praised their valiant defenders,
especially Joan the Maid who, from the night she had arrived in the city,

had offered consolation and told them God would aid them.[5] As Joan was preparing to leave the city the next day, men and women came to thank her and offer gifts. But the citizens who testified in 1456 said that Joan never attributed to herself any of the glory for the victory and refused as much as possible the honors people tried to shower upon her.[6]

Once the siege was lifted, Joan, the Bastard, and the other captains rested for a few days at Blois before heading to the king's castle at Loches on May 13. There townspeople tried to grab the legs of Joan's horse and embrace her hands and feet. She was warned that such behavior was idolatry, to which she responded: "In truth, I do not know how to protect myself from such things if God will not protect me."[7] At her trial Joan said that many people came up to her and tried to kiss her hands, but she discouraged them as much as she could. However, she added that "poor folk gladly came to her, for she did them no unkindness, but helped them as much as she could."[8]

When Joan and the Bastard arrived at the king's chamber, she went down on her knees and begged Charles to help them maintain the momentum by providing more soldiers so that they could retake Jargeau, Meung, and Beaugency. Her mission was advancing by the day. She originally said her voices told her simply to go to France. After the siege of Orléans was raised so quickly, Joan was anxious to continue the fight. Her honor had been repeatedly challenged as the English soldiers called her a whore and a cowherd while her soldiers and the people of Orléans came to believe she was the prophesied Maid. If she had not done so earlier, Joan now began to see herself as France's savior.

It would be almost a month before the next stage of the Loire campaign began. What was happening in these weeks? Despite their success in lifting the siege the French army had suffered significant loss of life, and there may have been only 2,000 soldiers left in the army. Moreover, Fastolf had not yet moved from Paris so there was no urgency.[9] But there was another reason to wait. The surprising leadership Joan had displayed at Orléans and the military victory made her supporters at court more determined than ever to give her the skills she needed to be a soldier. While her insistence on attack had helped change the course of the siege, she had spent most of her time on horseback urging her men on. What skills she had needed to be honed to make her even more frightening to the English, who had reportedly trembled when they saw her back on her horse after the arrow wound.[10]

Charles now appointed the duke of Alençon, relieved of the requirement not to fight at Orléans imposed upon him as part of his earlier ransom, as leader of the French army.[11] From May 13 to 23, Joan stayed with the duke, his wife, and his mother at Saint-Florent-lès-Saumur, near the castle where her greatest advocate, Yolande of Aragon, often resided. Alençon, married to the daughter of duke Charles of Orléans, recalled that his wife, who had had to pawn her jewels to pay the enormous ransom after he was captured at the battle of Verneuil in 1424, worried about what might happen to him. When he left to rejoin the army she told Joan that she feared greatly for her husband, since he had already been a prisoner and great sums of money had been spent to gain his release, and that she would rather he remain at home. Joan responded: "Lady, have no fear! I will return him safely to you in the same state he is now or even better."[12]

While Charles, Yolande, and the king's counselors discussed her future role, Joan was undoubtedly practicing her skills. When she traveled to Selles-en-Berry she made the acquaintance of Gui and André de Laval, grandsons of the widow of the great French war hero of the late fourteenth century, Bertrand du Guesclin. They wrote to their mother and grandmother about their meeting with Joan, who was fully armed except for her head and carried her lance in her hand. Why was she armed if not as part of her continuing training? After they followed her to her lodgings she offered them hospitality and wine, telling them she would soon have them drinking in Paris. Later they saw her mount a great black courser that had been thrashing around only moments earlier. She turned it toward the door of a nearby church and said: " 'You, priests and churchmen, make a procession and say prayers to God.' Then she went back to the road, saying 'Go forth!' with her standard deployed and carried by her page." She informed the Laval brothers that she had sent their grandmother a little gold ring as a token of her esteem.[13] By making such a gift, however small, Joan showed herself increasingly confident of her military and chivalric role. That Joan so impressed the men, and remarked to them that soon they would be celebrating in Paris, demonstrates her growing poise. Although she spoke with a "feminine" voice, she gave orders to the priests and behaved as an equal to men who were superior to her in status and class. Joan increasingly saw herself as a knight. "Joan chose, with her brilliant instinct for effectiveness, to dress herself in two intertwined uniforms of positive virtue, maleness and knighthood."[14] Yet it was more than role-playing; knighthood with all its attributes and clothing was becoming central to Joan's identity.

Part of Joan's proficiency and self-assurance came from Yolande but much of it resulted from the compliments and adulation she received from the men around her. Joan was most comfortable with men, especially soldiers. Although for the sake of propriety as well as protection she always lodged with women during the course of her mission, the women's recollections of her centered on her piety and good behavior. None said that she clapped them on the shoulders or told them jokes, as she did when she was among her men. One nobleman claimed that she always preferred to sleep with young girls "and did not want to sleep with old ladies." She also grew irritated when women greeted her with a kind of devotion.[15]

At Selles-en-Berry on June 6, dissension about how to proceed surfaced immediately. Some of the captains were in favor of an attack on Jargeau while others were opposed, saying that the English were too strong. Whether or not Joan knew of English preparations, she told the captains not to worry and to stop making difficulties about attacking for God would lead them; she added "that if she had not been sure that God was on their side, she would have preferred to keep watch over sheep and not expose herself to so many dangers."[16]

Too often, Joan's words have been taken at face value. As she would demonstrate at her trial, Joan was exceptionally adept at wordplay. Not only did she do all that was necessary to raise troop morale, but she also used every means necessary to achieve her ends. Here, as during the relief of the siege of Orléans, Joan had no intention of allowing the troops to waver from their ultimate goal. By invoking God and saying that if *she* did not believe she would not expose herself to danger, Joan shamed the French leaders and soldiers who feared superior English manpower and armaments. That they had reason to feel apprehensive after the disastrous battles of earlier years mattered not at all. Joan had by this point – at least from the perspective of the soldiers – become the de facto war leader. Besides accomplishing what many considered to be miracles, she had worked together with the soldiers to attack the English positions, even when the governor of Orléans and others had tried to forestall military action. One priest who had come to know her during the siege stated that "in the face of diverse opinions expressed by the captains, she had often intervened, giving them her counsel and telling them to show courage."[17] The major decisions taken from late May to August were made by Joan, in consultation with the other leaders, but often against the background of increasing dissension at court between those who supported Yolande – and Joan's mission – and counselors such as La Trémoïlle and Regnault de Chartres, who sought political solutions.

Joan and Alençon arrived at Jargeau with their soldiers and artillery on June 11 to confront Suffolk and his garrison of 700 to 800 men. That night, holding her standard, she warned the people inside the town to hand it over to the King of Heaven and good King Charles, telling them that if they did so they would not be harmed.[18] When she was asked at trial why she had not concluded a treaty with the captain at Jargeau, she answered "that the lords of her party replied to the English that they would not get the delay of a fortnight which they asked for, but they and their horses must depart immediately. She added that for her own part, she told the people of Jargeau to retire if they wished, with their doublets or tunics, and their lives safe; otherwise they would be taken by assault."[19] Joan's account is consistent with what the other commanders later said. She was determined not to give the English breathing space that would allow Fastolf and his men in Janville to join up with Talbot, Suffolk, and Scales. Speed was vital.

At first the French forces were repulsed, but Alençon described what happened next. "Joan took her standard and left to attack, exhorting the soldiers to be courageous." They accomplished so much that that night the French army was able to set up camp in the surroundings of Jargeau. Their numbers included over 2,000 soldiers and an equal number of urban militiamen.[20] The next morning the army began to set up the artillery, directing cannon and bombards toward the village, at which point rumors reached them that the mercenary captain La Hire was in talks with Suffolk, who commanded the garrison.

Learning of La Hire's negotiations, they decided to make an attack on the town. Alençon was hesitant, arguing with Joan that an attack was premature. She responded: "Go, gentle duke, to the assault! . . . Do not hesitate! The hour is ready when it pleases God [to go forth]!" She went on:"You work and God will work [for you]." She even goaded him, asking: "Ah! gentle duke, are you afraid? Don't you know that I have promised your wife to return you to her safe and sound?"[21] The picture that emerges from this encounter as well as the disaster of the Battle of the Herrings is of a group of high-ranking military leaders who procrastinated, waiting for the perfect situation. Joan was much more like La Hire, when he had

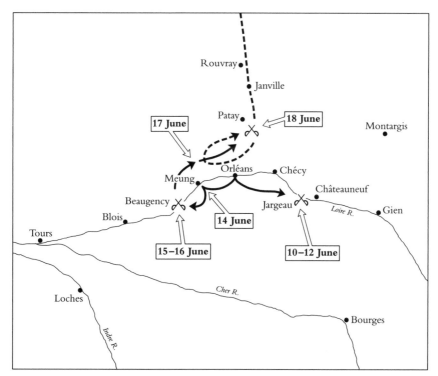

Map 7 The Loire campaign.

wanted to attack the convoy at Rouvray in February but had been delayed disastrously by the count of Clermont's excessive caution. Now Joan demanded action. While she could act the part of an inspirational leader at times, she was just as likely to shame or belittle even her favorite comrades when they showed weakness.

Joan played an active part in the fighting at Jargeau. At one point she warned Alençon to move away from the place where he was standing, "pointing to artillery in the village and saying 'it will kill you.' He moved, and a short time later, Monseigneur de Lude was killed in that very spot." When Joan left to join the attack, Alençon followed. She headed for the ditches, where ferocious fighting took place for about three to four hours. Here she received her third wound. "Joan was up on a ladder, holding her standard in her hand, when she was hit on the head with a stone. It broke on her helmet and knocked her to the ground. Getting up she said to the soldiers: 'Friends! Friends! Up! Up! Our Lord has condemned the English. At this hour they are ours! Be of good courage!' "[22] According to Alençon, Jargeau was taken almost immediately after Joan spoke these words.

The entire town, including its church, was pillaged and local militiamen undertook a wholesale massacre of those who had been defending it. As they began slaughtering those of knightly status who should have been ransomed, Joan and the other leaders escorted the captured earl of Suffolk and his brother to Orléans on the night of June 12 to avoid the general melee and keep them safe. A second brother of Suffolk had been killed in the fighting. Estimates of the dead on the English side range from 300 to 1,100. Why did Joan, who was said to hate the sight of bloodshed, allow this to happen? The leaders may have already left for Orléans before the worst atrocities occurred. It is more likely that while she could effectively restrain the actions of most of her own soldiers, this control did not extend down to the lowest ranks of local men-at-arms who had suffered huge casualties and wanted to exact revenge.

When Joan and the captains returned to Orléans they were greeted by a joyous celebration.[23] In 1456 the Bastard added a titillating postscript to the victory. He said that two weeks after taking Suffolk prisoner, he sent the earl "a small piece of paper that contained four lines that made mention of a Maid who would come from the oak wood (*bois chenu*), riding toward the backs of the archers."[24] Just in case the English and their allies did not yet recognize that Joan was the prophesied Maid, such a short note sent to an important military leader was intended to leave no doubt in their minds.

After the imprisoned duke of Orléans learned of the victories, he ordered Jacques Boucher, the treasurer of his city with whom Joan had been staying, to pay:

> Jean Luillier, merchant, and Jean Bourgeois, tailor, both of Orléans, for a long man's coat and a short surcoat to be worn over armor . . . for Joan the Maid . . . in consideration of the good and constructive services that the Maid rendered for us against the English . . . [as well as] two ells of fine Brussels crimson for the coat and doublet . . . and one ell of dark green[25] for the surcoat . . . and white satin, sandalwood, and other cloth.[26]

Except for being female, Joan looked the part of a knight and reveled in the finery that was now integral to her identity. One chronicle written by a Burgundian loyalist claimed that en route to the coronation "the Maid rode in front of the king, completely armed, her standard deployed. When she took her armor off, she wore the clothing and bore the state of a knight, including slippers with laces on her feet, a quilted doublet called a pourpoint, and hose, with a little hat on her head. She wore very noble clothes made of cloth of gold and silk, along with fur."[27]

After the victory at Jargeau the army marched from Orléans to Meung, twelve miles downstream, arriving on June 15. On learning of the victories, increasing numbers of recruits began to join up with the royal forces. Approaching from the east the French stopped briefly at Meung, where Talbot, Scales, and their men were lodged. The French did not need to attack. Crossing the poorly fortified bridge they stationed a large contingent of men there, cutting off any chance for Fastolf's 4,000 troops to join up immediately with Talbot and Scales. As a result, Talbot and his troops headed for the stronghold at Beaugency, a little more than five miles further downstream, where they took refuge in the castle.

At this juncture, a dangerous political situation developed in which Joan's leadership capabilities were tested. As Alençon and Joan joined their men in front of Beaugency castle, they learned that the constable of France, Arthur de Richemont, was arriving with over 1,000 troops. Richemont personified the problem of conflicting loyalties that bedeviled Charles VII's efforts to regain his kingdom. Born in 1393, he was son of the duke of Brittany, but his mother had remarried – King Henry IV of England – when Arthur was only ten years old. Still, he fought for the French side at Agincourt but was taken prisoner and lived in England for five years. After the Treaty of Troyes that had disinherited Charles, he joined the side of Henry V. When in 1423 he married Margaret, the sister of both Philip the Good and Bedford's wife Anne, his loyalties seemed set. However, after Bedford refused him a key military post, Yolande of Aragon had him appointed constable of France in 1425. But the factionalism at court, especially the enmity of La Trémoïlle and Regnault de Chartres, frustrated his ambitions and he was effectively exiled from court and denied all contact with the king.[28] At the time Charles listened more to his counselors than his mother-in-law, so Richemont grew disaffected. Still, he was anxious to participate in the war, probably even more so after hearing of the major French victories. His arrival at Beaugency thus posed a dilemma for Joan, Alençon, the Bastard, and their men. They did not want Richemont's help since La Trémoïlle had made it clear that the constable was not welcome at court or in the army.

Alençon later testified that the royal forces began to disperse when Richemont arrived. Even Joan had declared that if the constable came, she would leave. She knew enough about court politics to wish to avoid a confrontation. But the day he appeared they learned that Fastolf and about 4,000 English troops were ready to join up with Talbot at Beaugency. Hearing of this, Joan sided with La Hire, who argued that they needed the constable's men. Although Alençon still wanted to leave, she now decided that they must help one another.[29] Guillaume Gruel, who was in the service of Richemont at the time, recorded that when Joan and the constable met she "dismounted, as did he, and she embraced him by the legs. And then he spoke to her, saying, 'Joan, I have heard that you want to fight me. I do not know if you come from God or not. If you are from God, I fear nothing, because God knows my goodwill. If you come from the devil, I will fear you even less.' "[30] Such bold language appealed to Joan.

According to a Burgundian nobleman fighting on the English side at the time, Joan was now always involved in the war council and wanted everything to be directed as she pleased.[31] Joan declared Richemont welcome, even though many of her soldiers remained fearful of the consequences. Militarily the decision to include the constable and his men was the only valid option, since the combined forces of the English were now much larger. By this time, Joan's opinion was decisive when the military command differed. Alençon did not want Richemont's troops, but she overruled him, understanding that with the arrival of Fastolf there was no time for political considerations. Fastolf himself was cautious, but Talbot and Scales were determined to avenge the loss of Orléans. English reinforcements were only a few miles from Beaugency on June 16.

Largely thanks to the arrival of Richemont and his troops, some of whom stationed themselves in the forests of the Sologne so that they could attack the English from all sides, no battle was necessary. Even now, Joan was always at the forefront of the soldiers, with her standard deployed.[32] Monstrelet records that "the principal English captains in Beaugency, seeing that, by the renown of the Maid, fortune had turned entirely against them . . . did not know what to do. . . . Having considered these things, they negotiated with the French."[33] The English sued for peace and it was agreed that at midnight they would hand over the castle and the bridge. At sunrise on the next day they would depart along with their horses and armor and some of their moveable goods, which were of little value. The agreement included a provision that the English and their allies would not arm again until ten days had passed.[34] On June 18, Talbot, Scales, and Fastolf retreated to Meung after the French entered the castle in Beaugency. Fastolf tried to regain the bridge but, fresh from their recent success, the French army returned to Meung, forcing the English to begin the march back toward their headquarters at Janville.

The French could not allow the English command and army to escape and regroup. Joan cried out, "In the name of God, we must fight [the English]! Even if they were dangling from the skies, we will have them, because God sent them so that we could punish them." In line with what La Hire had urged, she now told her men that "the noble king will today have a greater victory than ever."[35] When Alençon, ever indecisive, asked her whether they should hold back or pursue the English, she yelled: "In the name of God, set upon them. . . . They will be beaten, with hardly any loss of our men, and for this reason you must pursue them." He ordered runners in the vanguard along with La Hire, Sir Thibauld d'Armagnac, and some of the leading captains to follow.[36] The Bastard confirmed the hesitancy of Alençon, the recently appointed leader of the army. When Alençon asked Joan what he should do, she responded in a loud voice: "Do you have good spurs?" The men around her turned to Joan, completely mistaking her intent, and asked: "What are you saying? Should we turn on our heels?" She shouted: "No! The English will not defend their positions but will be vanquished. You must spur them on and make them run."[37] Thibauld d'Armagnac later remembered Joan saying "Strike them boldly. They will take to flight and will not linger here."[38] Jean Wavrin de Forestel, a Picard fighting under Fastolf during the Loire campaign, wrote that the renown of Joan the Maid greatly undermined English courage. "They seemed to see fortune turning its wheel against them . . . principally by the enterprises of the Maid."[39]

The English had reached Lignerolles in the valley of the Retrêve by noon on June 18, not far from the village of Patay. Learning that part of the French army was rapidly closing in from behind, Fastolf arrayed his forces in defensive formation, hoping to trap the French as in times past, but they did not have enough time to do so effectively. The English captains ordered their vanguard, as well as the merchants, victuallers, and artillerymen to go ahead to take their place near Patay. Talbot, considering the site advantageous, dismounted with 500 elite archers to await the arrival of the main army and rear guard. There the troops took up their positions between two large hedges through which the French would have to pass, intending to trap them. According to Wavrin de Forestel, who was present, at that moment the French army saw a stag run out of the woods heading in the direction of Patay. It darted straight into the midst of the English army, who cried out loudly, not realizing that the French were so close by. Alerted to the location of their enemies, the French fell upon them in the passage where Talbot had hidden. Initially the English troops tried to fight but realized it was hopeless. At that point, Fastolf saw that all was lost. He decided to save himself and fled.[40] Talbot and Scales were captured. The French sustained few casualties, while the English death toll was 2,000, with 200 more captured.[41] Even Janville, the site where the English had been headquartered, now closed its gates to fleeing soldiers.[42] Since it was the scouting party that fell upon the English position, Joan was not present at the actual battle.

Over in less than two hours, Patay, more than Orléans, was a decisive French victory, the result of a culmination of victories that had begun when Joan first set foot in Orléans on April 29. Less than six weeks later, the Loire Valley had largely been cleared of the English. According to Perceval de Cagny, who served Alençon, after the battle Joan said to the duke: "Have the trumpets sounded and get on your horse. It is time to go to the noble king Charles to lead him to his coronation at Reims." But Richemont would not join them because Alençon did not dare bring him to the king; instead, the constable returned to his château at Parthenay, "content and joyous about the victory God had given the king but very angry that the king did not want his services."[43]

Convincing Charles that he must be crowned was difficult. Arriving at the castle at Gien on June 24, Joan found herself embroiled in court intrigue. A majority of the king's advisors were in favor of sending the army to Normandy in pursuit of the English.[44] Many were looking out for their own interests rather than those of the king; La Trémoïlle and his circle wanted the army to cleanse the region of Berry, including La Charité-sur-Loire, areas where he had substantial holdings.[45] But Joan prevailed with her "pressing demands," telling Charles that even though he was called king he had not yet been crowned.[46] Joan insisted that he go to Reims, the traditional site for French coronations, arguing that "once the king was crowned and anointed, the power of his enemies would continue to diminish and in the end they would no longer be able to harm him or the realm."[47] Witnesses later said that Joan admonished the king and his soldiers to go forth boldly and have no fear because all would go well and they would meet no resistance. While at Gien Joan dictated a letter to the people of Tournai, playing on what might be considered proto-nationalistic sentiments:

+IHESUS MARIA+
Good and loyal Frenchman of Tournai, the Maid sends you news that it has been eight days since by assault and other means she has chased the English from all the places they held along the River Loire. Many were killed, captured, and defeated in battle. You should know that Suffolk, de La Pole, Talbot, Scales, Fastolf,[48] and several knights and captains were captured, and the brother of the earl of Suffolk and Glasdale are dead. Be strong, loyal Frenchmen.

I demand that you be ready to come to the coronation of the noble king Charles at Reims, where we will soon be. And come before us when you know that we are approaching. I commend you to God, and God will keep watch over you and give you the grace to maintain the good cause of the realm of France.[49]

Still Charles delayed. Impatient with the wrangling at court, Joan left out of vexation and went to camp in the fields, two days before the king's departure. Although the king still lacked the money to pay the army, more and more knights, squires, and common soldiers expressed their desire to serve "in company of the Maid, saying that they would go wherever she wanted." Joan could ask for no more. In most accounts of her stated mission, the second goal after relieving the siege of Orléans had been to have Charles crowned. She told her men, "By my Martin [her baton], I will lead King Charles and his company safely, and he will be crowned in the city of Reims."[50]

Finally, on June 29, the army left for Auxerre in Burgundian-controlled territory, possibly with as many as 12,000 men. Despite being under the nominal control of either the English or Burgundians, many of the cities in northern France had only small garrisons, which facilitated the royal progress. En route Joan dictated another letter, to the people of Troyes. While greeting them as very dear and good friends, Joan pressed them to side with Charles and recognize him as the king of France. She called them loyal Frenchmen, assuring them that after the coronation Charles would be in command of his capital in Paris, no matter who came after him. But she warned, "If you do not, I promise and guarantee on your lives that we will enter with the aid of God into all of the cities that ought to be part of the holy kingdom, and there we will make a lasting peace."[51]

The city of Auxerre offered almost no resistance. By July 5 the royal army was at the gates of Troyes. Regularly in contact with their fellow citizens at Reims, the people of Troyes, a large city that had a particularly strong garrison of men, were unwilling to submit. Instead, everyone went to their post on the walls with the intention of resisting to the death.[52] When Charles arrived before Troyes, he took counsel with the princes of the blood and his captains to decide if they should stop at the city and besiege it or whether it was preferable to pass by. Not surprisingly, their opinions were again divided. They had some reason to worry, as one of the king's leading financial advisors reported, for "the troops saw that they did not have enough provisions. They were in despair, and almost ready to go back."[53] But the Bastard recalled that Joan once again spurred them into action after two and a half days of indecision: she entered the room where they were debating what to do and told Charles: "Order your troops to besiege the city of Troyes without all these endless deliberations. . . . Before three days have passed, I will have you enter the city either by love or by force."[54] Without waiting for Charles's answer Joan advanced with the army and began to set up tents around the city, preparing for a siege on July 8. Simon Charles gives the fullest account of what happened next. "Joan took her standard, followed by many foot soldiers, and ordered that each one make bundles of sticks to fill in the ditches. [They camped overnight and] the next day Joan cried: 'To the assault!' "[55] Some of the townsfolk fled while others took refuge in churches. The bishop and citizens of Troyes, "frightened and trembling" at the prospect of an attack, sent an emissary to negotiate their capitulation. Finally the city submitted and on July 10 the king entered with great pomp, Joan riding at his side bearing her standard aloft. Just as in the past decade so many French cities had fallen to the English and Burgundians with little resistance, so they now fell back into the French camp. Thanks to Joan the Maid, momentum was now on the French side. Throughout Europe and beyond, people spoke of her deeds with wonder and awe.[56]

Joan had received so much attention from the people and soldiers of Orléans, followed by the successive victories in the Loire Valley, that she had come to expect a certain level of respect. At trial she said that the people of Troyes paid her no special honor when she entered the town, although she did serve as godmother to a child there.[57] She also made the acquaintance of the famed Franciscan Brother Richard, a hellfire-and-brimstone preacher who had attracted crowds in the thousands to his sermons in Paris a few months earlier. There he had told his listeners that he came from Jerusalem, "where the Jews had announced to him the birth of the 'Messiah,' that is, the Antichrist." He would continue his loud harangue about the end of the world, which seemed possible to many since the harvest had been bad and people were hungry. His sermons sometimes lasted from five in the morning until eleven, by which time "he had stirred up the crowd so much that they lit bonfires of the vanities, throwing their table games, cards and billiards into the flames; their women burned their headdresses and . . . their trains."[58] So inflammatory were his sermons that, combined with his Armagnac leanings, he was banished from Paris. From there he headed to Troyes.

Joan was both amused and annoyed at how he greeted her, and not in the least taken in by his fervent tirades. "The people of Troyes, she thought, sent him to her, saying that they were afraid she was not a thing sent from God; and when he drew near her, he made the sign of the Cross and sprinkled holy water, and she said to him: 'Come boldly, I shall not fly away'."[59] Driven by his millenarian tendencies as well as by a healthy dose of egotism, Friar Richard hoped to make Joan one of his disciples in a mission that would later be deemed heretical. But even though he followed Joan and supported her for a time, she was not about to let him manipulate her. Joan's self-confidence and pride had swelled in these past months and she was not willing to be anyone's follower. It is remarkable that for all her pious behavior, including attendance at mass, confessing her sins, and speaking openly of the tasks with which God had charged her, Joan showed little interest in speaking with bishops, priests, or mendicant friars except for her personal confessors, whom she associated with her military endeavors. By this time she had probably come to associate important churchmen – or at least those who claimed to be – with those at court who tried to impede her efforts.

After the surrender of the city of Troyes, others fell in line. Charles sent criers ahead to towns to announce his imminent arrival. All along their route, the fortresses of the region surrendered, because Joan sent her men to tell them: " 'Hand it over to the King of Heaven and noble King Charles' [which most of them did]. . . . For those who refused, she went there in person, and all obeyed."[60] Châlons-sur-Marne was gained without a fight and the bishop gave Charles the keys to the city. But now deep in Burgundian territory, Charles hesitated because he had no siege engines or artillery. When he expressed reservations, Joan said to him: " 'Do not fear, because the burgesses of the city of Reims will come to meet you.' [And so it happened that] as the troops began to approach the city, they came out to greet the king."[61] On the evening of July 16, they arrived in the city. The archbishop, canons, bourgeois, and others came out in large numbers, crying "*Noël!*" Throughout the night the king's council and officers planned for the coronation the next day. For Joan, it would be a moment of supreme triumph.

Joan, with counsel from Yolande and others, was determined to accomplish her goals as quickly and effectively as possible. Repeatedly her personal interactions with members of the king's council – and the king himself – had led her to question their motivations and doubt that they shared her goals. Alençon said that he sometimes heard Joan say to the king that "she would only last a year, and not much more, and so it was important to consider how to accomplish the most during that year because she had four responsibilities: to chase the English out of France; to have the king crowned at Reims; to deliver the Duke of Orléans from the hands of the English; and to relieve the siege of Orléans."[62] Ever since he had first met her, Alençon, Joan's gentle duke, had fallen under her spell; when he hesitated or showed fear, she urged him on and told him not to worry. Her deeds, which had included saving his life at Jargeau, must have astounded him and he now believed that she would succeed in whatever she attempted. His description of Joan's direct involvement in terms of leadership, strategy, military skills, and expertise in artillery is echoed throughout the accounts of all Joan's military comrades as well as many hostile chroniclers. From the relief of the siege of Orléans until her capture at Compiègne, Joan was usually in the thick of battle. Contrary to some depictions of her as a mere standard-bearer,[63] she was actively involved whenever possible. While "her voices" and her piety motivated many, it was her deeds that astonished her men as well as her intuitive sense of timing and strategy that began to turn the tide of the war. According to Joan, her colleagues, and her enemies, she scaled ladders, set artillery, and received battle wounds. Most importantly, she demanded action in the face of constant hesitation and inactivity. Two of her favorite sayings were: "Go boldly!" and "God helps those who help themselves." For those around her, that was new.

Joan's contemporary, Christine de Pizan (d. 1429), who celebrated the Maid in her famous *Ditié de Jeanne d'Arc*, also wrote military and political manuals. In her earlier *Book of the Body Politic*, she outlined six key qualities for nobles and warriors that Joan personified:

> The first is that they ought to love arms and the art of them perfectly, and they ought to practice the work. The second condition is that they ought to be very bold, and have such firmness and constancy in their courage that they never flee nor run from battles out of fear of death, nor spare their blood nor life, for the good of their prince and the safe keeping of their country. . . . Thirdly, they ought to give heart and steadiness to each other, counselling their companions to do well, and to be firm and steadfast. The fourth is to be truthful and to uphold their fealty and oath. Fifthly, they ought to love and desire honor above all worldly things. Sixthly, they ought to be wise and crafty against their enemies and in all deeds of arms.[64]

As Joan ensured proper discipline among her men, forbidding them to consort with loose women (a command that they did not always heed), prohibiting them from swearing, and urging them to confess and hear mass, she fulfilled another of Christine's conditions: that of convincing her soldiers to maintain good manners and morals. When some disobeyed her orders, she would brandish her sword and threaten them.[65] By doing so, Joan maintained high standards of conduct. Christine adds that boldness – practically Joan's watchword – "often achieves more than great physical strength."[66] Using the example of an ancient Greek knight, Christine insisted that "by these wise and good exhortations he gave them heart and boldness to attack their enemies, which they had never dared before. And so they conquered them and broke the siege."[67] So too had Joan. Finally, Joan met Christine's sixth criterion. Like Master Jean, the great culveriner of Orléans, Joan showed in her actions that she acknowledged the necessity of craft and trickery to achieve military goals.

The nullification testimonies from her military colleagues and those who met her make it clear that Joan's demeanor, her eagerness to take part in battles and sieges, and her sense of urgency, inspired in them a spirit of loyalty and camaraderie that led them to follow her even when her actions began to conflict with those of the king and his counselors. Joan was a warrior, a soldier, and a general.[68] Although she claimed she never used her sword in battle or to shed blood, she wielded it often. She also managed to convince herself that she was not responsible for the enormous casualties of English, French, and allied soldiers at Orléans and during the campaigns of the Loire.[69] When Joan said at trial that she always preferred her standard to her sword, she was choosing to distance herself from the realities of the warfare that she had pursued even in the face of those who privileged diplomatic over military solutions. But even in this she resembled lords and knights. It was rare for leaders and soldiers of the period to emphasize their direct role in killing or shedding blood, since there was no honor or glory attached to such behavior. Instead, just as at Jargeau, they assigned that role to urban militias or lower class men-at-arms. Most descriptions of nobles' behavior on the battlefield refer admiringly to valiant charges, beautiful feats of arms, and chivalrous deeds; the ugly side of war usually appears only in exaggerated estimates of death tolls and casualties or in the deeds of lesser men. Nowhere in their testimonies do the Bastard, Alençon or others describe killing or taking pride in individual acts of violence.

Some have seen Joan's legacy in the holiness and spirituality that encouraged her men to believe in themselves. But when we look more closely, we find a girl better able to describe her sword than her standard and who liked a sword she had won from a Burgundian for its ability to give good whacks. However sanitized and chivalrous the depictions or recollections were, the fact remains that bloodshed and violence were almost everyday parts of Joan's life during this period. She had the courage and conviction of youth, of someone who believed in herself and was unwilling to tolerate either the lack of discipline or the ineffective tactics that had so often paralyzed French armies. Joan learned quickly, whatever task faced her. Ironically, Joan's class, age, and gender allowed her to act in ways that would have been much more difficult for the great nobles who had recently been fighting the English. Unlike them she was not tied to a past of failed leadership, inactivity, or inertia; rather, she saw and acted based not on what others advised but on her own intuition and confidence as a leader. As an outsider she thought more like the mercenary captain La Hire, with whom she often agreed. She was able to get "down and dirty" with those who manned the guns, while at the same time understanding the need for surprise. "She was obsessed by the knowledge that she would have to work fast or fail. She knew that she must allow the English no rest between battles to recover and reorganize themselves. . . . She also conducted the assaults one after the other as rapidly as possible to fulfill her larger strategic need for speed."[70]

The accounts of Joan's fellow commanders, soldiers, page, and squire, as well as of members of the court, along with the chronicles written from both hostile and friendly perspectives, emphasize rather than downplay Joan's role. Her fellow soldiers usually said they believed she came from God because of her amazing abilities, but that often seemed an after-thought in their accounts. Joan comes across as an active, sometimes angry, presence, a soldier to the core. Some, including Alençon, minimized his own role or described his behavior in ways that made him appear foolish. Had they been speaking in 1429, the reasons would have been obvious: to spread fear among the English and Burgundians. But by 1456, we would expect the opposite. Charles's attitude to the nullification proceedings was ambivalent at best, for he had no desire to emphasize Joan's role in the events of 1429. One would have expected men such as the Bastard, Alençon, and Aulon to highlight or exaggerate their own part in events rather than attributing the victories to a peasant girl who would later be discredited at court and get herself executed for heresy.

The victories in the Loire and the route to the coronation would be the high points of Joan's career. At the same time, there can be little doubt that Joan's independence in pushing for the attack, allowing Richemont to join up with the French army – even if it made the difference for victory – and her increasing desire to dictate strategy to the king and his counselors began to change her fortunes at court. She had already provided much more than the sign that she had promised the churchmen at Poitiers; La Trémoïlle and others now believed it was time for them to take over. But Joan had other ideas.

CHAPTER 6

The King and the Maid

Aﬀ ter the surrender of Troyes, Charles sent heralds throughout
the region to announce plans for his coronation. By July 14 the army, led
by Joan in full armor, had reached Châlons-sur-Marne, which opened its
gates immediately.[1] Waiting to see her were five people from Domremy,
including her godfather Jean Morel, whom she presented with a red vest
that she had worn during her travels[2] and Gérardin d'Épinal. Gérardin
recalled Joan telling him that the only thing she feared was treason.[3] She
sensed that some of the king's counselors, never friendly to her cause, had
grown increasingly uneasy about her ascendancy after the unbroken string
of victories that led to her marching toward Reims alongside the king at
the head of a large army. Throughout Europe most of those who had heard
of the extraordinary recent events, even those hostile to the French cause,
attributed the changing tide of the war to Joan. A Burgundian chronicle
stated that "the dauphin began to conquer cities and regions, thanks to the
exploits of the Maid and the renown that had begun to spread everywhere
about the young girl."[4] While Yolande still supported Joan, Georges de La
Trémoïlle and Regnault de Chartres had been wary of her from the start
and now openly advocated a different military strategy.

On July 15 the army left Châlons, stopping about fourteen miles
from Reims at the château of Sept-Saulx, owned by Regnault de Chartres,
archbishop of Reims. The pope had appointed him to the position in
1414, but because of his role at Charles' court, he had not been back to his
city during the Burgundian occupation. On Saturday morning, July 16,
the king, the archbishop, Joan, and several lords entered Reims without
opposition.[5]

Joan appreciated what others did not. Even as she pursued military goals, she realized that for Charles to be recognized as king he had to be crowned and anointed with the oil of Clovis. Considered the first French king, Clovis I (466–511) converted to Christianity after winning a major battle. In 496, the bishop of Reims baptized him using a holy oil or chrism believed to have been brought from heaven by a dove. Thereafter the holy oil was kept in the Abbey of Saint-Rémi. Reims had also been a capital of Charlemagne's (*Charles* the Great's) empire. In Joan's mind, the tradition of consecrating French kings with holy oil that came from God and the political imagery associated with Charlemagne – and as a consequence, Charles – made the ceremony essential at a time when the crown was contested and much of France occupied. As a result of the Treaty of Troyes, the child Henry VI had been named king of France, although he would not be crowned in Paris until 1431. Philip the Good could also stake a claim based on blood.

Unlike many members of Charles's court, Joan intuitively understood the political and symbolic necessity of the ceremony. Perhaps growing up not far from Reims in a frontier region torn by fragmented allegiances, she grasped better than others the necessity of making Charles king *by the grace of God*, anointed with the chrism unique to French monarchs. Once Charles had been crowned and anointed, it could not be undone. He would still have to prove himself as king, but the ceremony at Reims was the first step.

The time Joan spent at Châlons and Reims was as close as she would ever again get to home. Although Reims offered no resistance to the entry of the king, the Maid, and their army, the coronation was not in all respects normal and had to be hastily organized. Several peers of the realm and bishops, including the duke of Burgundy and bishop Pierre Cauchon of Beauvais, were absent because they favored the other side. But churchmen, nobles, and military men who supported Charles attended, as well as members of Joan's family, including her brother Pierre and father Jacques d'Arc, who stayed at an inn known as the Striped Donkey.[6] Durand Laxart, who had helped make her mission possible, was also present. Isabelle Romée and Joan's other brother Jean, who had fought alongside her and Pierre, may have been there as well.

The regalia kept at the royal abbey of Saint-Denis just outside of English-controlled Paris were unavailable, but suitable substitutes were found. Four captains, including La Hire, were sent to retrieve the vial of holy oil and bring it to the cathedral. Fully armed and mounted, their banners aloft, they entered the cathedral on horseback, dismounting at the entry to the choir. Bishops wearing their mitres and holding large crosses surrounded the altar. But there was one notable absentee who had fought for the king. The constable of France, Arthur de Richemont, should have borne the sword that was held in front of the king during the ceremony. But to Joan's chagrin, Richemont was barred from attending; Charles d'Albret, La Trémoïlle's half-brother, took his place.

The ceremony was splendid, lasting from nine in the morning to two in the afternoon. With the archbishop of Reims presiding, the king was anointed according to the traditional formula. Wearing only a simple shift, Charles prostrated himself before the altar. Then as the king knelt, the archbishop anointed the top of his head, followed by his breast, shoulders, and arms. After each, the archbishop uttered the words: "I anoint you for the realm with holy oil, in the name of the Father and the Son and the Holy Spirit." Those gathered sang a hymn that related how the priest Sadoch and the prophet Nathan anointed Solomon, which was followed by a shout of "Long live the king for eternity!" The archbishop prayed that Charles would show himself worthy of the power now vested in him.[7] The ceremony nearly complete, the king then changed into royal regalia, marking his transformed status as God's lieutenant on earth. The archbishop then slipped the royal ring onto the king's finger, symbolizing his union with the French people. Bishops and peers in attendance took the crown from the altar and, bearing it aloft, processed with it above Charles's head as he was led to his throne.

A letter sent that day to Charles's queen, Marie, and her mother Yolande at Saumur related that "it was quite wonderful to see such a beautiful mystery. It was very solemn, with all things having been found that were necessary, from the crown and royal habit to other essentials. . . . When the king was anointed and the crown was placed on his head, everyone cried 'Noël!' and the trumpets sounded in such a manner that it seemed that all the vaults of the church would splinter. During the ceremony, the Maid stood by the king, holding her standard in her hand. It was a wonder to behold the beautiful bearing of the king as well as the Maid."[8] Once the ceremony was concluded, Joan embraced the king by his legs and kissed his foot. She wept with joy, causing others to shed tears as she addressed Charles: "Noble king, at this hour, God's will has been fulfilled that you would come to Reims and be anointed, showing that you are the true king and the one to whom the realm must belong."⁹ Gui and André de Laval, who had been so impressed with Joan when they met her in June, received the title of count that day along with La Trémoïlle. Thanks to Joan's resolve, Charles was now king of France in more than name. Yet even as he publicly displayed his new status by touching for the king's evil,¹⁰ Charles and La Trémoïlle were secretly negotiating a fifteen-day truce with the duke of Burgundy, Philip the Bold. Having achieved her most important goals, even Yolande now advocated a peace policy.

Joan was of another mind. On July 17, she addressed a letter to the duke of Burgundy, advancing her plan for a France united under Charles:

Joan the Maid asks you by the King of Heaven, my rightful and sover-eign lord, that you and the King of France make a good and lasting peace, each pardoning the other entirely with good heart, as loyal Christians ought to do. If it pleases you to fight, then go fight the Saracens. Prince of Burgundy, I ask and demand that you no longer make war on the holy realm of France, and make your men withdraw from whatever places and fortresses they hold in this holy realm. On the part of the noble King of France, he is ready to make peace with you, saving his honor. ... All those who fight against the holy realm of France make war against Jesus, King of Heaven and all the world.¹¹

Whether it was Joan's decision or that of others to send this letter, it marked a new and ominous stage in her career. Joan did not understand the world of high politics. Although she was a quick study and demon-strated extraordinary skill among both theologians and military men, she had neither mastered nor shown herself particularly interested in court intrigues or dynastic struggles unless they directly affected her mission. She had done what was necessary when she accepted Richemont and his troops at Beaugency, but had incurred the displeasure of La Trémoïlle and Regnault de Chartres. Her anger that Richemont was not given his place of honor at the coronation did not help her standing with those around Charles. Moreover, Duke Philip had never been part of her original or even evolving plan and she did not comprehend the complexities that divided him and the king of France. She had done damage to Philip when she had helped the king retake towns that had been under Burgundian control and had Charles crowned in one of its most important cities. Writing to Philip was both provocative and undiplomatic.

The interests of Joan and those around Charles now began to diverge seriously. But for the moment at least, Joan was triumphant. Unknown to her, the poet Christine de Pizan would soon pen a poem celebrating her success.

> In the year 1429 the sun began to shine again. . . . [Everything has changed] because the rejected son of the legitimate King of France [is now] crowned with great majesty. . . . You have recovered it by the intelligent Maid who, God be thanked, has opened it to you. . . . Can one praise [the Maid] enough for having given peace to this land, so long laid low by war? . . . Esther, Judith, and Deborah were ladies of great renown through whom God restored his people from great oppression. [God] has accomplished more miracles through this Maid. . . . A girl of sixteen years (is this not a force beyond nature?) on whom arms do not weigh heavy, so that her whole upbringing made her this, so strong and hardy! And her enemies flee from her, not one of them can last. . . . [She] drives them out of France, recovering castles and cities. . . . She is the leader of our worthy and able men.[12]

Joan's confessor Pasquerel was as astonished as everyone else. He stated in 1456 that when he would say to her that " 'never have we seen things such as you have done nor in any book have we read of such feats,' she would respond: 'My Lord has a book that no clergyman has ever read, no matter how perfect he is.' "[13] Now, more than before, Joan began to set herself apart as someone privileged with special knowledge that God had communicated to her alone. Her increasing self-importance showed in her actions, setting her on a collision course with the La Trémoïlle-dominated court. Joan's mission, as she had originally envisioned it, was complete. But she intended to make good on the outlandish claim she had made in her first letter to the English – that she was going "to kick [them] out of all of France, body for body" – whether Charles and his counselors agreed or not.

In the aftermath of the coronation the king wended his way toward Paris, too slowly for Joan's taste. Towns fell one after another to Charles and the Maid, including Laon, Soissons, Compiègne, Château-Thierry, Senlis, Beauvais, and Lagny. "The English and other adversaries were so astounded and disconcerted that the great part of them did not dare either to appear or defend themselves, hoping to avoid death by flight."[14] On

July 31 at Château-Thierry, Charles tried to placate Joan when he granted "his very good friend Joan the Maid, considering the great, high, noble, and profitable service she had and continued to provide each day for the recovery of the realm, [a tax exemption] for the inhabitants of Greux and Domremy."[15] As they continued toward Paris, they reached the towns of La Ferté and Crépy-en-Valois. There they were greeted as saviors.

> The people came to the king, full of elation crying: "*Noël*." Then Joan, who rode between the archbishop of Reims and the Bastard, said these words: "Here is a good people! I have never seen a people who so rejoiced at the coming of a noble king. If I could be so happy at the end of my days, I would like to be buried in this land!" Hearing this, the archbishop said: "O Joan! In what place do you want to be buried?" She responded: "That where it pleases God, because I do not know the time or the place. And if it would please God, my creator, that I retire, giving up weapons, I would go serve my mother and my father, guarding the sheep with my sister [sic] and my brothers, who would so rejoice to see me."[16]

The Bastard's reminiscence seems retrospective, though Joan often said when angry that she would rather be home with her family if she did not have such important work to do. Did she really use phrases like this? If she did, she may have been trying to situate herself within the context of salvation history.[17] In the garden of Gethsemane, Jesus had prayed: "My Father, if it is possible, let this cup pass from me; yet not what I want but what you want."[18] Nothing suggests that Joan had any real desire to return to Domremy.

From Provins in early August, Joan dictated another letter to the people of Reims to express her displeasure at the sluggish royal pace and her knowledge of behind-the-scenes maneuvers by La Trémoïlle to make peace with Burgundy.

> My dear and good friends, loyal Frenchmen of the city of Reims, Joan the Maid sends news to you, and asks that you have no doubts about the good fight she wages for the blood royal. And I promise you that I will never abandon you as long as I live. It is true that the king has made truces with the duke of Burgundy lasting fifteen days, by which he will give up the city of Paris peacefully at the end of that period. However, do not marvel if I go there very soon, for no matter how many truces are

made, I will not be at all content and I don't know if I will keep them.
But if I do so, it will be to guard the king's honor, for no matter how
much they abuse the blood royal, I will keep the royal army together so
that it will be completely ready at the end of fifteen days if they do not
make peace. For that, my very dear and blameless friends, I beg you not
to feel any uneasiness as long as I live.[19]

Joan had come to believe that she was the woman of legend, the savior
of France. She had rescued Orléans and the cities along the Loire and
led the king to his coronation. Was he going to give that up for a truce
with the duplicitous duke of Burgundy? Joan intended to guard the king's
honor even if he would not. She reassured the people of Reims (and
people in all the other cities in Burgundian-controlled territory that had
opened their gates to the king) that *she* would not disband the army. *Her*
honor depended upon it.

In August, more towns in Burgundian and English-controlled territories surrendered to Charles even as he negotiated with Philip. A few major
skirmishes took place before the royal forces neared Paris. By August 15,
the English and French armies, both with about 8,000 soldiers, camped
close to each other near Montépilloy. Joan and Alençon, expecting a
confrontation, fortified their position during the night. But when the
English made no move, Joan took her standard and rode to the vanguard,
making several feints against their fortifications to try to provoke an
engagement. Joan wanted to fight. However, when it became clear the
English would not be drawn out, the French army returned to its camp.
The next day the English marched for Paris. On the 17th, the king
received the keys to the city of Compiègne, where he took up residence
rather than pursuing Bedford's army. Joan expressed her irritation at the
king's complacency, telling Alençon: "My gentle duke, get your men and
the other captains ready," adding, "By my Martin, I want to see Paris up
close."[20]

Finally, on August 23 the royal army left Compiègne – without the
king – heading for Paris. They arrived in the northern suburbs between
La Chappelle and Saint-Denis, site of the royal abbey, on the 26th. But
even as they made preparations for an attack on the capital, which Charles
had authorized, the king and his counselors at Senlis began to negotiate a
continuation of the truce until Christmas. The king's plans no longer
converged with those advocated by Joan.

The assault on Paris was doomed to failure, not only or even mainly because of Charles's reluctance to fight. Joan probably assumed that, like so many towns had before, Paris would embrace Charles, willingly or after a show of force. But Paris was heavily fortified with 30-foot high walls and two moats surrounding the city. The one closest to the walls was filled with water, while the outer moat was dry, more like a trench. The Bastille was stocked with arms and gunpowder, and cannon and large crossbows atop it made defense of the city relatively easy.[21] The captain of Paris and the Bastille had prepared his men for the assault, stockpiling weapons and supplies to hold them through the winter if necessary. Joan and Alençon sent out scouts each day after their arrival, which led to numerous skirmishes around the gates of the city. She frequently rode to the walls trying to assess the best means of attack. Finally, Alençon was dispatched to bring Charles to Paris. The king eventually arrived at Saint-Denis on Wednesday, September 7.

The anonymous author of the *Journal of the Bourgeois of Paris*, whose notes cover the years from 1405 to 1449, was a churchman affiliated with the cathedral of Notre Dame or the University of Paris rather than a merchant. His descriptions of living conditions in Paris, including harvest failures, omens, and the cost and quality of wine, offer a vivid inside look at the city before and during the brief siege. The Parisians had learned to fend for themselves, viewing the dukes of Burgundy, whom the Bourgeois characterizes as neglectful to a fault, as only slightly better than the despised Armagnacs and English. According to him, the king's faction does "nothing day or night but lay waste all his father's land with fire and sword and the English on the other side do as much harm as Saracens."[22] Because of his distrust of all sides, his year-by-year accounts are especially valuable. He relates that earlier the duke of Alençon had sent letters to the city's leaders, hoping to divide the people and instigate a popular uprising. Exaggerating the size of the French army at 12,000 men, the Bourgeois exclaims that they were "so full of foolish belief that on the word of [a] creature in the form of a woman who was with them and whom they called the Maid, what it was God alone knows, that the day of the Nativity of Our Lady they formed the resolution to attack Paris." The feast of the Nativity of the Virgin, one of only three birthdays celebrated in the liturgical year – the others being those of Jesus and John the Baptist – was an important holy day. On September 8, between eleven and twelve in the morning, the large French army arrived at the moats in front of the city walls. The notary of the Paris *parlement* wrote tellingly that the Parisians saw Joan as "the woman who led the army with the other captains."[23]

With its large number of horses, wagons and carts filled with bundles of straw and wood, the French army assembled in the field near the Saint-Honoré Gate across from a place called the Pigmarket. They arrayed themselves in front of the shallow outer ditch. As the two sides exchanged insults, Joan took her standard and from a high point between the two moats shouted to the defenders parading atop the walls: "Hand yourselves over to us promptly in the name of Jesus, because if you do not do so before nightfall, we will enter by force, whether you like it or not, and you will all be put to death without mercy." They responded in kind: "Whore! Slut!"[24]

A thunderous crash of cannonballs and culverins fired from inside Paris filled the air as Joan, Alençon, and a large number of knights, squires, and other soldiers made their way into the ditch with bundles of sticks and branches. Arrows rained down on the attackers. Considering the strength of the defenses, surprisingly violent clashes continued until sunset when Joan was struck in the thigh by an arrow shot from a crossbow. Although she was wounded, she remained adamant that if the soldiers got closer to the walls, Paris would be taken. But because it was nightfall, she was hurt, and the men were weary from the long assault, Gaucourt and others came to get Joan, grabbing her and dragging her back from the trenches. Joan was furious, shouting "By my Martin, the place would have been taken!" They sat her back on her horse and led her back to her lodgings in La Chappelle.[25] By this time Joan was nearly out of her mind with fatigue, frustration, and pain.

Still Joan wanted to fight on, remembering the victory at Orléans which had been won late in the day, after she was wounded, when she rallied the troops. But even though Joan admitted at trial that it took about five days for her wound to heal, she woke up early the next morning and sent for the duke of Alençon. She asked him to have the trumpets sounded. They began to resume the attack, even though some of the troops were unwilling to return to the siege. At that moment Charles called it off, commanding that Joan, Alençon, and the other captains desist. They were exasperated but obeyed the king's will, hoping that they would be able to find a way into Paris from the other side by passing across the Seine on a makeshift bridge the duke of Alençon had constructed over the river from

Saint-Denis. When they returned the next day they were sorely disappointed "because the king, knowing the intentions of the Maid, the duke of Alençon, and others, had spent the night having the bridge broken into pieces."[26] Charles sent Yolande's son René of Anjou and the count of Clermont, the same man who had been largely responsible for the disastrous loss at the Battle of the Herrings, to make sure that they stopped the attack. The Bourgeois claims that the French troops cursed Joan bitterly, because she had promised "that without fail, they would take the city and that each one of them would become rich from the city's goods and that they would put to the sword all people and burn down all houses where they met with opposition." He added that after they were given a safe conduct, the French returned to claim their casualties – according to him at least 500 dead and 1,000 wounded.[27]

Could Joan have urged her troops on using such words? This account has usually been dismissed because the Bourgeois was hostile to Joan, but elements of it ring true. "Without fail [sans faute]" was, according to the villagers in Domremy, one of her favorite sayings. She believed they would take Paris, so why would she not communicate that to her men? Joan spurred her men on and urged them to act boldly whenever an opportunity presented itself. And whether or not she was present after the assault on Jargeau, when the town was pillaged and its inhabitants massacred, she bears some responsibility. At the same time, in view of so many different witnesses' descriptions of her as simple and good, it is unlikely that she offered such explicitly violent descriptions of what they could expect in reward for the capture of the city. While the captains around her, especially Alençon, were as eager as she was to take Paris, it is equally possible that many of the foot soldiers and others understood how foolhardy an undertaking it had been. In any case, Joan was an angry woman by the end of the attack on Paris.

After the assault was called off, Joan left a suit of armor and sword in the abbey of Saint-Denis. It was not her sword, but one she had won at Paris along with a suit of armor.[28] The offering was strange, for one normally left a personal item as an *ex voto* out of gratitude. But Joan was not grateful. By leaving an unknown soldier's armor and sword, her action could only have obscure symbolic value.[29] It was a devotional gesture that cost Joan little. At trial, when asked about this incident, she maintained that it had not been the sword of Saint Catherine, telling her judges that she would not answer that question for the time being.[30] Joan had good reason to sidestep the issue, for it was with "very great regret" that Joan left the attack on Paris and in her frustration she took out her anger on a camp follower. Alençon recalled that at Saint-Denis he saw Joan, "her sword unsheathed, pursue a woman living with soldiers, to the point that she broke her sword [on the woman's back]."[31] It was not the first time Joan had had a nasty encounter with camp followers. Her page recalled that only a short while before, near the city of Château-Thierry, Joan had seen the concubine of one of her soldiers on a horse. She followed the woman with her sword drawn and although she did not strike her, she advised her never again to be in the company of soldiers.[32] The king was furious and told her she should have used a stick rather than the sword that had come to her divinely.[33] The Bourgeois of Paris claimed that Joan carried a large baton (her Martin) "in her hand and when one of her men made a mistake she used it to give great whacks, showing herself to be a very cruel woman."[34] Although probably an exaggeration, Joan's anger and belligerence were real.

Gauging Joan's mood at this moment is not difficult. She had languished for the better part of six weeks after the coronation and felt that Paris could be taken. When the king called off the attack and destroyed the improvised bridge, her hopes began to collapse since she believed that the kingdom could not be unified without its capital. Alençon's chronicler says Paris broke Joan's will.[35] His assessment may be too strong, but Paris did change Joan. She had come to believe that she could do anything, even in the face of insurmountable obstacles. Indeed, she had already accomplished what to many had seemed impossible, so why not Paris? Almost immediately after the coronation her faith in Charles had been shaken when he negotiated a truce with Burgundy. Calling off the siege was, to her, treachery by the man she had made king. Did she also begin to question her invincibility? Up until Paris Joan's military judgments and leadership had been superior to that of many of her fellow captains, but in attempting to take the heavily fortified and populated capital, she miscalculated. It was a failure of her leadership.

When Joan was asked at trial if she had followed the counsel of her voices when she attacked Paris, "she answered no, but she went at the request of nobles who wanted to make an attack . . . or an assault-at-arms; and she intended to go beyond and cross the trenches of the town of Paris."[36] Joan's evasiveness reflects frustration and anger at her first failure, which she could at least partially blame on the king. Yet she also unfairly deflected the blame onto her military comrades. When her questioners pursued the issue, asking if it was right to attack Paris on the feast day of the Virgin, she said "that it was good to observe the Festival of the Blessed Mary; and it seemed to her in conscience good to keep the Festival of Our Lady from beginning to end."[37] Even when speaking about a holy day on the church calendar, Joan responded with flippancy.

The only way Paris could have fallen would have been treason from within, which sometimes happened during sieges of smaller towns and cities. Sympathizers of Charles VII had spread defeatist rumors in hopes that some of the guards would let them in or there would be a popular uprising. But the Parisians preferred the more neutral, if neglectful, rule of Philip the Good to the possibility of Armagnac reprisals that the Bourgeois mentions in such detail.[38] They wanted to carry out their mercantile activities unimpeded, without having their crops destroyed or trade disrupted. The Parisian notary Clément de Fauquembergue, the same man who drew a small sketch of Joan in his notebook, confirms the solid defenses of the city and the presence of some Armagnac supporters: "At this time in Paris there were men who were scared or corrupted, who let out cries throughout the city, here and there from the bridges, crying that all was lost, and that the enemies had entered into Paris, and that everyone should surrender and save themselves. . . . But for all that, there was no other disorder among the inhabitants of Paris."[39]

The king and his counselors continued to pursue negotiations with the duke of Burgundy after the disastrous blow to the army's morale at Paris. By this point Joan had become a liability to the king. She had served her purpose – men had clamored to join the French side after the victories in the Loire. At the same time, English soldiers had increasingly lost their heart for war, and desertions, recruiting, and getting financial support from England had, and would continue to pose, serious problems for the duke of Bedford and strain relations with his brother Humphrey of Gloucester's regency government in England. After the coronation it was logical for Charles to look for a diplomatic solution that could heal the breach between the Armagnacs and Burgundians and perhaps allow them to present a united front against the English. As a result of the debacle at Paris, Joan's image was tarnished *and* she stood in the way of reconciliation with Philip the Good. La Trémöille and Regnault de Chartres were now free to work against her. No longer would Yolande help her.

Charles retreated to the Loire and on September 21 disbanded the army, sending Joan's favorite, the duke of Alençon, back to his wife, and the other commanders to their separate regions. Joan was devastated. When Alençon assembled men to fight against Bedford and his positions in Normandy, Brittany and Maine, he asked the king to send Joan to fight alongside him. Charles was mistrustful and cynical by nature, not surprising in view of his early life. In this case, he and his counselors were probably right to refuse the request, saying "they did not want to allow Joan and Alençon to be together again."[40] At Paris, even if they felt their actions had been justified, Joan and Alençon had come close to insubordination. Headstrong Joan, who had become something of a loose cannon, and her favorite Alençon – who later in Charles' reign would be found guilty of treason for plotting against the king[41] – were too dangerous a team to be left to their own devices. At the same time Charles could not simply get rid of her, as support for Joan remained strong among soldiers and townspeople in places such as Orléans and Compiègne.

Joan was put in the care of Charles d'Albret, the king's lieutenant general in Berry. She was sent to Bourges, where she stayed for three weeks with Marguerite de La Tourolde who, like so many others, was deeply impressed by Joan's piety. Marguerite recounted to Joan some of the tales she had heard about her; she told how some people said that Joan "went without fear to the assault because she knew that she would not be wounded. But Joan answered that she had no more guarantee of that than other soldiers."[42] This directly contradicted Joan's statements at trial as well as her confessor's testimony, but Marguerite's version more accurately reflects what Joan believed before her capture and trial. If Joan truly believed God directed her efforts, would that not have been a guarantee? Marguerite considered Joan a simple girl except in the art of war and said she loved giving alms to the poor. While Joan stayed in Bourges some women "brought their rosaries and medallions to her, wanting her to touch them, but Joan laughed and said 'Touch them yourselves, because your touch will be as good as mine!' "[43]

Toward the end of her stay Joan was told that Catherine de La Rochelle, a disciple of Brother Richard, the strange preacher Joan had met in Troyes, wanted to talk to her about visions she had had of a white lady who came to her wearing cloth of gold. Joan expressed skepticism when Catherine said to her that the white lady told her "to go through the good towns with heralds and trumpets which the king would give her, to proclaim that whosoever possessed gold, silver, or hidden treasure should immediately bring it forth . . . and it should go to the paying of Joan's men-at-arms." Hearing that, Joan told Catherine to go back to her husband and children and take care of her household, calling her plan sheer folly. Brother Richard and Catherine were not pleased. Catherine persisted until Joan finally agreed to spend a night with her to see if the "white lady" was real. Joan saw nothing, but Catherine claimed the lady had come. When Catherine told her the lady would come again, Joan "slept by day, so that she might stay awake the whole of the succeeding night. And that night she went to bed with Catherine, and watched all night; but she saw nothing, although she often asked Catherine whether the lady would appear, and Catherine answered, 'Yes, presently.' "[44] Joan once again saw nothing.

Why was Joan so dismissive of Catherine's visions? Why did she demand signs from Catherine that she refused to provide herself? Her trial judges wanted to know. Joan answered that she would not have pressed to know the sign "if it had been as well shown before notable ecclesiastics, and others [as her own had]. . . . Moreover, she already knew through St. Catherine and St. Margaret that the affairs of this Catherine were nothing."[45] To Joan, Catherine de La Rochelle was a charlatan distracting her from the work at hand. That she told her to go home is revealing, for Joan recognized nothing of herself in Catherine. Catherine was a wife and mother, not a special warrior with a mission. Joan admitted that she told Catherine, who wished to go to the duke of Burgundy and make peace, that it seemed to her "that peace would not be found, except at the lance's point."[46]

Once Joan had fully healed from her thigh wound, La Trémoïlle found a way to occupy her by avenging a past insult he had suffered. A mercenary captain, Perrinet Gressart, who had prospered as a result of his services to all sides in the conflict, controlled La Charité-sur-Loire, Saint-Pierre-le-Moutier, and many other towns on the eastern borders of Berry. In 1427, while on a mission to the Burgundians, La Trémoïlle had been captured by Gressart despite being assured of safe conduct. He was forced to agree to an enormous ransom before being freed. La Trémoïlle ordered his half-brother Charles d'Albret, along with Joan and a small army, to make their way in the first week of November to Saint-Pierre, a walled town that at the time had few inhabitants because of Gressart's depredations.

The siege proved surprisingly difficult. They had besieged the city for some time before the order was given to attack. A large number of soldiers inside resisted so strongly that the French army had to retire. Joan's squire, Jean d'Aulon, received an arrow wound to the heel. But when he saw that Joan and a very small group of men had remained behind, he pulled himself up onto his horse and rode up to discover why she had not retreated with the others. Joan removed her helmet and told him she was not alone. She said that "she still had 50,000 men in her company, and that they would not leave until she had taken the town. And when she said that, she did not have with her more than four or five men, which he knew for certain, as did several others who saw this as well. For this reason, he told her to retire to the rear like the others had done." As she had so many times before, Joan paid him no heed, but started gathering bundles of branches and sticks to make a bridge over the town's moat. She shouted: "Everyone get the faggots and the sticks!" The soldiers did so, which stunned Aulon because the town then fell after little resistance.[47]

Others present at the siege said that when the town was taken on November 4, soldiers wanted to seize and loot the twelfth-century church, but Joan forbade them to take anything at all.[48] Her confessor reported that even when they were camping in the countryside with few provisions, she would never eat any food that her men had gained from pillaging.[49] How do these versions tally with the Bourgeois's account of Joan's words to her soldiers at Paris? Saint-Pierre was a small town and, once it had been taken, Joan could afford to be magnanimous. Yet in the heat of a fiercely fought battle like the one at Paris, she may well have used incentives to encourage the troops, thinking that she could deal with the results later.

What was Joan thinking when she stayed behind with only a few men? The danger was obvious. Was she delusional? It is more likely that, as she did so often, Joan knew exactly what was happening around her but believed strongly in her own abilities to turn the situation around. Although Paris had been a failure, she could blame that on Charles. By contrast, Saint-Pierre would have reminded Joan of some of her earlier victories in the Loire, when she had to goad her men on. Whenever another commander – or the king – called for retreat or disengagement, Joan grew impatient and frustrated. When she could, she countermanded orders to delay. Saying she had a great multitude with her – far more than she had ever had – was more about confidence and conviction than delusion.

Three days after the victory, Joan sent a request to the city of Clermont-Ferrand for gunpowder, arrows, and artillery to prepare for the siege of La Charité. They complied, sending in addition "a sword, two daggers, and arms for Joan."[50] On November 9 Joan wrote to the people of Riom, recounting the victory at Saint-Pierre-le-Moutier and telling them that "with the aid of God, I intend to empty those places that are against the king. But because of the great cost of powder, arrows, and other war needs to besiege the city, and how little the lords who are in this city with me have to besiege La Charité, I request . . . that you immediately send help for the siege, including powder, saltpeter, sulfur, arrows, strong arbalests, and other equipment. Without them, the siege will be long."[51] Joan the warrior was back in full form.

Joan and Albret had insufficient men and equipment to take La Charité. She would have preferred to work alongside Alençon, who still wanted her with him in Normandy. Joan blamed their failure, rightly so, on La Trémoïlle, who had sent her there in the dead of winter, although she admitted that Catherine de La Rochelle had told her that it would be too cold to besiege the city. On one occasion Joan said that the king had sent her, and on two others that "she wanted to come to France, but the soldiers told her it was better to go first to La Charité."[52] She denied that she had done so by counsel of her voices. Joan always credited her voices with her victories but blamed defeat on the king or his council. By November of 1429, Joan knew and was unhappy about being kept out of the way while Charles's negotiations with Burgundy continued. But as a good soldier, she fought on.

The exact dates when Joan and Albret were at La Charité are unknown. The king's chronicler says only that they besieged the town, setting up some bombards, cannon, and other pieces of artillery. It went on for some time, but they ended by lifting the siege without having accomplished anything and losing most of their artillery.[53] Since the king did not send enough provisions or money to sustain her company, she had to lift the siege and retire, to her great displeasure.[54] It had lasted about a month before they left in shame.

By late December 1429, Joan was unhappy and disillusioned. For Christmas she returned to Jargeau, perhaps trying to revisit the triumph of only six months earlier. Charles knew of Joan's displeasure, and as king of France he could reward Joan for her successes, hoping she would take the hint and retire. He ennobled her and her lineage, appealing to her vanity.

> In praise of the outpouring of such astonishing grace that the Divine
> Majesty gave to us by the signal assistance of our dear and beloved Maid,
> Joan Darc of Domremy. . . . We raise Joan and all her kin and their
> posterity to the level of other nobles of our realm . . . despite the fact
> that, as has been said, they are not of noble origin and that they are
> perhaps of a condition other than free.[55]

Joan apparently cared little for the honor, since she never mentioned it.
However, her brothers and their descendants made the most of the opportunities it provided. By this point Charles, the anointed and crowned king
of France, wanted Joan out of the way. She had become a hindrance to his
and La Trémoïlle's plans by continuing to pursue war while they negotiated for peace.

January through March of 1430 was the winter of Joan's discontent.
She remained at La Trémoïlle's castle of Sully-sur-Loire, presumably
so the king's men could watch her movements. Requests she sent to the
city council of Tours show how little she had to occupy her time. On
January 19 and February 7, the city fathers deliberated her request to pay
for the wedding expenses of the daughter of the painter who had made
her standard and pennons. They agreed to pay for a wedding dress but
refused anything else beyond a special blessing for the girl, in view of
money they had to spend on repairs to the city.[56]

Finally, in March, Joan took matters in her own hands. She began by
dictating more letters. One of these letters, the authenticity of which has
been questioned,[57] addressed the Hussites of Bohemia. It seems likely
however, that having little else to do, Joan now directed her attention to
enemies of the faith. If so, she was treading on dangerous ground, acting
as a spokesperson for the Church. She wrote:

> It has come to my ears, to me, Joan the Maid, that you have become
> heretical Christians, like blind people and Saracens. You have extin-
> guished true belief and . . . [have instituted] a revolting superstition that
> you defend by blood and fire. . . . You destroy holy images and reduce
> churches to rubble. You are completely mad! What insane fury possesses
> you? You want to persecute, destroy, and extirpate the true Faith. . . . As
> for me, Joan the Maid, I tell you truly that I would have come among
> you long ago with my avenging arm, if the war against the English had
> not kept me busy here.

She warned that if she did not hear in the near future that they had returned to the Church, she might leave the English and come against them "to destroy your horrible superstition, breaking it with the sword and taking from you either your heresy or your life."[58] Joan's confessor may have inspired the letter, but its language is consistent with the threats she voiced in her letters to the English as well as her earlier suggestion to Bedford that he join her in a holy enterprise. If she could not fight an actual war, she could at least threaten one. Sending her on a crusade might have been tempting for Charles, yet he could not be sure that he would not need her again. Even if she had become a problem for him, she still inspired fear and loathing on the other side.

Joan also dictated two letters to the people of Reims in the same month. There had been rumors within the city that some citizens were planning to go over to the Burgundian side. All of the northeast had reason to be wary. Although the truce was not set to expire until Easter, Burgundian actions against cities that had surrendered to Charles were already under way. At the beginning of April, Philip the Good traveled to Péronne where he gathered his soldiers,[59] while the English garrison at Calais waited for the arrival of the young King Henry VI. At the same time Jean of Luxembourg, one of Philip's allies, prepared to besiege the city of Compiègne. The Rémois had written to tell Joan that seditious activities were taking place in the city. In her first letter she acknowledged their fears, advising them to "shut your gates, because I will soon be with you. And if they come, I will have them chased by their spurs so fast that they will not know how to stop, and their destruction will soon follow. The other thing I will add for now is for you always to be good and loyal. I pray God will watch over you."[60] Less than two weeks later she wrote again, saying that she had heard evildoers were in their midst who planned to betray the city to the Burgundians. She assured them that if they were in need Charles would come to their aid. How could Joan believe that would happen? By now she realized that her king did not want to make war. She ended the letter with a warning: "you should know that you would suffer greatly because of the harshness these treacherous Burgundians show to their enemies." She promised they would hear more from her shortly.[61]

By late March Joan had had enough of her enforced inactivity. Without the king's knowledge or leave, Joan left the castle on the pretense of taking some recreation.[62] She had started to hear stories of English and Burgundian brigands pillaging cities that had surrendered to the king the previous summer. Upon learning that 300 to 400 English troops were heading for the Île-de-France, she took to the field with captains and soldiers from the Lagny garrison. Equally matched in troops, they met up with the English who ranged themselves along the length of a long hedge. The French immediately decided to fight, probably at Joan's insistence. The English were defeated and a large number killed and imprisoned. Many French soldiers also died or were wounded. Joan then led the prisoners into Lagny.[63]

One of the more accurate chroniclers of the time, a Burgundian, went on to describe an event that would attract great attention at Joan's trial.

> A gentleman soldier named Franquet d'Arras, of the Burgundian party, had gone to Lagny-sur-Marne, accompanied by other valiant soldiers and archers, about 300 in number. [There] he met up with the Maid whom the French had made their idol, with 400 Frenchmen, all good combatants. From the moment they encountered each other, neither could by honor flee the battle. However, the name of the Maid was so great and so famous that everyone dreaded her as a thing about which one could not judge whether she was good or evil. But she had already undertaken and led to a successful conclusion so many campaigns that her enemies feared her, while those of her party loved her. . . .
>
> Now, Franquet was a courageous man who was astonished by nothing. He saw the only remedy in his case was to fight the Maid. . . . [Eventually] Franquet, without thought of saving himself by flight, hoping to escape and save his men by his valor, was captured, while his men were killed and completely defeated. Led [away] prisoner, he was later decapitated by the cruelty of this woman who desired his death.[64]

Another Burgundian wrote that Joan had fought "very courageously and vigorously" against Franquet. He too said that Joan had ordered Franquet's head cut off.[65]

Joan did not personally kill Franquet but neither did she stop his execution. Questioned about his death at her trial, Joan answered cagily that she "consented to his death if he had deserved it, since he had confessed himself a murderer, a thief, and a traitor. She said his trial lasted a fortnight and he had for judges the bailiff of Senlis and a jury of the people of Lagny." She added that she had asked that Franquet be exchanged for a man from Paris, the landlord of the Bear Inn.[66] But when she heard the latter was already dead and was told by the bailiff that it would be a great injustice to ransom or free Franquet, she said: "As the man I wanted is dead, do with this fellow as justice demands." When she was asked if she sent money, or had money sent, to the man who had captured Franquet, she responded that she was "not Master of the Mint or Treasurer of France that she should pay out money."[67] Did Joan have Franquet summarily executed? It is possible, considering her flippant response. In any case she made no effort to save him, even if there was talk of prisoner exchange. All of Joan's actions, at least since Paris, suggest that she was not particularly bothered by bloodshed. Many French and English had died when she and her men attacked at Lagny, which she never mentioned at trial. Instead she replied with sarcasm.

Some people in Lagny thought Joan had performed a miracle. When she was asked about a child she had supposedly resuscitated, she said that it had been three days old. Learning that other women of the town were praying before a statue of the Virgin, Joan joined them, asking God and the Virgin to bring the child back to life.

> At last life appeared in the child, which yawned thrice, and was afterwards baptized: and immediately it died and was buried in consecrated ground. Three days had passed, they said, with no sign of life in the child, which was as black as her coat. But when it yawned, the color began to return. . . . Asked whether it was said in the town that she had brought about the resuscitation, and that it was due to her prayers, she answered that she did not inquire about it.[68]

Earlier Joan had rejected attempts by others to treat her as an idol, as when she told the women at Bourges to bless their own rosaries. There is no evidence that this case was any different, yet she made no effort to downplay the event. Joan's cleverly noncommittal response accurately reflects her changing personality in the short period since she had become not only France's heroine but also a European phenomenon.

The victory at Lagny rejuvenated Joan and the soldiers around her. It also heightened English fears.[69] On May 3 Bedford issued an edict in the name of King Henry VI against captains and soldiers who refused to embark for France. Bedford was by now seriously worried about his own standing and personal fortune in France. He wrote that many captains and soldiers were dilly-dallying in London, contrary to their orders.

Wanting to put an end to this perverse disorder, which shows contempt for our authority and prejudice to our cause, we enjoin you . . . [to proclaim] that each and every captain and soldier in the city of whatever rank or condition who has been retained to make the voyage with us to the continent go to the coasts, to Sandwich and Dover . . . as hastily as possible. . . . All those who are found delaying in London will be seized immediately and arrested with their horses and armor kept as surety, and they shall be imprisoned.[70]

While Bedford does not mention Joan, the edict shows that recruiting and desertions posed an increasing problem for the English, who were nervous following the loss of Lagny. In addition, a major plot in Paris in March threatened their hold on the capital. The Bourgeois of Paris describes the late winter as a time of great poverty and despair in the city that made it ripe for rebellion. The Parisians, who had once "loved the Duke of Burgundy," grew increasingly disenchanted with him when he did not come to their aid in 1430 and 1431, preferring the company of his new wife. "Some of the important men of Paris, of the Parlement, the Châtelet, merchants, and craftsmen put together a plot to let the Armagnacs into Paris." But one of the conspirators, a Carmelite friar, was captured and under torture revealed the names of the conspirators. In the week before Palm Sunday more than 150 were taken into custody. Six were beheaded at Les Halles, some were drowned, and others died as a result of torture.[71] Although the conspiracy failed, it showed the mounting discontent of the Parisians with their Burgundian and English overlords.

The truce with Burgundy officially expired on Easter, April 16. By May a new French offensive was being organized. King Charles issued a manifesto to French-held towns in the northeast. Joan felt triumphant at the prospect of the policy of appeasement coming to an end. The king accused " 'Our adversary of Burgundy' of having 'diverted and deceived us for some time with truces', while behind this mask of good faith he had consistently favored the English, and obviously lacked any genuine peaceful intentions."[72] But French actions against Burgundy in 1430 were hollow, a series of "scattered, uncoordinated, and sometimes ill-conceived raids," for Charles was not yet in a position to wage a war of conquest. His government was "weak, disunited and engrossed in court intrigue or private warfare." La Trémoïlle cared far more about his personal rivalries and augmenting his power and wealth than about fighting England or Burgundy.[73]

The subtleties of court politics, especially those of La Trémoïlle, were lost on Joan, pieces of a puzzle she never figured out. She heard what she wanted to hear, that the king would no longer make truces with Burgundy and that she would be able to take the fight to them. The increasing disjunction between the royal strategy concocted by Charles and his counselors and Joan's continuing desire for military action and success was instrumental in her marginalization and eventual downfall. She could not understand why Charles did not see the larger picture, even though it was Joan who, for all her amazing accomplishments in war, did not see why reconciliation with Burgundy was vital.

Joan spent the remainder of April and early May in Soissons, Crépy-en-Valois, and Senlis, to the south and southwest of Compiègne. She had waited for a long time to confront her enemies again, and after Lagny her confidence − at least in herself − was restored. Throughout May, Joan stayed in Compiègne several times, including on May 14, when a reception was held in her honor. Regnault de Chartres and Louis de Bourbon, count of Vendôme, attended. She may have believed that once again she had the full confidence of Charles. Yet Joan said at trial that she knew she would be captured:

> In Easter week last [year], when she was in the trenches at Melun, she was told by her voices . . . that she would be captured before St. John's Day [June 24]; it had to be so; and she should not be distressed, but take it in good part, and God would aid her.
>
> Asked if since Melun she had been told by her voices that she would be taken, she answered yes, several times, nearly every day . . . but they did not tell her when.[74]

This statement was most likely a reconstruction she made at trial, intended to recall Jesus' entry into Jerusalem and his capture, which led to his crucifixion. Was Joan really convinced her capture was imminent in May of 1430? Probably not. She still believed in herself and many remained loyal to her. Joan would spend the last weeks of her freedom doing what she did best − leading a war effort.

CHAPTER 7

Captivity

In April of 1430, Henry Beaufort, cardinal of Winchester, and the young King Henry VI landed at Calais with a large English force. Ironically, Beaufort had returned to England after a failed campaign against the Hussites. At odds with other members of the English royal council, he took the troops he had planned to use for a crusade to help relieve the faltering English efforts in France. At the same time, after the expiration of his truce with Charles VII on April 16, Philip the Good and his ally Jean of Luxembourg, count of Ligny and St.-Pol, began preparations for an attack on Compiègne for its strong French garrison hindered passage to Paris. Relations between Burgundy and England had grown somewhat closer as a result of Philip's marriage to Bedford's cousin Isabelle of Portugal five months earlier. At this point, Joan's single-minded determination to unify France under her king had guided her for almost two years. The danger of increasing cooperation between Burgundy and England and a renewal of the conflict provided her once again with an opportunity to take the fight to her enemies.

Compiègne was surrounded by thick stone walls that were punctuated by forty-four towers. The bridge across the Oise measured 450 feet long, with a fort at the end and a rampart that blocked access to the bridge.[1] The people of Compiègne held a reception and banquet for Joan, providing a sign of their faith in her: she had been steadfast even when others had failed them. Early on the day after the reception, Joan made a sortie outside of the city, but had to retreat because of the presence of a large contingent of Anglo-Burgundian troops. Instead, accompanied by Regnault de Chartres, Louis, count of Vendôme, with whom she had fought at Orléans, and several other captains, she left for Soissons, twenty-three miles to the east. She hoped to use Soissons as a base to separate the English and Burgundian armies. But unknown to Joan, the captain and bishop of the city had decided to turn it over to Jean of Luxembourg. When they arrived the captain refused them entry, so the soldiers prepared to sleep in the field. With night approaching the captain led Joan, the archbishop, and the count, along with a small company, back into the city. But as soon as they left Soissons the next morning the captain sold the city to the duke of Burgundy and put it in the hands of Jean of Luxembourg.[2] Joan was furious. When asked at trial if she had said she would have him drawn and quartered if she got her hands on him, Joan wisely did not answer.[3]

Joan had no choice but to head back to Compiègne by way of Crépy-en-Valois, where she awaited reinforcements. On May 22, she was notified that the duke of Burgundy and a large number of English soldiers, including John, earl of Arundel – a man whose "cruelty no less than his success had made him exceptionally odious to French patriots"[4] – had arrived before Compiègne. When she was told that she had too few men to head toward the middle of the Anglo-Burgundian army, she responded: "By my Martin, we are enough, I am going to see my good friends of Compiègne."[5] Joan left at night and slipped back into the city after midnight. The decision changed Joan's life.

Skirmishes between the French and the Anglo-Burgundian soldiers besieging the city were the norm, but the events of May 23 changed everything. Joan rose early and went to pray in the pilgrimage church of Saint Jacques. Around nine in the morning, with heavy fighting across the river, Joan armed herself and with her men crossed the great bridge to join the melee. She presented a daunting figure:

> Mounted on her horse, armed just like a man, she wore over her armor a doublet of crimson cloth of gold. She rode a dapple-grey horse, very beautiful and proud, and held herself in her armor and with gestures just like a captain leading a great army. With her standard raised high and blowing in the wind, accompanied by many noblemen, she left the city.[6]

As soon as she joined the fight the enemy retreated. At first things went well when she attacked the followers of Jean of Luxembourg and twice drove them back to the camp of the Burgundians. On the third attack the

Map 8 Joan's last campaigns.

French troops pushed them to the middle of the road leading away from the city. But seeing their soldiers in disarray, a group of Anglo-Burgundian soldiers lying in wait emerged and, kicking their spurs, rode between the bridge to the city and Joan and her company. It was about six o'clock in the evening. One large contingent headed straight toward Joan. Her men lost hope that they could sustain an attack. When they urged her to return to the city she was furious, saying: "Be quiet, for it is only necessary to hold fast until they are defeated. Think only of striking them!" But the soldiers saw it was a lost cause and turned back toward the bridge. When the Burgundians and the English saw that she was heading back to the city, they posted a large number of men at the end of the bridge. Captain Guillaume Flavy, seeing the English and Burgundian troops ready to cross into the city, ordered the drawbridge raised and closed the gate. Joan was trapped outside with only a few men.[7] At her trial, Joan said that as she retreated to the fields on the Picardy side near the road, she was taken, and between the place where she was captured and Compiègne there was nothing but the river and the boulevard with its ditch.[8]

Even Burgundian chroniclers accorded her respect, saying that Joan had remained at the rear in order to save her company.[9] Whether it was the result of courage or foolhardiness, Joan was captured. Many of the enemy soldiers did not share such appreciation for Joan's behavior. One archer, "out of spite that a woman of whom he had heard so much would try to

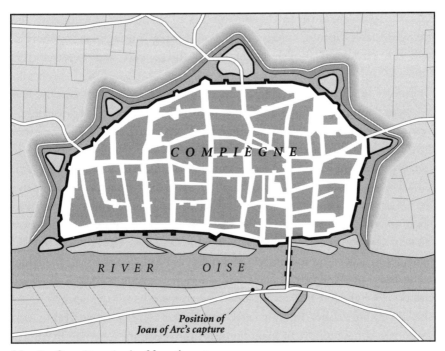

Map 9   Compiègne in the fifteenth century.

repulse so many valiant men, grabbed her from the side by her cloth of gold doublet and pulling her from her horse, made her fall to the ground." Although Joan struggled to remount, she could not. She surrendered to the Bastard of Wandomme, one of Luxembourg's men who commanded a contingent of about seventy men. "More joyous than if he had a king in his hands,"[10] he led her away from the fray until combat was over. By putting herself in the hands of a nobleman, Joan was proclaiming to all present that she was his equal. Her comrade Poton de Xantrailles, her brother Pierre, her squire Aulon, and a small number of others were also seized.

News of Joan's capture elated the Burgundians and English, "more than if they had taken 500 soldiers, because they feared no captain or war leader up until that day as they had dreaded the Maid."[11] For the French side her captivity was potentially disastrous. As much as the king and his counselors wanted to be rid of Joan, they did not want her in the hands of the enemy. Joan was a very special prize. Wandomme handed Joan over to Jean of Luxembourg, who kept her in his custody for three or four days. The duke of Burgundy came to see her and spoke with her, but there are no accounts of the words they exchanged. On the same day, Philip the Good wrote jubilantly to the inhabitants of nearby St. Quentin to tell them of Joan's capture, saying that it would make "big news everywhere as will the error and foolish belief of all those who had followed this woman."[12]

Philip's letter is as revealing about Joan's moral leadership and the fear it inspired among the rank and file as are the English edicts against desertion. He mentioned Joan first among those captured. Although the other prisoners would be ransomed, she was too valuable – and dangerous – to her captors. Nor could she expect help from the court of Charles VII. Charles himself said little or nothing about Joan's capture, but Regnault de Chartres wrote to the city of Reims asserting that she had deserved such an unhappy outcome. "She had too much confidence in her own powers and opinions. . . . She did not want to believe the council, but did everything according to her own pleasure. . . . God allowed Joan the Maid to be taken because of her pride and the rich clothing she wore. She had not done what God had commanded but followed her own designs."[13] At the beginning of her mission, at Chinon, the archbishop of Reims had given grudging support to Joan, but after the coronation he had become a strong proponent of peace with Burgundy. Even though he had had little choice but to be at her side when she had left for Soissons – probably to keep an eye on her – her actions endangered the king's diplomacy.

Philip and his allies had every reason to hope that the French would now lose heart and return to the bargaining table. Instead, he faced a number of setbacks in the summer of 1430 that he blamed on the English. The following November he wrote to Henry VI, care of Bedford, that:

> it was at your urgent request that I took part in the French war. For my part, I have so far accomplished everything that I agreed to. . . . It is a fact that, as a result, all my lands both in Burgundy and Picardy have been and are at war and in danger of destruction. . . . Moreover, it was at your request and command that I undertook the siege of Compiègne, though this was contrary to the advice of my council and my own opinion.

Philip, desperate for money, added that he would not continue military operations unless the English provided him with adequate provisions and payments that were owed to him.[14] Relations between Burgundy and England would continue to deteriorate. Charles and Philip began to negotiate once again, but it would take until August of 1435, when the Treaty of Arras was signed, to put an end to hostilities between the French and Burgundians.

In the meantime, Joan proved a good bargaining chip for Philip and his ally Jean of Luxembourg. They moved Joan from Clairoix to Beaulieu-lès-Fontaines on May 27, where she would remain for six weeks. But if the Burgundians hoped Joan's captivity would break her spirit, they soon found out otherwise. At Beaulieu, Joan tried the first of her two attempts at escape. At trial, she was asked to tell "how she expected to escape from the castle of Beaulieu between two pieces of wood: she answered she was never a prisoner in any place but she would gladly escape; and being in the castle she would have shut up her keepers in the tower, had not the porter seen and confronted her."[15] Thanks to her ingenuity and indomitable spirit, Joan came very close to escaping, although she would almost certainly have been recaptured.

In June, the English-controlled University of Paris demanded that Joan be handed over to them, but the duke of Burgundy and Jean of Luxembourg did not accede to their requests. Chronicles of the time make it clear that England was right in fearing that Joan would try to escape or

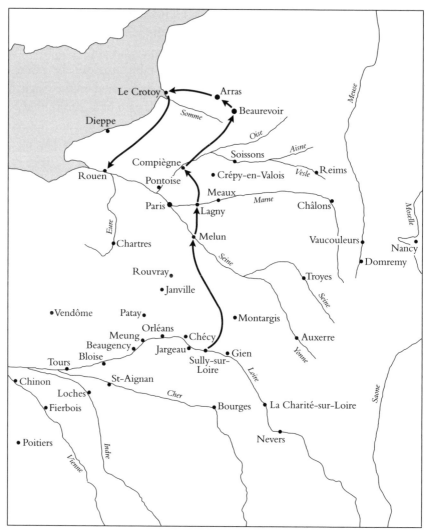

Map 10   Joan's route to captivity and execution, March–May 1430.

be ransomed, indicating the strained relations they now had with her Burgundian captors. The English council wrote to the two men on numerous occasions, urging them to hand Joan over.

The bishop of Beauvais, Pierre Cauchon, an important diplomat and former rector of the University of Paris, wrote offering money. When they refused, he threatened that "although the taking of this woman is not similar to the capture of a king, of princes and others of high estate . . . the bishop summons and requires the abovesaid in his name and [Henry VI's] to deliver the Maid to him."[16] Not similar to the capture of a king!

Jean of Luxembourg had good reason to procrastinate. Joan was a very important prisoner. But in view of her attempted escape from Beaulieu, she was transferred to the much more secure fortress of Beaurevoir, where she enjoyed a relatively comfortable captivity in the tower from July 11 until mid-autumn. The duke's aunt, Jeanne of Luxembourg, was the main reason he did not hand Joan over to the English. First, as godmother to Charles VII she had close connections to the French royal family. Secondly, the elderly countess had willed her estate to Jean rather than his older brother, so he had every incentive to remain in her good graces. Along with Jean's wife Jeanne of Béthune and his stepdaughter Jeanne of Bar, Jeanne of Luxembourg seems to have done everything in her power to make Joan's confinement at Beaurevoir as pleasant as possible. They may well have enjoyed the opportunity to get to know the girl about whom practically everyone in Europe was talking.

Joan may have appreciated the women's kindness but it did not make the loss of her freedom any more agreeable. Perhaps to make her more acceptable to their male relatives, the three Jeannes asked her to give up her male clothing. Joan responded that she would not change her clothes without God's permission. She told them she appreciated their offer of a dress or cloth to make a new one, adding that she would rather have done it for these ladies than any others in France, save her queen.[17] Although Joan claimed that she could not change her clothes because God had not given her leave, at Beaurevoir she had no good reason to continue wearing the clothes of a soldier. More importantly, Joan rejected the offer because she knew that her clothing had made her "the Maid." Everything she had accomplished since her departure from Vaucouleurs had been done wearing simple male clothing and a man's haircut, followed by suits of armor, chain mail, and finally the sumptuous and symbolic clothing given to her by the duke of Orléans after the victory. Joan had come to equate her male attire with power and honor. To give it up was not possible without losing her identity.

Accustomed to activity, Joan could not have been happy. Moreover, while the ladies at Beaurevoir protected her, she was subjected to occasional harassment. A knight later admitted that "several times, joking around, he tried to touch her breasts, doing his best to put his hands on her bosom but Joan would not allow it and pushed him away as hard as she could."[18] Whether Joan's virginal status was the result of a vow to God or an excuse to escape from her parents, she had learned early on that it endowed her with the characteristics of the prophesied Maid. Even if the knight had only been trying to fondle her breasts, Joan did not want to be reminded of her female body.

Joan was determined to escape, even though, as she told her trial examiners, her voices had forbidden it. At Beaurevoir she devised a dangerous plan to escape through the window. She probably tied bedding to the windows, trying to climb slowly down the castle walls, but either the fabric or part of the window gave way and she fell to the ground. Although Joan sometimes said she leapt, dramatizing her attempt at escape, it is clear that she fell; she could hardly have expected to survive such a high jump from the tower's keep. She nearly broke her back and was sick for a long time as a result of her other wounds.[19] When her captors found her, Joan appeared to be dead and only came around when they told her what had happened. She could not eat for several days[20] but when questioned, she acknowledged that the jump was prompted by rumors that the English were going to come and take her. Joan insisted this had not been an attempt at suicide, although she admitted she would rather die than fall into the hands of the English.[21] She later told her judges that she did so in "hope of saving my body and going to the aid of many good people in need."[22] She, Joan the Maid, had to rescue Compiègne and other cities that needed her. Joan saw herself as the *only* hope for a unified France. She had put her faith in Charles but now she had to rely on herself. She insisted repeatedly that she would try to escape again if given the chance. Joan always said that God helped those who helped themselves.[23]

The refusal of Philip the Bold and Jean of Luxembourg to deliver Joan up enraged the English.[24] As early as May 26, the Vicar General of the Inquisition at Paris had written to both men, demanding that she be turned over to them. Lawyers and theologians of the University of Paris, who would play the leading roles in Joan's trial, warned the duke of Burgundy that his adversaries would do everything in their power to take possession of her, through means foul or fair.[25] They warned Jean of Luxembourg that if Joan were set free or "lost to us, which certain of our adversaries would endeavor to obtain" it would be to his peril, and he was ordered to hand her over to bishop Cauchon of Beauvais.[26] But the appeals and threats fell on deaf ears, at least until count Jean of Luxembourg was freed from his aunt's influence and power.

Jeanne of Luxembourg left for Provence in the autumn and died near Avignon in mid-October. As his aunt lay dying, the count began to negotiate terms for Joan. Already, in September, the English had levied a tax on the Normans of "10,000 *l.t.* to pay for the purchase of Joan the Maid, said to be a sorceress and warrior, leader of the armies of the dauphin."[27] Finally, the English would have their prize.

In the first weeks of October, the famous prisoner began the lengthy journey that would take her to Rouen. The route chosen was not the quickest, but it was the safest, avoiding the cities that had been reclaimed by France and hugging the borders of Burgundian territory until they reached Normandy. This procession also allowed people in the towns along the way to witness the Maid in captivity. However, it did not always work to her captors' advantage. When Joan was taken to the castle at Drugy, near St. Riquier, the "old religious of the abbey visited her with honor . . . along with the important people of the city, and everyone felt compassion at seeing her persecuted."[28] Joan was treated well, and when they reached Le Crotoy, she was housed in the castle along with the chancellor of Notre Dame of Amiens, who was also a prisoner. Thanks to his presence she was able to confess and receive the eucharist. While there, a group of women visited her from Abbeville, almost eighteen miles away. They viewed her as "a marvel of their sex." Although most women did not aspire to a military role like the one Joan had chosen, she was an inspiration to many. Joan thanked them for their visit and asked them to pray for her. She reportedly said after their departure: "Ah! These are good people. May it please God that if I am so lucky when I end my days, I will be buried in this region."[29]

Joan seems to have been relatively content – probably for the last time – in Le Crotoy, and it was there that she said she had her last vision of St. Michael. After that, they traveled not far from the coast to Saint-Valéry, Eu, and Arques. Moving westward toward the sea, Joan may well have feared that she would be taken to England. But from Arques they headed south. In Bruges at the time of these events, the Venetian nobleman Pancrazio Giustiniani wrote: "what will happen to her, nobody knows, but it is feared the English will have her put to death."[30] That a knowledgeable and well-placed foreigner believed that the English intended to execute Joan shows the high stakes involved in her capture.

On November 21 the rector of the University of Paris announced that Joan was in their custody, but chastised bishop Cauchon about the length of time it had taken to deliver her. As a great prelate of the Church, it was his duty, according to the university, to rid the world of scandals to the faith, especially since the girl had been taken in his diocese. They urged him to deliver Joan to Paris as soon as possible.[31]

Rouen was the second choice for Joan's trial: the risks of taking her to Paris were simply too great. Since Henry VI was in Rouen, the duke of Bedford decided that the trial would be conducted there. The capital of English-held Normandy, it was undoubtedly safer than Paris. After leaving Bosc-le-Hard and d'Isneauville, Joan's escort probably skirted the Verte forest, the last wooded area from which an ambush was possible. Only one source, the Venetian nobleman, mentioned that Charles threatened the duke of Burgundy that he would take revenge for handing her over to the English.[32] In fact, the king had no intention of using more than idle threats to try to get Joan back. In view of her earlier attempts at escape, as well as the fear she inspired, her captors were unwilling to take any unnecessary risk. At dusk on Christmas Eve they reached the village of Bihorel, where Joan first glimpsed the skyline of the city where she would die.[33]

Rouen was at the heart of the dynastic struggles among the Armagnacs, the Burgundians, and the English. For its citizens, the past decade had been the worst of times. As a result of fighting in the region after Agincourt, famine was a constant of daily life, the scarcity of food being so great that people were forced to eat horses, dogs, cats, and rats.[34] Epidemics of dysentery, whooping cough, and plague struck the city in the decade from 1409 to 1419.[35] Prior to his assassination, Duke John the Fearless had courted the people of Rouen who, like those of Paris, had suffered considerably at the hands of the Armagnac faction. In response to excessive royal demands that amounted to what one historian has called a military dictatorship,[36] the Rouennais led a pro-Burgundian revolt in which the bailiff, who was also the dauphin's chamberlain, was assassinated outside his house. Several others suspected of sympathy for the dauphin were drowned in the Seine. By early 1418, Burgundian sympathizers were at least in nominal control of the city, but with little to no support from the duke.

The arrival of Henry V boded ill for Rouen. His troops began to encircle the city in the summer of 1418. When it became clear that Burgundy would not help, the citizens put up a strong resistance during a six-month siege but eventually had to pay an enormous "ransom" to the

English king. The city was devastated by January 20, 1419, when Henry V made his solemn entry. A Dominican chronicler of Rouen noted that "they had besieged the city up to the convent of Saint-Jacques, forcing many of the friars to flee."[37] The people were skin and bones, with hollow eyes and shrunken noses, barely able to breathe or speak. Their complexions were so ashen that some said they looked like the figures of dead kings on tombs. Cadavers lay in every street, while hundreds cried out for bread. People died so fast that there was hardly time to bury them.[38]

So began what would be a thirty-year occupation, until Charles VII's troops reconquered the city in 1449. In January 1422, Bedford admitted that "many of [the Rouennais] say that our men and officers have committed many wrongs, abuses, and excesses under the cover of their positions. . . . Churches are broken down, married women and others are taken and raped, and the poor people are beaten inhumanly."[39] By 1425, there were riots and "murmuring" about the royal justice, but after the death of Henry V, Bedford controlled England's holdings in France from Paris to Rouen. The situation in the city improved considerably under his administration and as a result of his building programs, but memories of the days of the siege would have a lasting effect on some of those who played principal, if unwilling, roles at Joan's trial.

This was the city Joan and her escort entered through the Beauvoisine Gate. Joan was taken to the Château de Bouvreuil, an impressive castle that had been built in the time of Philip Augustus. A credible reconstruction places Joan in a hexagonal room with a small Romanesque window facing the countryside that was eight steps above ground level.[40]

On January 3, 1431, Bedford issued a letter in the name of the king that announced the news of the trial:

It is well known how for some time a woman calling herself Joan *the Maid*, putting off the dress and habit of the female sex (which is contrary to divine law, abominable to God, condemned and prohibited by every law), has dressed and armed herself in the state and habit of man, has wrought and occasioned cruel murders, and it is said, to seduce and deceive the simple people, has given them to understand that she was sent from God and that she had knowledge of His divine secrets, with many other dangerous dogmatizations most prejudicious and scandalous to our holy faith. . . . And because she has been reputed, charged and defamed by many people on the subject of superstitions, false dogmas, and other crimes of divine treason.

She was to be examined by bishop Pierre Cauchon of Beauvais along with learned examiners from the University of Paris. Already in this letter there are foreshadowings of how the trial was to be conducted and the charges that would be leveled against Joan; they were going to use every ecclesiastical and inquisitorial tool at their disposal. But most ominous was one of Bedford's last sentences. "Nevertheless it is our intention to retake and regain possession of this Joan if it comes to pass that she is not convicted or found guilty of the said crimes."[41] The regent would allow no possibility of an innocent verdict and broadcast this intent to all. By so doing, he made certain she would never again campaign against the English.

Despite his orchestration of the trial, Bedford sought to minimize his personal involvement as much as possible so that it would not appear to be tainted by English animosity. He and his wife, Anne of Burgundy, were living in the castle when Joan arrived, but on January 13 they left for Paris. The eight-year-old Henry VI would remain in Rouen along with the earl of Warwick and the cardinal of Winchester. Bedford did not return until September 18, nearly four months after Joan's execution.[42]

Cauchon first had to be given jursidiction in Rouen. Although Joan had been captured in the diocese where he served as bishop, it was then in French hands. In theory he had no standing to preside over a trial in English Normandy. At Bedford's bidding, the cathedral chapter took over since the archbishopric of Rouen was vacant. They appointed Cauchon to conduct an "inquiry against a woman commonly called Joan the Maid, who abandoning all modesty, has lived a disorderly and shameful life to the scorn of the estate proper to womanhood." They informed him that it was his duty to institute inquiries against "this woman who, suspected of heresy, had committed so many misdemeanors against the Catholic faith. . . . and to institute proceedings in the city of Rouen."[43] The constant refrain about Joan's contempt for "the estate proper to womanhood" would set the stage for some of the key charges brought against her.

The letter demonstrates several important aspects of how Joan was to be tried and where. Paris was out of the question. Although there is no solid evidence to support the idea, the English feared Charles or some of Joan's military comrades would try to save her. Granting Cauchon jurisdiction in Rouen was of no great concern to them since the verdict had been preordained. More importantly, the letter begins to establish *fama publica* (public notoriety), a requirement of canon law in undertaking inquisitorial trials. Before an inquisition began, a defendant had to be charged with a specific crime; otherwise he or she had the right to remain silent. By the time of Joan's trial, judges could proceed if there was belief "by reputable persons that the defendant was guilty."[44] Bedford, no doubt supported by the University of Paris theologians as well as canon lawyers in England, knew this when he began his own letter-writing campaign after Joan was captured. Although certain assessors would judge the trial invalid in March because these charges of public notoriety had never been presented to Joan, the letter of December 28, 1430 expresses the opinion that her many sins against the faith and womanhood made such a proceeding appropriate for an inquisitorial process. After all, most of the European world knew of Joan, even though many admired her. But this letter set out in writing the probable cause of *fama publica*.

Following the succession of letters, officials were appointed. Cauchon, earlier accused of laxity, now zealously followed orders, declaring Jean d'Estivet promotor of the trial on January 9. Estivet's role was to accuse and denounce Joan, to examine and interrogate her, and to bring the case to an end.[45] On the same day, Master Jean de La Fontaine was named counselor and examiner of witnesses. He questioned witnesses under oath, drew up depositions, and in some circumstances took Cauchon's place. Jean Massieu, a priest of Rouen, was designated executor of mandates; one of Massieu's roles would be to lead Joan to and from her cell to the chamber where she was interrogated. In this capacity, at least during the first month of the trial, he allowed Joan to pray in the chapel of St. Romain before she was escorted to the Robing Room next to the Great Hall in the eastern end of the castle.[46] Massieu said that on several occasions Jean Beaupère, a close friend of Cauchon and one of the leading examiners, reproached him:

> "Miserable one, who makes you so brave to allow this whore excommunicated by the Church to pray in the chapel? I will have you put in such a tower that you will never see the moon or the sun for a month if you do this again." And when he saw that Massieu would not obey, Beaupère stood several times in front of the chapel, between the witness and Joan, to make sure that she did not pray there.[47]

Two notaries of the archiepiscopal court of Rouen, Guillaume Manchon and Guillaume Colles (known as Boisguillaume), were appointed and granted access to Joan as often as necessary to question her and write down her "confessions," receive the oath of witnesses, and record the opinions of witnesses such as theologians and canon lawyers, word for word. Cauchon was determined to have all the facts of the case put into writing and draw up the proceedings in proper form.[48] The notaries, along with Jean Beaupère, sat at the feet of the judges where they noted down their questions and Joan's answers. Manchon said that they did not always agree. "There was a great difference, to the point that they quarreled. For this reason, on the points where he saw a difference, he put down *Nota*, in order that Joan could be questioned again."[49] As a result of the desire to make the charges against Joan stand in accordance with canon law and the court of popular opinion, Cauchon wanted to dot all the i's and cross all the t's.

From January 13 to 23, evidence was gathered to proceed against Joan. On the 23rd it was decided to conduct an inquiry into Joan's actions and sayings. La Fontaine was put in charge of this phase and from February 14 to 16 he and the two notaries compiled the information and presented it to Cauchon. A few days later, seven doctors of theology, two canon lawyers, three bachelors of theology, a canon of the cathedral, and Cauchon deliberated, concluding that they "possessed sufficient evidence to proceed against this woman and summon her in matters of faith."[50]

In spite of the procedural and legal failings later charged against those who proceeded against Joan in 1431, Cauchon, an extraordinarily well-qualified University of Paris canon lawyer and theologian, believed he was conducting an exemplary trial. However, three immediate mistakes are obvious. While Rouen may have been safer than Paris, witness depositions and willingness to serve would present major problems, as would the lack of any counsel from Joan's "party." She had no defense except her own words, which more often than not were used against her to *create* the case. Even so, Joan would receive help at the trial from a most unlikely source. The second mistake was appointing the conscientious scribe Guillaume Manchon as head notary under the apparently mistaken assumption that he could be either bought or intimidated. The final mistake was assuming that in spite of her fame, Joan would crumble before such a prestigious assembly of theologians, canon and civil lawyers, medical doctors, and judges. Instead Joan showed that she was a modern-day incarnation of

Catherine of Alexandria in her eloquence, conviction, and stamina. Just as Joan had done in battle, she now showed that she could be wise and crafty against her enemies in a different kind of test. Although the result was a foregone conclusion, Joan would go down fighting like a lion rather than a lamb.

CHAPTER 8

Judging the Maid

❧

Although Joan's trial generated almost as much interest as her battles, much less information reached the public until after the publication of the trial record in the summer of 1431. The occasional merchant in Rouen or the experts who were called there but refused to participate in the trial may have told others what they had learned, but for the most part what went on during the proceedings was kept secret. This led to rumors, especially in Rouen, where with few exceptions the people only saw Joan twice, at her abjuration and execution. Joan, too, was kept in the dark. Unlike her judges, who probably expected convicting Joan would be child's play in view of her simple manner, Joan did not know the degree to which the odds had been stacked against her. She may even have believed she would be rescued. Joan had been through many tests before – several times at Vaucouleurs, twice at Chinon, Poitiers, and, of course, in battle. In all these instances, against the odds she had emerged victorious, at least until Paris. She therefore approached the trial as she did any battle: with skill, boldness, audacity, and ruses.

Joan once again had to undergo physical inspection of her virginity. The English hoped that evidence to the contrary would undermine all her other claims, which had proved so essential to the French victories. A citizen of Paris who was in Rouen at the time of her recantation and execution reported that he heard that Bedford's wife had Joan examined to know whether or not she was a virgin. She was found to be physically intact.[1] Passing the test of virginity would prove to be the simplest of Joan's battles in Rouen. A servant of Jean Beaupère, one of Joan's leading antagonists at the trial, remembered the visit "because they said afterward that Joan had been injured in her rear end as a result of riding horses."[2] But while Joan would allow women to examine her, she would take no nonsense from men. A dressmaker reported that the duchess of Bedford had asked him to make a proper dress for Joan. When he tried to fit her, taking her gently by the breast, she became indignant and slapped him in the face.[3]

While Cauchon had no difficulty gathering his allies from the University of Paris, who were eager to participate, a trial that was intended to convict Joan for heresy rather than for war crimes had to be conducted as an inquisition. Such a trial needed an inquisitor. Surprisingly, finding someone both qualified and willing to serve proved to be one of Cauchon's first and greatest challenges. When on February 19 he summoned Jean Graverent, the Inquisitor of France, Cauchon was informed that he was occupied elsewhere. Graverent, who was firmly on the English side, was involved in another case, but surely that would not have prevented his presence at such an important trial if he had wished to preside? On learning that the inquisitor was unavailable, Cauchon demanded that the Vice Inquisitor for Rouen, Jean Le Maistre, prior of the Convent of Saint-Jacques, attend in his stead. Immediately Le Maistre raised problems. Saying that he was only appointed for the diocese of Rouen, he doubted that his commission could be interpreted to include the present trial.[4] Cauchon, not pleased, ordered him to appear the next day. Le Maistre did so, along with one of the brothers of his convent, Martin Ladvenu. When Cauchon and several University of Paris theologians again invited him to participate, Le Maistre answered that "for the serenity of his conscience and the safer conduct of the trial" he would not participate in the matter unless he received special authority.[5] Cauchon was forced to write to Graverent asking him to grant such authority. Although Le Maistre attended some of the early sessions, Cauchon was frustrated by the Vice Inquisitor's lackluster involvement, worrying that it might affect the outcome.

On March 12, Le Maistre was called to Cauchon's residence. For the first time, Ysambard de La Pierre, another Dominican of Saint-Jacques, came with him. La Pierre would henceforth attend all the sessions and play a vital role in making sure that the trial was not a complete sham. Cauchon, exasperated at the Vice Inquisitor's reluctance, reminded Le Maistre of all the difficulties he had raised from the beginning. Still Le Maistre hesitated, saying that he would look over the commission and then give his reply. Cauchon reminded him that he had already been present for much of the proceedings, asking him why he needed more time to decide.[6] Why did a Dominican prior, entrusted with inquisitorial powers, try to evade his responsibility? Only on March 13, over two months after the other officers of the trial had been appointed, did Le Maistre agree to become a full participant in the case.[7] The next day, presumably at Le Maistre's insistence, another notary, Nicolas Taquel, joined Guillaume Manchon and Boisguillaume. Since Cauchon assumed the trial would proceed smoothly and without difficulty, he was determined to follow correct procedure[8] – at least at the beginning.

From the time he officially joined the other trial judges, Le Maistre played a subordinate role, without special rank among the expert witnesses and doctors forming the tribunal, his part largely limited to rubber-stamping Cauchon's decisions and appointments.[9] Although he has been charged with cowardice and weakness, his position as prior and protector of the convent of Saint-Jacques constrained him. The convent had already suffered considerably at the hands of the English in the years after the siege and a complete refusal to take part in the trial would not have helped Joan and would probably have brought ruin to the community.[10] The only significant role Le Maistre would play in the trial, besides having his name included as the bishop's "We", was to protect those threatened by Cauchon, the English, or their University of Paris collaborators. He may also have tried to help Joan as much as he could, along with other Dominicans of Saint-Jacques.

Despite these unexpected difficulties, Cauchon was determined to press forward. Joan would be his next problem. The first session was held on February 21 at eight o'clock in the morning in the royal chapel of the castle. Without presenting any articles against her, Cauchon demanded that she take an oath, her hands on the gospels, to answer truthfully all questions put to her. Joan replied, "I do not know what you wish to examine me on. Perhaps you might ask such things that I would not tell."[11] Joan's response was not only shrewd but canonically correct, far more so than could be expected from a nineteen-year-old peasant girl. Canon law stated that requiring an oath was unreasonable if charges had not been presented, the requisite ill fame established or the defendant objected.[12] Joan objected strenuously.

While some aspects of inquisitorial and canon law procedure were often ignored by the fifteenth century, Joan's right to protest that she had not been charged with any specific crimes should have been respected.

Cauchon knew inquisitorial rules from his days at the University of Paris. He had surrounded himself with numerous theologians and canon lawyers who could have corrected this oversight. No one did. As much as he wanted to follow proper procedure, Cauchon knew that the English were watching over his shoulder and could halt the trial at any moment. If that happened, Joan would have been sent to England, where she would have had no chance at all. Cauchon was neither the villain nor the semi-sympathetic judge often portrayed in popular literature and films. He was an ambitious man, not only a servant of the Church but also of the State. For the past fifteen years he had served the dukes of Burgundy and kings and queens of England, and in 1431 he acted as secretary to the duke of Bedford. He would continue to serve their interests until his death. Seven months after Joan's execution he would be present as a peer at the coronation of King Henry VI in Paris.[13] Cauchon fully understood English intentions regarding the trial of Joan of Arc, what it could mean for him, and also his obligations as a man of the Church. Still, he knew what he had to do. That was to put together a trial that at least on the surface appeared to be well conceived, followed correct procedure, and produced a judgment based on expert witness testimony and deliberations. On some issues he followed the letter of the law, allowing the notaries to have Joan verify or correct her testimony at the end of the day. Yet at the beginning of the trial, after his frustrating attempts to involve the Vice Inquisitor, he had to make an important decision: what had Joan done wrong except make war against the English and Burgundian occupying forces? Even Burgundian chroniclers seemed to admire her as often as not. So Cauchon made a conscious decision to bypass the canon law rule that charges must be presented before a trial could commence. He had to find a way to make Joan incriminate herself in words that could later be used against her.[14]

After considerable haggling about what she would or would not reveal, Joan, kneeling, with her two hands upon the missal, swore to answer truthfully whatever should be asked of her "concerning matters of faith," but would remain silent and "would not tell or reveal to any person the revelations made to her [by divine sources]."[15] Joan realized that Cauchon and the other questioners were trying to entrap her so she began to set conditions for what she would or would not tell them. That she particularly exempted her voices and revelations is significant. The voices she claimed to hear had become part of her persona, even her legend, gaining her respect and admiration even as she engaged in bloody battles. If she really did hear voices, she would have felt it was important to keep their directives secret. If, on the other hand, they had been an excuse for her to leave her home and go to the king, how could she possibly speak of them? Joan was damned if she did and damned if she didn't, and she intuitively understood the dilemma facing her. So she stalled.

After some questions about her childhood, Cauchon admonished her not to try to escape. Joan refused. As the session ended, Cauchon sent her back to her cell, where she was to be guarded by John Grey, one of Henry VI's personal guards, along with Jean Berwoit and William Talbot. She had five bodyguards in all.[16] At night three of them stayed in her cell and two outside the door. Joan slept fettered with two pairs of irons binding her legs, attached very tightly to a chain from the foot of her bed to a long piece of wood, about 4 or 5 feet long and locked with a key. As a result, she could barely move.[17] No one was allowed to speak with her, with one exception.

Cauchon planted a spy. Nicolas Loyseleur, one of the bishop's closest friends from the university, told Joan that he was a priest from Lorraine. He would enter her cell in layman's clothing and the guards would withdraw so that the two of them were alone. An opening had been made in the adjoining room where the notaries were told to listen as Joan spoke to Loyseleur. Sometimes Cauchon and Warwick also eavesdropped. Loyseleur began to question Joan, pretending to give her some news of the state of the realm. Joan answered him, believing that he was from her region and loyal to the king of France. Unfortunately she believed him and made her confession to him several times. Generally Cauchon did not begin a session without first having spoken to Loyseleur.[18]

On the few occasions when Joan was offered limited counsel, she may have refused because of Loyseleur's advice. One of the notaries stated that "sometimes Loyseleur entered Joan's cell and told her not to believe the churchmen 'because if you believe them, you will be lost.' He assumed the bishop of Beauvais knew about this, because otherwise Loyseleur would not have dared do such things.' "[19] It is impossible to know exactly what was going on behind the scenes but Loyseleur undoubtedly realized that for all her simplicity, Joan was very smart. His advice would have helped gain her trust while at the same time making her more uncooperative at trial.

The next morning, February 22, when a large number of theologians and civil and canon lawyers gathered with Cauchon in the Robing Room, the bishop may have hoped the previous day's interrogation would have

1 Joan of Arc's house, Domremy. Surrounding peasant houses were torn down during restoration work in the late nineteenth century.

2 The church of St. Remy, Domremy. After being partially destroyed during the Thirty Years War, the church was rebuilt with an opposite orientation so that the current entrance would have been behind the altar. In Joan's time the entrance to the church, in which Joan was baptized, could be seen from the small window in her room.

3 Statue of Joan in the *bois chenu*, at the site of the "Fairy" or "Ladies" Tree. Great lords and ladies, as well as village boys and girls, went to celebrate the advent of spring by picnicking, placing garlands on the tree, and dancing. At Joan's trial the English claimed the tree was associated with sorcery.

4 Chapel of Notre Dame de Bermont, the hermitage in Greux to which Joan made pilgrimages on Saturdays. The interior contains a wall painting that some believe depicts Joan.

5 Gate of France through which Joan rode into Vaucouleurs to meet with Sir Robert de Baudricourt to convince him to send her to Chinon. The remains of the castle are to the right.

6 The church of St. Catherine of Fierbois, to which Joan sent for her special sword. The church, on the pilgrimage route to Santiago de Compostela, had become a major repository for relics after French crusaders returned from their defeat at Nicopolis in the late fourteenth century.

7 Chinon Castle in the Loire Valley. Joan traveled here to meet Charles VII to convince him of her mission to save France.

8 Portrait of King Charles VII by Jean Fouquet (1447). Before Joan's victories in the Loire Valley, Charles had been nearly penniless and had few supporters. Following the victories and his coronation at Reims, he went on to become a successful king by late medieval standards. Despite Joan's unswerving loyalty, Charles made no efforts to save her after she was captured and put on trial.

9 Castle of Saumur, frequent residence of Yolande of Aragon, an early supporter of Joan and the mother-in-law of Charles VII.

10 House of Jacques Boucher, where Joan lodged during the siege of Orléans, reconstructed after World War II.

11 *The Entrance of Joan of Arc Into Orléans on May 8, 1429,* Jean-Jacques Scherrer, 1887. The painting accurately captures both the curiosity and the excitement inspired in the people of Orléans upon Joan's arrival in the city.

12 Jean, count of Dunois, the Bastard of Orléans and military leader of the operations to relieve the siege. Although initially skeptical of Joan and her mission, he became one of her staunchest supporters.

13 Beaugency Castle, from which the English retreated after being confronted by the combined forces of Joan and the constable of France.

14 Reims Cathedral, where Joan led Charles to be crowned. Reims was the traditional site for the coronation of French kings. Here, with great ceremony, the king was anointed with the "oil of Clovis," which made him God's specially appointed ruler.

15 Statue of Joan of Arc with her banner in Notre Dame Cathedral, Reims. Joan almost never wore a dress after she left Vaucouleurs, but she was depicted that way in most artworks in the centuries after her execution. The words and scenes on the banner are accurate.

16 Equestrian statue of Joan of Arc on the north side of Reims Cathedral. This statue accurately portrays Joan in armor with her hair cut short, more than the statue in the previous photograph.

17 Joan of Arc at the siege of Paris, in Martial d'Auvergne's *Vigiles de Charles VII c.* 1470. Despite the depiction, Joan was not wearing a dress during the siege.

18 Sketch of Joan of Arc by Clément de Fauquembergue, notary of Paris, who had never seen her when he drew this picture in his account book.

19 Joan threatening camp followers with her sword, in Martial d'Auvergne's *Vigiles de Charles VII c.* 1470. Throughout her short career Joan expressed contempt for prostitutes and camp followers and was said to have broken her special sword on the back of one woman. She forbade the men in her army to consort with "loose" women.

20 Sully-sur-Loire, the castle of Georges de La Trémoïlle where Joan stayed in nearly forced confinement during the winter of 1430.

21 Church of St. Jacques, Compiègne. Joan prayed inside this south transept the morning before she was captured on May 23, 1430. A wall now blocks the exact site in the interior.

22 The remaining keep of the Château de Bouvreuil in Rouen. Joan was not imprisoned in this particular keep but it was here that she was threatened with instruments of torture.

23 North garden of Saint-Ouen, Rouen, general site of the former cemetery where Joan recanted on May 24, 1431.

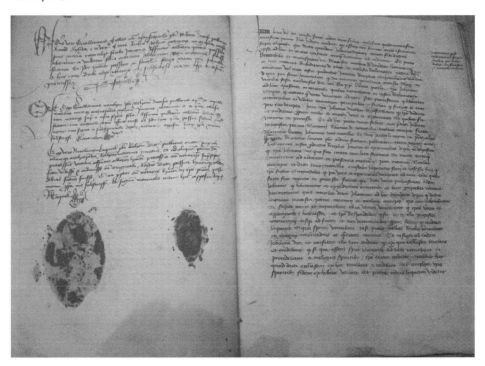

24 Trial record signed by the three notaries.

25 Mock-up of Joan's execution scene, with an accurate depiction of the height of the platform. The high platform was erected so that all those in the Old Market could see the execution and be certain that she died on May 30, 1431. Joan stands at the base of the ladder with the two Dominicans, Ysambard de la Pierre and Martin Ladvenu, who stayed at her side until the end. The executioner, Geoffroy Thérage, complained afterwards to the Dominicans that because of the height of the platform he had not been allowed to put Joan out of her misery by knocking her out.

26 The base of the enormous cross is the exact location where Joan was executed. The nearby sculpture by Maxime Real del Sarte (1926) is at the side of the new Church of Joan of Arc.

convinced Joan to be more pliable. He soon found otherwise, when he pressed her to swear once again. After listening to the admonition, she replied that she had taken an oath yesterday and that should suffice. Cauchon reminded her that not even a prince could refuse to take an oath when it was required in a matter of faith. Joan said: "I swore yesterday; that should be quite enough. You overburden me." Finally she appeared to agree that she would speak the truth on matters concerning the faith. But when Beaupère, who often led the questioning, pressed her to answer truly, as she had sworn, what he should ask her, she replied, "You may well ask me such things, that to some I shall answer truly, and to others I shall not."[20]

The exchange is revealing. Joan had not been accused or defamed, at least not directly. Although oaths were commonly required before presentation of charges in the fifteenth century, forcing the accused to do so violated canon law. Moreover, no defendant could be forced to swear more than once.[21] While Joan's apparent knowledge of her rights is intriguing, her unwillingness to swear is understandable. Joan stated outright that she would conceal the truth.[22] Since oaths were taken seriously in the Middle Ages, most believed that breaking one would lead to damnation. Joan understood canon law and inquisitorial procedure rather too well and was trying to avoid self-incrimination, even as Loyseleur tried to trick her into damning admissions.

Joan lied outright several times at the trial, having announced she would do so from the beginning by stating that she would neither tell the whole truth nor say something that she "could not" without perjury. On March 3 she stated that "I would rather have you cut my throat than tell you all I know."[23] She justified her stance by mentioning village proverbs, restrictions placed upon her by her "voices," and matters relating specifically to King Charles. She told her judges repeatedly that they should not force her to commit perjury. When at the third session they urged her to remove all reservations to her oath, she responded with asperity: "It should be enough to have twice taken the oath." When they pressed her to swear simply and absolutely, she answered: "You may well do without it!"[24]

Even before the trial there is evidence that Joan lied when it suited her purposes. Going to church or to Notre Dame de Bermont when her parents believed she was in the fields was deceptive, but asking Durand Laxart to lie to her parents on her behalf was a much more serious matter. It is also probable that she learned of the location of her special sword when she heard mass during the two days she spent at St. Catherine of Fierbois, even though she denied prior knowledge of its existence when asked by Charles. Also, she admitted that "sometimes she put a cross [in her letters] to warn some of her party not to do as her letters said."[25] As she had learned in battle, tricks and ruses were a necessary and strategic part of warfare. Now she would apply that knowledge to try and defeat the English – through their French collaborators – one more time. Joan could justify her lies by the perfidy of her enemies. Since she had refused to swear to answer all their questions truthfully, God would surely understand.

In her persistent unwillingness to take an oath, or in adding qualifications to it, Joan negotiated a tricky path between qualified truths and outright lies. By doing so she bought time. In the second session the question of her clothing arose. When she was asked on whose advice she "took to man's dress, she usually refused to answer. Finally she answered that she charged no one with that; and several times she answered variously."[26] After her experience with the ladies of Luxembourg, Joan had become conscious that not everyone approved of her male clothing, especially when she was not involved in war. She realized, in ways that she probably did not yet understand, that any information she provided on the subject could be damaging. However, there was an element of truth in Joan's response. The many witnesses in 1456 who spoke about her adoption of male clothing offered contradictory testimonies. Jean de Metz, Bertrand de Poulengy, Durand Laxart, one of his friends, and the people of Vaucouleurs all took credit for having provided her with male clothing. Her king had given her a full suit of armor and Duke Charles of Orléans had given her a knight's attire. She could have named all of them or none. That Joan did not attribute the choice to someone else may indicate her loyal nature; it might also be that Joan *wanted* the credit for choosing the clothing herself. It was part of who she was.

Joan's tactics were nothing short of brilliant. On almost everything they asked except basic facts about her childhood, she stalled or took the offensive. The following Saturday, February 24, as they pushed her to describe her voices, she answered one question with her signature phrase: "The voice told her to answer boldly." She followed that immediately by saying that when the voice told her things, she often did not understand the meaning. Then she turned to Cauchon: "You say that you are my judge; take good heed of what you do, because, in truth, I am sent by God, and you put yourself in great peril."[27] Joan sensed that in some ways she was winning this battle of wits with those who sought to judge her. She forced them to ask the same questions over and over again, then did not answer or said she would do so at a later time. As Joan's trial continued, she began to take the measure of her judges and learned how to evade their questions or mislead them. Often she used her voices as an excuse. Even though she said that the voice told her to answer boldly, when asked about her revelations, she said, "I have not been advised upon that. Give me a fortnight and I will answer you. . . . She said that she would not answer that day; and that she does not know if she ought to reply, or not, until it has been revealed to her."[28] Her confidence grew as she assessed her enemy and began to understand that she could threaten them just as she had the English garrison at Les Tourelles and in her letters.

Joan demonstrated her quick intelligence and wit throughout the trial; even though she often complained that the questions put to her were subtle or inappropriate, she handled them deftly. On February 24 Joan was asked if she was in a state of grace. "She responded that it was a difficult thing to respond to such questions; but she ended by saying: 'If I am, I hope God will keep me there, and if I am not, that God will put me there! Because I would rather die than not be in God's love.' "[29] Some of those in attendance said the interrogators were stupefied, and they left it there, without questioning her more.[30] The bishop of Demétriade, who complained that it was not right to put such a question to a woman, said that she responded very prudently and extricated herself from difficult situations adroitly, even though the examiners sometimes interrupted her with new questions, passing from one thing to another to see if she would change her answers. He felt the sessions were far too long, so much so that even the theologians who attended were worn out.[31] If they were fatigued, how much more so would Joan have been, considering that she was chained at night and surrounded by guards?

Yet Joan astonished the judges and witnesses with her stamina and memory. The lead notary, Manchon, testified that:

During the trial she was worn out by numerous and diverse questions. Almost every day there was an interrogation in the morning that lasted three or four hours. And sometimes, based on her testimony, they chose some especially tricky and subtle questions, which they questioned her about after lunch for three or four more hours. Often they went from one question to another, changing the subject. But in spite of this, she responded with wisdom and had an amazing memory.[32]

The goal of these early sessions was to distract and disorient Joan so that she would incriminate herself. "In spite of that, she responded well for a weak woman and sometimes, questioned again about certain things, she even referred to the day on which she had already answered the question."[33] Cauchon was so eager to trap Joan into admissions that many of those present commented about the unfairness of his tactics. Yet for Joan it was a challenge. One theologian said that she responded so astutely that she would have made an excellent cleric![34]

A bourgeois of the city who only saw Joan during the abjuration and execution, heard from the local Dominican Raoul Le Sauvage, whom he said only spoke to him with great reticence, that he had never seen a woman of that age give so much trouble to those who questioned her. Le Sauvage, one of the main spokesmen for the Convent of Saint-Jacques, admired her responses and her astonishing memory. One time, after the notary had transcribed her answers, he read back to Joan what he had written. She said that she had not responded that way and referred it to those present. She was right and they corrected the response.[35]

Joan had little tolerance for the interrogation methods. She complained vigorously of the content and difficulty of the questions, with a barrage of them asked at the same time and repetition of those she had already answered or sidetracked. Yet she handled the subtle and often deceptive questions masterfully, although some were so incoherent and complicated that several of the theologians and lawyers were confused. When Cauchon and the promotor Estivet interrogated her at the same time, Joan told them: "Do one after the other!"[36]

In the first four sessions Joan feigned ignorance, especially when the subject of her voices was raised. It was only on February 27 that Joan finally identified her voices as coming from anyone other than God or an angel. Even after she identified Catherine, Margaret, and Michael as her saints, the judges tried to get her to reveal more. But she played dumb, saying that she did not know whether she was permitted to answer, since sometimes the voices were unclear.[37] Defiantly, Joan said that sometimes St. Catherine would try to communicate with her, but she "failed to understand on account of the noise in the prison and the noise made by her guards."[38] Even as she decided to name her saints, she stalled by insisting that conditions in the prison were such that the instructions of her voices were drowned out.

Again hoping to entrap her, the judges asked her to name the true pope. Joan sarcastically demanded to know if there were two of them. As a result of correspondence she had received in 1429 from the count of Armagnac, she knew of the Great Schism (1378–1415) and the two and then three competing popes. When the count had asked which of the popes he should obey, Joan deferred, saying she would tell him when she was in Paris.[39] Joan had learned early in her military campaigns only to divulge information she knew to be true or that would inspire her men. But now, at trial, she answered that her personal belief was that the pope in Rome was the one who should be obeyed. It was a savvy answer. Even as the trial proceeded, events in Rome were taking center stage. The Council of Constance that ended the Schism in 1415 had ensured that future councils would meet regularly so that such a disastrous situation could not recur. The Council of Basel was set to begin meeting soon and a number of the University of Paris doctors at the trial would attend later that summer. Two days after Joan answered the question about the true pope, Eugenius IV was elected pope "at Rome."[40] Whatever Joan did or did not know about papal politics, saying she accepted the "pope at Rome" was an almost generic answer, at least in 1431.

At times Joan's responses dripped with sarcasm or feigned astonishment. Her comments about the angel Michael's hair and clothing and St. Margaret's language could only be described as mockery. It was well, she said, to know that Michael had hair, but she left it to God whether her saints had arms or legs. And as to St. Margaret speaking French, of course she did! Why would she speak English when she was on the French side?[41] Whenever the voices came to her "there was a great deal of light on all sides, as was most fitting." Turning to Cauchon, she said "that not all the light came to him alone!"[42] In so saying, she challenged this particular church court's right and ability to judge her voices. The judges again turned to the appearance of the angels. Did they all look alike? Joan's answers were deliberately vague. She said that "some of them were fairly like one another, and some were not, as far as she could see; some had wings or were crowned, others were not."[43] Questioned about whether she prayed for her sword to "have better fortune, she answered: 'It is well to know that I could have wished my armor to have good fortune.' "[44] In all of these exchanges, Joan did not answer the questions that were asked. As often as not, her responses were non sequiturs that provided no information at all.

Joan equivocated throughout the trial. She said simply that she would not answer now, or that she needed time to consult her voices. On other occasions she claimed she did not have leave to speak of certain subjects. When asked whether the angels "were long with her, she answered that they often came among the Christian folk and were not seen, and she often saw them amongst the Christian folk."[45] Joan was letting her judges know that she had special knowledge that they did not. Yet her ambiguous word choices always left her room to answer in different ways.

Joan also added conditions that must have exasperated her examiners. Whenever she was asked to swear an oath she made stipulations before agreeing to do so. She had often requested to hear mass, so the judges offered a compromise. Would she be willing to wear a dress in order to hear mass? She again played a cat-and-mouse game with them:

> "Promise me that I may hear mass if I wear a woman's dress, and I will answer you." Then the examiner said to her: "I promise that you may hear mass, if you are in a woman's dress." She answered: "And what do you answer, if I have sworn and promised to our king not to put off this dress? Yet I will tell you: have made for me a long dress reaching down to the ground, without a train, and give it to me to go to mass; and then, on my return, I will put on once again the clothing I have."[46]

At least in the first months of the trial, Joan viewed her interrogations as a game she thought she could win. And verbally she did just that. She toyed with her judges, seeming to give them what they wanted, only to snatch it back. Giving up her male clothing was not an option for Joan, but it was something she could dangle before them as a possibility. The clothing she wore had proved its worth many times. It had given her the courage to scale ladders, lead attacks, and try to climb down castle walls. It had made her the Maid of Lorraine. Could it not now make her the St. Catherine who had defied and outwitted her learned judges?

When asked questions she did not want to answer, Joan redirected them, twisted words to her advantage, or changed the subject. Asked if her angel had not failed her, she said "How should he fail me, when he comforts me every day?"[47] When the judges tried to pin her down about the supposed sign she gave to the king, she responded sharply: "I have

JUDGING THE MAID 141

always told you that you will not drag this from my lips. Go and ask him."[48] She did add with respect to the sign that she "thanked Our Lord for her deliverance from the trouble arising from the opposition of the clergy of her party."[49] On the last point, although she did not answer the question, she told the truth. Although many theologians gave at least limited support to her mission from the beginning, the churchmen with whom she dealt on a regular basis had often tried to obstruct her based on their political designs. As a result, she had come to rely more and more on her own judgment, her understanding of what God wanted for her – or of what Joan wanted for France.

Joan regularly expressed her self-righteousness by referring to God or the saints. She told the judges that she came from God, saying that there was nothing for her to do here. In her numerous threats or innuendoes aimed at Cauchon, she made it clear that he was not her judge. "I tell you, take good heed of what you say, that you are my judge, for you assume a great responsibility, and overburden me."[50] Joan's justification of herself and her mission arose from her belief that God was on France's side. She taunted Cauchon, saying that before seven years had passed the English would lose everything they had in France. "It will be a great victory which God will send the French."[51] The examiners followed up, asking if God hated the English. "She answered that of God's love or His hatred for the English, or of what He would do to their souls, she knew nothing, but she was certain that, excepting those who died there, they would be driven out of France, and God would send victory to the French and against the English."[52] Her reply was a verbal summary of what she had said in her Letter to the English almost two years earlier. Joan felt on solid footing when she spoke of the war.

On other issues, having deflected or deferred her answers, she formulated responses that fit her mission. On March 13, returning to the subject of the sign, she claimed that an angel assured Charles by bringing him the crown, telling him he would possess the whole kingdom of France by the help of God and the labors of Joan. Charles learned he was to put Joan to work by giving her soldiers; if he did not, it would take much longer for him to be crowned and consecrated.[53] Her interrogators turned back on her, asking if God was on the English side when they prospered in France. She answered that she "did not know whether God hated the French, but she believed it was His will to suffer them to be beaten for their sins, if they were in a state of sin."[54] The same argument had been put forth by leading theologians, who had wrestled with the problem of why God would favor one side over another. So too had the poet Christine de Pizan. In her poem praising Joan she had asked: "Who could see what would come to pass in the future (which will be remembered well everywhere) that France (of whom it was said that she had been brought down and ruined) would, by divine command, go from so many evils to such great good. . . . God came to the aid of His people so that our enemies were no more able to help each other than dead dogs."[55] The English occupation had brought France so low – to a state where its leaders and people recognized their sinfulness – that only God could assist them. With Joan's help, of course.

Joan's view of Burgundians had not improved since her childhood experiences, especially since she had fought against them and been captured by a vassal of the duke. She was asked about the assassination of John the Fearless, in 1419, the act that had led to the rift between France and Burgundy. Her response was typical. It was a great pity for the kingdom, she said, but God had sent her to aid the king of France.[56] Although she claimed she had only known one Burgundian in her youth, Gérardin d'Épinal, she said "she would have been quite willing for him to have his head cut off, that is if it pleased God." Joan lied again. She was godmother to Gérardin's son and he had attended the coronation of Charles VII to see her. By saying she would have approved of his beheading, she was describing her feelings about the Burgundians generally. Had she hated the Burgundians since her youth? She did not hesitate. Only since she had known God was on the side of France, but the Burgundians would have war "unless they do as they ought."[57] Once more, Joan felt comfortable. Whenever she could speak of fighting or of specific, concrete events in the war, she expressed herself with ease. In her letter to him after the coronation the previous July, Joan had let the duke of Burgundy know that he must make a lasting peace, but that if he chose to fight against the "holy realm of France" he would be committing a sin against God.

Cauchon had serious reason to be alarmed at what should have been a simple trial with an easy verdict. His inner circle included a number of his close friends and associates from the University of Paris, some canons of the cathedral at Rouen, and a few bishops and abbots. But many of the 131 expert witnesses or assessors were unwilling attendees. An atmosphere of fear, intimidation, and threats surrounded those who did not have a personal stake, or chose not to participate, in the trial. In mid-March, as

Cauchon compiled the transcripts to present them to the assessors who would draw up articles of accusation against Joan, he summoned a Norman cleric named Jean Lohier to give his opinion about the conduct of the trial. Lohier argued that because the trial concerned the king of France, someone from his side should have been a party to the proceedings. Since Joan had no counsel, as a simple girl she could not be expected to respond to so many masters and doctors in great matters, especially touching her revelations.[58] Lohier told the notary Manchon: "you see the manner in which they proceed. They will get her by her words. If she says: 'I know something for certain that touches on the revelations' or 'it seems to me,' they will substitute 'I am certain.' It's my opinion that no man could condemn her."[59] Manchon asked him if he had seen the transcripts. Lohier responded that the proceedings were "worthless and insupportable because it was being conducted in the castle, a place that was not safe for the judges, counselors, or assessors." Lohier told Manchon that he would leave Rouen because he saw that their intention was to kill Joan. Two days later, Cauchon reported to his closest associates that Lohier wanted to put their trial into an appeal phase and fight them, that he would do nothing to help them.[60]

On March 17, the day before Cauchon called together his allies to apprise them of Lohier's comments and decide how to proceed, Joan had engaged in an interesting exchange as part of the interrogation in her prison cell that suggests that she had, against the bishop's command, received help on points of canon law. Also present were Le Maistre, La Fontaine, La Pierre, Massieu, and two doctors of theology. When asked whether she would submit all her deeds to the judgment of the Church, Joan said "she loved the Church and would support it with all her might for the Christian Faith."[61] That same afternoon the trial transcript, correlating almost exactly with Manchon's 1450 testimony, states that when asked if she would answer the bishop and his delegates as she would the pope himself, Joan "demanded to be led before him, and then she would answer all that was required."[62] Cauchon feared that the trial would be derailed. Combined with Lohier's simultaneous comments, Joan had claimed a right that was hers according to canon law. Defendants could appeal to the pope at any point in a trial.

More than ever, Cauchon was determined to suppress dissent, threatening those who disagreed with him or tried to stand up for Joan. A physician, one of at least three who had been part of the trial to make sure Joan remained healthy – presumably in case there was any question of foul play later – testified that he was forced to attend by the bishop of Beauvais. Several times he had given excuses to Cauchon, saying it was not his job to give an opinion on such a subject. Finally he was told that if he did not go along with the others, bad things would happen to him. He added that "Master Jean Lohier and Master Nicolas de Houppeville were threatened with drowning if they refused to attend."[63] Houppeville, a bachelor and master of theology, had participated in a few deliberations at the beginning of the trial but disagreed with the procedure, pointing out that Joan had already been questioned by the clergy of Poitiers and the archbishop of Reims. By saying so, he incurred Cauchon's fury. Called before him, Houppeville reminded the bishop he was not his judge and so he would remove himself from the process. Jean de La Fontaine, one of the officials at the trial, managed to send him a note warning him, but not before Houppeville was taken to the castle and then the royal prison. When he asked why he had been seized, he was told it had been done on Cauchon's orders because of what he had said. Fortunately the abbot of Fécamp, who was close to Cauchon, intervened on behalf of Houppeville, who had heard that he would be exiled to England or elsewhere far from Rouen. He took no further part in the trial but later testified that the Vice Inquisitor Le Maistre attended only out of fear, often complaining that they harassed Joan with their questions.[64] Massieu agreed, saying Le Maistre told him: "I see that if one does not proceed in this matter according to the will of the English, death is near."[65]

Guillaume Duval mentioned another incident that suggests that he and his fellow Dominicans from the local convent of Saint-Jacques were trying to help Joan in whatever way they could. He had been present at one session with Brother Ysambard de La Pierre. Finding no place among the assessors, they sat at the middle of a table near Joan. "When she was questioned, Brother Ysambard advised her as to what she should say, nudging her or making some other sign." After the session, when he, La Pierre, and La Fontaine were sent to visit Joan in prison, they went together to the castle of Rouen. There the earl of Warwick attacked Brother Ysambard with "rage and indignation, biting insults, and harsh epithets, saying to him: 'Why did you touch that wicked person this morning, making so many signs? *Mort Bleu*! Villain! If I see you again taking trouble to save her and to advise her for her good, I will have you thrown into the Seine.'" Duval and La Pierre fled in fear to their convent.[66]

Despite the human tendency to want to forget participation in a shameful event, it is clear from the quantity and overlap of testimony that the trial was conducted in a climate of fear and menace. Le Maistre and some others intervened to prevent threats to Houppeville, La Pierre, and others from being carried out, but the message was clear that those called to trial were expected to behave in a manner that suited Cauchon and his masters. Even the Vice Inquisitor knew what would happen to those who caused trouble.

The consultation on canon law made after Lohier's departure changed the course of the trial. The lack of establishment of public notoriety (*fama publica*) before proceeding to trial was the most serious problem for Cauchon, who knew inquisitorial procedure well. On March 18, Cauchon, scrambling to preserve his trial, called together several doctors of theology and canon and civil lawyers, asking them to deliberate on the best way to proceed. They gathered over the next week and a half to draw up charges in preparation for an "Ordinary Trial," the phase in which a defendant was formally presented with charges. On March 27, seventy articles were read to the group. The content of most of the articles was summarized, describing Joan as someone:

> vehemently suspected, denounced, and defamed by honest and sober people; to the end that she should be denounced and declared by you her said judges as a witch, enchantress, false prophet, a caller-up of evil spirits, as superstitious, implicated in and given to magic arts, thinking evil in our Catholic faith, schismatic . . . and in many other articles of our faith, accused and working evil, blasphemous towards God and his saints, scandalous, seditious, perturbing and obstructing the peace, inciting to war, cruelly thirsting for human blood, encouraging it to be shed, having utterly and shamelessly abandoned the modesty befitting her sex, and indecently put on the ill-fitting dress and state of men-at-arms; and for that and other things abominable to God and man, contrary to laws both divine and natural, and to ecclesiastical discipline, misleading princes and people; having to the scorn of God permitted and allowed herself to be adored or venerated, giving her hands to be kissed; heretical or at least vehemently suspected of heresy.[67]

Joan was expected to defend herself. But defense was never her strong point. Since she did not believe she had done anything wrong, her best defense was a good offense.

On March 28, in a grueling full day session, Joan was asked to respond to each article. It was obvious to all that she recalled her earlier responses with great accuracy, for she accepted some of the articles, completely denied others, and modified or altered the text of yet others. The summaries blatantly distorted and falsified much of what Joan had stated during the previous five weeks. For example, one article said that she "bore a mandrake in her bosom,"[68] an allegation she repudiated. There had been no such question or answer during the sessions; they had only asked if in Domremy she had had a mandrake, which she had vehemently denied. One of the strangest articles claimed that Joan had been intimate with Robert de Baudricourt, saying that she had told him that after she accomplished what God demanded of her, she would have three sons by him. The first would be a pope, the second an emperor, and the third a king! The level of fabrication is stunning, including an imagined conversation between the two: "Now then, I should like to give you one [sic] if they're going to be such powerful men, because I should be better off." To that, she supposedly answered: "No, gentle Robert, no, this is not the time; the Holy Spirit will find a way!"[69] At first, Joan's correction appears equally bizarre: "As for having three children, she never has boasted of it." Although the answer seems on the face of it to support the allegation, Joan was simply parroting the word "boast" that had been used in the article. She meant that she had never said it. Many times she referred to her previous answers or made small corrections. Yet the fact that her denials and references are recorded is further proof of the basic accuracy of the transcript.

Despite the wearisome and time-consuming reading, Joan remained strong. Sometimes she bluntly informed her judges that they would get nothing more from her about a given subject. Other times she responded stubbornly, as when they harped on about her clothing, declaring that she behaved more like a man than a woman. She persisted in her refusal to change her clothes, adding that "as for other womenly duties . . . there are enough women to do them."[70] Although by the end of the morning and afternoon sessions Joan was obviously weary, almost always saying "I refer me to my earlier answers," her consistency is noteworthy. She knew what she had said, repeated it, and corrected mistakes. Witnesses twenty-five years later commented on her intelligence and memory.

The repeated interrogations began to take their toll on Joan by late March. On the 31st, she had to answer articles that she had deferred. Many revolved around the meaning and her understanding of the Church Militant. The Church Militant was defined as the full community of believers on earth, led by the pope and his Church. By contrast, the Church Triumphant comprised Christians who had triumphed over sin and death and were in Heaven. Not surprisingly, Joan assumed the Church Militant was the church court in which she was being tried. Against the backdrop of this misunderstanding, her words became dangerous. She agreed to submit, as long as it was not against God's bidding. What if the Church Militant showed her that her revelations were illusions, "diabolical, super-stitious, and evil things?" Joan rejected the idea, saying only that she would submit to God. "If the Church Militant commanded her to do otherwise she would not submit to it for any man in the world, except Our Lord, whose good will she would always do."[71] The complicated theological concept eluded her, trapping her into making statements that suggested she relied solely on her own judgment rather than that of the Church.

On April 2, the judges and several assessors met to condense the charges based on Joan's replies. Nicolas Midi drew up twelve articles, which were to be taken to Paris for consideration by the university. They claimed that Joan's revelations were not from God but were "a fiction of the human imagination or proceeded from a spirit of evil."[72] The articles dealt with her male clothing, her descriptions of the saints and angels, her claims to prophecy about France and England, the "leap" from the tower, her insignia of JHESUS MARIA, and her duplicitous use of a cross and circle to indicate to her comrades that she was not telling the truth.[73] Potentially most damaging was her apparent unwillingness to submit herself to the Church Militant. While eleven canon and civil lawyers identified many sins in Joan, some were hesitant to proceed, pointing out that it was not easy to distinguish by what spirit a mind was directed. In the fourteenth and early fifteenth centuries, theologians wrote extensively about discern-ment, the ability to differentiate between whether revelations experienced by a man or woman came from divine or demonic sources.[74]

Many of those present, especially the local Dominicans, were critical of Joan but did not believe she should be condemned. La Pierre, who earlier had tried to signal answers to Joan, recognized that when she spoke about "war, she appeared moved by the Holy Spirit. But when she spoke of herself, she often used fictions." Nevertheless he did not think that was grounds for a charge of heresy.[75] The longest response came from Raoul Le Sauvage, a famed preacher from the convent of Saint-Jacques. He agreed that many of the statements Joan made appeared rash, suggesting she was given to fantasies, headstrong, boastful, presumptuous, and possibly heretical. But he ended:

> Nevertheless, my reverend father and my lords, it is meet to take into account the frailty of womankind; and the propositions and statements should be repeated to her in French, she should be charitably admonished to reform, and not to presume so much upon revelations which may be uttered and invented by the evil spirit or some other. Therefore, as I said, to bring this to a more certain and positive conclusion and issue, so that it cannot be suspect from any quarter, I think through submitting to higher opinion, that for the honor of his royal majesty and of yourself, for the peace and tranquillity of your conscience, the said articles should be sent with the appropriate comments to the apostolic Holy See.[76]

As the convent of Saint-Jacques's spokesman at the trial, Le Sauvage seems to have been trying to get Joan out of the hands of the English-run court.[77] Just like his prior Le Maistre, who had been coerced into serving as Vice Inquisitor, Le Sauvage used language that indicated proper form was not being followed. He further set forth arguments intended to have the trial removed from Rouen and heard before the pope, as Joan had requested. Like the others, he knew that the English intended to take Joan into their custody if she was not convicted, but he advanced arguments to make those present consider what they were doing. She was, after all, a young girl who could not be expected to understand some of the questions that had been asked of her.

On April 18 the judges went to Joan's prison to urge her to repent. This "charitable admonition" was a required theological formality intended to produce a recantation. When they arrived, Joan said she felt ill. Hearing that, Cauchon "in all friendliness and charity," said they had come to comfort and console her.[78] Listening to what she certainly believed to be a hypocritical exhortation to heed the advice of the judges and theologians who claimed to desire the salvation of her body and soul, Joan "thanked us for what we said of her salvation, and added: 'It seems to me, seeing how ill I am, that I am in great danger of death: if it be that God desires to do His pleasure on me, I ask to receive confession and my Savior also, and a burial in holy ground.' "[79] A physician was called in to examine her. He reported that:

[h]e took her pulse to find out the cause of her malady, and asked her what had made her ill. She said the bishop of Beauvais had sent her some carp, which she had eaten and she believed that had caused her sickness. At this, Estivet [the promotor of the trial] called her a slut, shouting, "You hussy, you have been eating fish and other pickled things that are not good for you." She answered she had not and then Joan and Estivet exchanged many insults.

The doctor learned from those present that Joan had been vomiting.[80] Other physicians, summoned by the cardinal of Winchester and the earl of Warwick, corroborated this account. They were told that under no circumstances did King Henry VI "want her to die a natural death since she was his and had cost him dearly." They palpated her right side and found her to be feverish. After concluding it was necessary to bleed her, they reported back to Warwick. He said to them: "Watch out while you're bleeding her, because she's tricky and could pretend to die." After being bled, Joan appeared to feel better. Then Estivet arrived, repeatedly calling Joan a whore and a slut. She was so irritated by him that she once again became feverish and fell sick.[81]

Whatever caused Joan's illness, she did not lose her spirit. Considering that she had twice been wounded by an arrow, stepped on a trap, been knocked off a ladder, and survived a long fall from a tower, it was unlikely that she was in danger of death when this event occurred. She was being worn down by the long trial sessions and her detention, which had become ever more strict, but she was not above using the ruses Warwick mentioned. Her illness struck fear into the hearts of Cauchon and the English, and gave her a respite from the incessant questioning.

No further sessions were held until May 2. Having received many of the responses requested from theologians and canon and civil lawyers, the judges and assessors called Joan into their presence for a Public Admonition. Warned that she must prepare to submit to the Church, Joan answered Cauchon: " 'Read your book', meaning the transcript he held in his hand, 'and then I will answer you. I trust in God my creator for everything. I love Him with my whole heart.' "[82] She was told she must reform her ways, lest "out of arrogant and haughty pride she desired to persist in her own views, and imagine she understood matters of faith better than doctors and learned men, she would expose herself to grave danger."[83] Cauchon continued, explaining that she must submit to the Church Militant, telling her that her male clothing showed contempt for the Church, that her revelations and prophecies were false, and that it was wrong to search curiously into things beyond human understanding, or to put faith in what is new without consulting the opinion of churchmen. When Joan was asked to reply, she hedged on the subject of the Church Militant, but when asked if she would submit to the pope, she answered " 'Take me to him, and I will reply to him,' and would make no other answer."[84]

Joan remained deeply suspicious of her judges' motives, and continued to equivocate. When, with no intention of granting anything of the sort, they asked her if she would submit to the church at Poitiers where she had originally been examined, she snapped back, "Do you think you will catch me in that way?"[85] Although during the course of the Preliminary and Ordinary Trials, Joan had referred her judges to the "book of Poitiers," she believed this was an attempt to trick her into submission to the church court at Rouen. She was right.

The question remains, how did Joan respond with answers that astonished and amazed so many present at the trial? What led her to believe that she did not need to swear an oath before charges were presented, or that she was not expected to swear more than once? How did she know that it was her right, which she repeatedly asserted, to be kept in an ecclesiastical rather than a secular prison? How did she know that she could appeal her case to the pope?

Nicholas Eymerich's Manual for Inquisitors of 1376 was based on his travels and examinations of men and women suspected of heresy and sorcery. It would later become the handbook used by the Spanish Inquisition. Eymerich warned that suspects used a wide variety of techniques to stymie inquisitors, listing ten in particular:

1. Equivocation
2. Adding a condition
3. Redirecting the question
4. Feigning astonishment
5. Twisting the meaning of words
6. Openly changing the subject
7. Self-justification
8. Feigned illness
9. Feigned stupidity or madness
10. Leading a way of life that is apparently holy.

Some, Eymerich added, even resorted to the simple expedient of threatening those who might testify against them.[86]

Joan used every technique mentioned by Eymerich – examples could be multiplied endlessly from the trial record. But how did she know? Was this the common sense of village folk who occasionally had to deal with heresy hunters? It is possible, though inquisitors were far less common in north-eastern France than in the southwest, where a crusade had been launched against the Cathar heresy in the early thirteenth century. An expert on canon law and inquisition argues that Joan came close to guessing what her rights were under the law.[87] But it was more than intuition. Most probably, Joan was cautiously advised by some unlikely allies at the trial, the Dominicans of Saint-Jacques. Most inquisitors were Dominicans, although bishops could also institute heresy proceedings. But because of the overtly political nature of the trial, Cauchon needed Le Maistre's participation to lend a semblance of credibility to the proceedings.

Joan's knowledge of tactics and inquisitorial procedure cannot be denied. Who better than the Dominicans of Rouen to have helped Joan, at least to the degree they could? A comparison of the trial transcript and the attendance records reveal that of the 131 assessors at the trial, only six Dominicans took part. Five of them, Le Maistre, La Pierre, Ladvenu, Le Sauvage, and Duval, came from the local convent of Saint-Jacques[88] and appeared sympathetic to Joan. They made cautious efforts to explain answers that could help Joan; they suffered threats, obviously not idle in view of what would happen to one of their brothers after Joan's execution; and the Vice Inquisitor Le Maistre intervened to help those threatened with exile, imprisonment, or even death. Raoul le Sauvage, hoping to have Joan delivered from the threat of English retribution that hung over the trial, had argued that the case should be turned over to the pope. Another Rouen Dominican, Jean Toutmouillé, did not attend, but reported in 1450 that "it was of common and public renown that her judges acted out of a spirit of vengeance."[89] La Pierre, who started attending only after Le Maistre was forced to participate, was rebuked by Cauchon and Warwick for nudging Joan, making signs to her, and trying to provide her with help. The Rouen Dominicans were not willing participants in the trial, but once they had to attend they did their best to help Joan. To some degree they succeeded, carefully giving her information about her canon law rights and ways to evade her examiners.

Why would the Dominicans more than others oppose the trial and/or be sympathetic to Joan? We can hope that they acted out of simple human compassion for a young girl. But three other factors may account for efforts to undermine Cauchon's trial. As Le Maistre suggested in his protests, there were double problems of jurisdiction, Cauchon's and his own, that masked a deeper antagonism toward "outsiders" and specifically to the English cause as represented by Cauchon, Bedford, Warwick, and others. Although he never showed any favor toward Joan and was close to Cauchon, the prior of Longueville, Pierre Miget, later testified that "if she had not been so frightening to the English she never would have been treated that way or condemned. They feared her more than a great army."[90] The dreadful English siege of Rouen in 1419 was still fresh in the Dominicans' memories, for their convent had suffered significantly. Furthermore, they did not like the idea of misusing an inquisition, typically their area of expertise, in a case that was overtly political.[91] Local feeling ran strongly against the University of Paris theologians and lawyers, many of whom were directly linked to Cauchon, who had come into *their* town to run a sham trial.

The Dominicans provided Joan with direct or indirect help but, as in so many other circumstances, she was also a quick student and skillful manipulator of her judges. She followed the motto she had used in war when she urged her men to "Go boldly!" Now she told her examiners that her voices told her to "answer boldly." That she did.

The French royal chronicler wrote of Joan: "More obediently than an innocent lamb, without murmur or recrimination in response to their iniquitous orders, she withstood the prolonged mockery of those who dishonored her, like Annas and Caiaphas had treated Christ."[92] His Joan is almost Christlike, an innocent lamb of God who would go to her death without recrimination. Nothing could be further from the truth. Joan did not know that she had only four weeks left to live after the public admonition, but the one thing she would not do was to "go gentle into that good night."[93]

CHAPTER 9

From Fear of the Fire

Near the end of the Public Admonition on May 2, Joan was warned that if the Church abandoned her she would be in great peril – her soul would be in danger of eternal fire and her body of temporal fire. She answered threat with threat: "You will not do as you say against me without evil overtaking you, in body and soul."[1] What was Joan thinking? Did she still hope for rescue or escape? Was she so convinced of the righteousness of her cause that she could not see what lay ahead?

A week later, on May 9, Joan's usher Jean Massieu led her to the Great Tower of the castle, the only part that still stands. There, in the presence of the judges and eight theologians and lawyers, she was told that if she did not confess the truth – what they wanted her to say – she would be tortured. According to medieval church law, torture could be carried out once and only under the condition that the individual was unclear in his or her statements. Although his actions did not always match his words, the fourteenth-century Dominican Nicholas Eymerich, who had written the manual for inquisitors, had argued that torture was largely ineffective. He also maintained that people who confessed under torture but withdrew the confession afterwards should be released.

Joan was led to the room containing the instruments of torture. Seeing them, she responded defiantly: "If you were to tear me limb from limb and separate my soul from my body, I would not tell you anything more: and if I did say anything, I should afterwards declare that you had compelled me to say it by force." Joan told them she had asked her voices if she would be burned, and they told her to wait patiently, that God would help her.[2] The man appointed to torture Joan later testified that she behaved with such dignity and displayed so much wisdom that those in attendance marveled at her composure.[3] At that point the judges, worrying that torture would be of little use, decided to postpone it until they could debate the issue further.[4] In all likelihood, Cauchon and the judges never intended to torture Joan but only to frighten her into submission. If word got out that the Maid had been tortured into confession the case would lose even more credibility than it already had. By stating that she would later deny anything she might say under torture, however, Joan made it nearly impossible for her judges to proceed, once again exhibiting an inside knowledge of church law.

On May 12, Cauchon called together several members of the trial to elicit their opinions about how to proceed. There was a considerable difference of opinion. When asked by Cauchon if it was fitting to put Joan to the torture, three answered yes, including the two-faced Nicholas Loyseleur, who argued it would be good for her soul; six said it was not appropriate, arguing either that it would cast doubt on the trial or that there was already enough evidence to convict her; five, including Ysambard de La Pierre said it was not expedient but that she should again be charitably admonished to submit to the judgment of the Church. Jean Le Maistre, Vice Inquisitor, did not even mention the word torture, saying only that "she should once more be examined on whether she believed she should submit to the Church Militant." Cauchon finally decided that torture was neither necessary nor advisable under the circumstances.[5] He feared that Joan would either withstand the torture, casting real doubt on his case, or immediately recant. For all that Joan would yet endure, at least her bold stance when threatened with torture, along with some support from the assessors, saved her from that.

A week later, on May 19, Cauchon called together most of the assessors to present the opinion he had received from the University of Paris, which was completely under English control. The university's letter, addressed to King Henry VI, congratulated the trial judges for their holy and just procedure, asking them to bring matters to a speedy conclusion for "in truth the length and delays are perilous."[6] Based on the information Cauchon had relayed to them, they declared Joan to be schismatic, malicious, heretical, an apostate, and a liar. They ended by condemning her belief that she knew she would go to paradise, saying that only God knew such things. If, they added, she would not willingly return to the fold, she must be abandoned to a secular judge to receive a "penalty proportionate to her crime."[7]

Most agreed with the university's stance. However, the Convent of Saint-Jacques' spokesman Raoul Le Sauvage argued "that Joan should be admonished again, *in private and in public*, before the people: if she would not return to the way of truth and salvation, he referred to the judges for the subsequent procedure."[8] His words differed only slightly from those used by others, but the significance of what he suggested was enormous. It would expose the proceedings of the trial to a wider public, allowing them to see and hear Joan for the first time since her arrival in Rouen six months earlier.

On May 23 Joan was brought to a room near her cell where some of the judges and assessors had gathered. The University of Paris' decision, broken down into six articles, was read to her. In addition to charging her as a heretic, schismatic, apostate and witch, one article drew attention to her male clothing. The indictment stated:

> You have said that you wore and still wear man's dress at God's command . . . and so you have put on a short tunic, jerkin, and hose with many points. You even wear your hair cut short above the ears, without keeping about you anything to denote your sex, save what nature has given you.

They went on, telling her it was blasphemous for her to have worn male garb, especially during the times she received the eucharist. Since she claimed she would rather die than change her clothing, she was charged with transgressing divine law, Holy Scripture and the canons of the Church. "You are full of vain boasting . . . given to idolatry and worship[ing] yourself and your clothes."[9] This charge would become the basis for Joan's conviction.

Two articles were especially damning: the male clothing that she refused to give up because it constituted her identity, and her supposed unwillingness to submit to the judgment of the Church Militant. Having found little else that could be used against Joan except her claim to hear voices, Cauchon and his partisans focused on the biblical prohibition in Deuteronomy: "A woman shall not wear a man's apparel . . . for whoever does such things is abhorrent to the LORD your God."[10] Although the subject had caused concern for some French theologians, most had come to the conclusion that her costume was necessary for her mission. Some had even argued that the New Testament replaced laws that had been in force before the coming of Jesus. Joan's most serious transgression was that she never viewed her male clothing as a *costume*.

As for her submission to the Church Militant, Joan had done so on a number of occasions, although La Pierre's testimony makes it clear that she still did not fully understand that the Church Militant was different from the church court in which she was being judged. "She asked: 'What is the Church? As to you, I refuse to submit myself to your judgment, because you are my mortal enemy.' "[11] La Pierre and Ladvenu told her that she must have no doubts at all about submitting to the pope and a holy council, where there would be important clergymen from her party in attendance. If she did not, she would be in danger. The day after she was so advised, Joan responded that she wanted to submit to the pope and the council.[12] Cauchon was incensed when he learned of her submission and Le Maistre had to intervene again to protect La Pierre. At that point, the earl of Warwick ordered that no one should be allowed to see Joan without his or Cauchon's permission.[13]

On the question of clothing, however, Joan was intransigent. Early in her military career she rightly claimed that she needed male clothing for battle. She justified doing so by saying God had commanded it in terms of practicality for her military expeditions, when she spent days and nights among men. She did not want to give her men any occasion for sin, which would have been impossible to avoid if she had been there while wearing female clothing.[14] Joan's position became more problematic during her stay with the ladies of Luxembourg but in Rouen she could once again insist that safety was her main concern. After all, she was incarcerated in a secular prison guarded by five men who favored the English cause. While Joan usually justified her choice by saying she wore it at God's command, several witnesses remembered Joan complaining that she had suffered many outrages and violence in prison.[15] It was not only that Joan wore male clothing that enraged the English and her judges, but also that she wore the sumptuous attire of a knight. Throughout the first months of the trial Joan had said that her clothing was unimportant but toward the end it had become "a crucial sign of her identity regardless of her circumstances at any particular moment."[16]

After Joan was once again admonished, the session on the 23rd ended with her repeating: " 'As for my words and deeds, which I declared in the trial, I refer to them and will maintain them.' . . . She said that if she were condemned and she saw the fire and the faggots alight and the executioner ready to kindle the fire, and she herself were in it, she would say nothing else and would maintain until death what she said."[17] With that, the judges declared the trial to be over. The University of Paris had given their decision and Joan had been told what she must do. But Raoul Le Sauvage's earlier comment that she should be admonished *in private and in public* must have made Cauchon and the English uneasy enough that they decided there would be one public ceremony in which Joan would be given the opportunity to recant. In view of her recalcitrance throughout the trial, even when shown instruments of torture, they probably thought there was little chance she would do so. It was a major miscalculation.

On May 24, Joan was taken to the cemetery of the abbey of Saint-Ouen, where a scaffold had been erected and kindling for the fire was set in place. This was the first occasion on which most of the people of Rouen could satisfy their curiosity by seeing the famous prisoner. Rumors abounded, with some saying that the English had gone to trial against Joan because of the hatred and fear that they felt for her.[18] Such a large crowd was packed into the small space that many, including trial participants, could not hear what was happening. Guillaume Érard, a University of Paris doctor of theology who had earlier served on missions for the king of England, first delivered a sermon, denouncing Joan for acting against the king (Henry VI), God, and the Catholic faith. If she did not immediately repudiate her views she would be burned.[19] A man who lived not far from where Joan had grown up happened to be in Rouen for the two public events. He remembered that Joan grew incensed with Érard's harangue, especially when in the midst of it he cried out: "France, you are much abused, you who have always been the bastion of true Christianity. Charles, who calls himself king . . . has adhered like a heretic and schismatic, as he is, to the words and deeds of this worthless, defamed woman full of dishonor." Turning to Joan he raised his finger and denounced her for heresy. Joan did not defend herself but rather the king who no longer wanted or needed her: "By my faith, sir, with due reverence, there is no more noble Christian to be found, nor one who better loves the faith and the Church. Charles is not at all like you say." The last thing Cauchon and his colleagues had wanted was a public disputation. Hearing her speak, the preacher shouted to Massieu: "Keep her quiet!"[20] Joan also repeated her appeal to be taken to the pope but was told that it was not possible because he was so far away. Besides, they claimed, each diocese had competent judges.[21] In so doing, they undercut their charge that she had refused to submit to the Roman Catholic Church.

Under no circumstances would the English, Cauchon, and their allies allow the case to be revoked to Rome. The trial was about politics and retaliation, with a good measure of fear mixed in. Theological opinion varied about Joan's clothing, and since she had submitted to the Church, she might well have been declared innocent. The judgment in Rouen was made not by the Church, but by a hand-picked group of men who represented the English side. There was no chance that Bedford or Warwick would allow her to escape, as they had announced at the beginning of the trial.

Massieu, the executor of writs and usher who had escorted Joan to and from her cell and who had appeared sympathetic on numerous occasions, read aloud a formula of abjuration, which Joan was asked to sign. She was warned that in the future she must not bear arms, wear men's clothing, or cut her hair short, along with several other restrictions. But he and others testified later that the document that was placed in the trial transcript[22] was *not* the same as the one he read to her. That one contained no more than eight lines whereas the one placed in the transcript was at least five times as long. Joan took the quill and was poised to sign.

The crowd, largely composed of English supporters, erupted in anger, as no one had expected Joan to give in. An Englishman shouted to Cauchon that he was wrong to accept her recantation because it was a farce. Massieu heard the bishop shout out furiously: "Apologize to me" saying that in matters of faith he would rather look to the salvation of Joan than her death. Otherwise he would not continue.[23] The cardinal of Winchester's Keeper of the Privy Seal shouted: "Finish up! You are too partial [to Joan]!" At that point the bishop threw the document to the ground saying he would do no more that day because it would go against his conscience.[24] When charged that he favored the English, Cauchon was said to have replied: " 'You lie! I would favor no one in such business.' The cardinal of Winchester then told his man to be quiet."[25] Was Cauchon having second thoughts? He has often been portrayed as the evil genius behind Joan's execution. But the bishop had long been a distinguished member of the University of Paris. His real guilt lay in his unbridled ambition to be appointed archbishop of Rouen, so he served his English masters as best he could. Yet by this point he too may have had some reservations about the trial, or even worries about Joan's threats.

In the midst of the commotion Joan spoke up, saying that she placed herself in the hands of the Church and would sign. Immediately Érard shouted: "Do it now! If not, you will die in the fire today." Joan answered that she would sign rather than be burned. There was a great uproar and people threw stones.[26] Many were infuriated at Joan's submission, doubting her sincerity. A knight who was present said that the secretary took from his sleeve a small written schedule that he gave Joan to sign. "She responded that she did not know how to read or write. . . . In a mocking guise Joan made a kind of circle."[27] Even though Joan could not read or write, she *could* sign her name. That she did not do so is revealing. Was this the cross in a circle that Joan admitted using to tell her followers not to believe what she wrote? Others said that she laughed when she made her mark on the paper.[28] The bishop of Noyon remembered that after the abjuration many said it was nothing more than a comedy and that she was only making fun of them.[29] He was probably right. Signing with a cross in a circle, laughing, and mocking displayed Joan's feelings about her captors and judges. This was her first opportunity to show herself off to the people of Rouen – and to show up her judges. But Joan was young. She did not grasp the fact that she had just signed her death sentence.

Anger at the possibility that Joan might escape death was palpable. After she had recanted, she listened to the sentence:

> Inasmuch as you have, after repeated charitable admonitions, by God's help through a long delay returned into the bosom of Our Holy Mother Church, and . . . with your own lips publicly abjured along with all heresy: according to the form appointed by ecclesiastical sanctions we unbind you by these presents from the bonds of excommunication . . . on condition that you return to the Church with a true heart and sincere faith. . . . But inasmuch as you have rashly sinned against God and the Holy Church, we finally and definitely condemn you for salutary penance to perpetual imprisonment, with the bread of sorrow and water of affliction, that you may weep for your faults.[30]

No evidence remains that Joan *had ever been* excommunicated. In any case, the sentence may have shocked Joan if the memory of one of her physicians was correct. He recalled that she had hesitated noticeably before signing. At that point the preacher Érard told her that she would be freed from her prison. The doctor thought she only signed under that condition.[31] Did Joan really believe she would be set free?

When the notary Guillaume Manchon was asked why Joan received such a harsh sentence after she was told nothing bad would happen to her, he responded that there were conflicting loyalties among those involved as well as fear that she might escape. The English were determined to impose the death sentence while some of the churchmen and friars hoped for mercy. A nineteen-year-old who was present said that after the earl of Warwick complained to Cauchon and some of the doctors that King Henry had been badly served by the recantation, one of them responded, "Lord, don't worry. We will get her yet."[32]

On the afternoon of the 24th, Joan was taken back to her secular prison where she was given a woman's dress. She donned it as soon as she had removed her male costume, allowing her head to be shaved as a sign of repentance.[33] What happened to change Joan's mind? Had she indeed played out a farce, all the while mocking her judges in the expectation that she would go free or be transferred to a church prison? Or was she simply afraid of dying? Did she believe that by some miracle she would be saved? It was probably a combination of the three.

Throughout the trial Joan had suffered insults and harassment in her prison cell. One of the notaries said that during her imprisonment, he had heard rumors around the city that at night the English would go to torment her, telling her sometimes that she would die and other times that she would escape.[34] Although the trial record is silent about what occurred between Thursday evening, May 24, and Monday morning, May 28, many witnesses recalled the events of that weekend vividly. Joan's spirit may finally have been broken. Although Joan was not raped, she was intimidated, humiliated, and entrapped. The Dominican Ladvenu claimed that Joan had told him that in prison that after she had recanted, she was attacked violently by a great English lord who tried to rape her. She said this was why she was forced to resume wearing men's clothes.[35] La Pierre agreed, for she had told him that "when she was in women's clothing she had suffered many outrages and violence in the prison. When she was led before them in one session, her face showed such fright, sorrow, and was so full of tears that he felt great compassion."[36] Massieu said Joan told him what happened in her own words. "When she was ready to get up, she asked the English guards to undo her chains. Then one of the guards tore off the women's clothing she was wearing and . . . threw the male attire to her, ordering her to get up. . . . She responded, 'You know that is forbidden to me. I will not put them on.'" But they would not return the other clothes. This went on for about an hour until finally, out of necessity, she was constrained to get out of bed and put on the clothing.[37] If the scene unfolded as Massieu claimed, it might have had almost the same effect on her psyche as physical rape. One thing alone is certain. The bundle of clothes was put in her cell deliberately. As churchmen, some of the judges, possibly even Cauchon, might have been satisfied with the events that had taken place in the cemetery at Saint-Ouen. But Bedford's intent had been clear even before the trial began; his threat that he would allow no possibility of an innocent verdict and would take her into English custody had not been an idle one. If those around Joan wanted her to keep the promises she made on May 24, all male clothing would have been taken from her cell. Instead, perhaps understanding Joan better than some of those who seemed more sympathetic, Warwick and his men knew that she would change her clothing given the opportunity.

The English, who had remained in the background throughout the trial, now assumed a more prominent role since Joan's recantation made her execution for heresy doubtful. A Venetian who had been paying close attention to events wrote home that "the English say among themselves: 'Once this girl is dead, Charles's affairs will prosper no more.' "[38]

A wide variety of witnesses corroborated what happened after Cauchon learned that Joan had resumed wearing male garb. The bishop dispatched two of his most trusted associates, Jean Beaupère and Nicolas Midi, to go to the castle and discover what had happened. After being bullied, threatened, and insulted in the courtyard, they returned without having interviewed Joan.[39] Later in the day Massieu and others went to the castle but were forced back by the English guards, who brandished hatchets and swords.[40] When Manchon, who probably accompanied Massieu, arrived in the courtyard, "about 500 Englishmen surrounded them, roughing them up and calling them traitors, saying they had behaved badly during the trial. Only with great difficulty and fear were they able to escape."[41] They could do nothing more for her.

Once Joan resumed male clothing, her fate was sealed. La Pierre reported that when Cauchon and Warwick learned she had changed her clothes, they responded exultantly, "We've got her!"[42] On Monday, May 28, when Manchon accompanied the bishop and earl to the castle to ask Joan what had happened to change her mind, they found her wearing a man's outfit, a short mantle, a hood, a doublet and other male garments. By this time Joan had changed her story, probably the *result* of once again wearing clothes that she felt expressed her identity. She said at trial that she had done so of her own will, under no compulsion, for she preferred men's clothing. When Cauchon reminded her of the document she had signed at Saint-Ouen, she said "she never meant to take such an oath. . . . It was more lawful and convenient for her to wear [male clothing], since she was among men, than to wear woman's dress. She said she had resumed it because the promises made to her had not been kept."[43]

On the one hand, Joan needed the strength and power her male clothing accorded her, but on the other she had to make excuses for breaking her word. She did so by invoking "her saints." By speaking through them she could justify her choices. She said "she had damned herself to save her life. . . . The voices told her, when she was on the scaffold or platform before the people, to answer the preacher boldly." She now called him a false preacher, one who had accused her of many things she had not done, adding that she said she would not go against the voices of St. Catherine and St. Margaret. "All that she said was from fear of the fire. . . . She would rather die than endure any longer the suffering of her prison." Besides, she added, she did not understand what was in the formula of abjuration.[44]

In her fright when she had seen the scaffold prepared for an execution, Joan had rejected all she had become by listening to those who kept urging her to sign the piece of paper. Some who had done so had her best interests at heart, which is why the English were so enraged. But back in her cell, intimidated and fearing physical assault, she jumped at the chance to go back to the way things had been even if it meant certain death. Perhaps by putting on male clothing again she hoped to regain the identity that had helped her win victories in the past. Could such a victory happen once again?

On Tuesday, May 29, most of the judges and assessors assembled in the archbishop's palace to deliberate, or at least make a show of doing so. Joan had relapsed, going back on the promise she had made, making her execution inevitable. That she did so by changing her clothing did not matter, since her renunciation of male attire was part of the document she had signed at Saint-Ouen. The end result was known to all present, but for the purposes of the trial, the assessors had to state their opinion for the record. Most tried to avoid direct responsibility by referring to the opinion expressed by the abbot of Fécamp, who had declared that Joan had relapsed. He recommended that they once again read to her "the formula she had recently heard, to explain it and preach the Word of God to her. After that the judges would have to declare her a heretic and abandon her to the secular justice, praying it to act towards her with gentleness."[45]

In theory the Church could never directly execute an individual who had been judged guilty. The abbot's words followed the traditional formula before a heretic was executed. All those present knew there would be no mercy and that what had been done could not now be undone. Even Ladvenu agreed with the abbot, as did La Pierre, who added that Joan "should be once more charitably admonished for the salvation of her soul and told that she had no further hope in the life of this world."[46] Le Sauvage, the spokesperson for the Dominican convent of Saint-Jacques, was noticeably absent. La Pierre said that at the end of the session Cauchon declared to the English who waited outside "Farewell! Farewell! Make a good face! It is done."[47] Joan was summoned to appear at eight o'clock the next morning in the Old Market of Rouen.

On Wednesday, May 30, at around seven o'clock in the morning, Ladvenu, accompanied by his Dominican brother Jean Toutmouillé, heard Joan in confession and brought her communion.[48] Why was a relapsed heretic allowed to consume the body of Christ the morning that she would be burnt at the stake? After she made the request, Cauchon consulted with the other judges and assessors to determine whether the sacrament of confession and communion ought to be given to her along with absolution. They decided to allow it. Even so, they expected it to be done quickly and without ceremony. Ladvenu complained of the irreverence and disrespect shown to the eucharist as a sacrament and the solemnity of the occasion. He sent for a liturgical stole, which marked the solemn office of a priest or friar, and surrounded by candles gave Joan the consecrated host. He remembered her great devotion and the copious tears she shed, so much that he could barely describe it.[49] Knowing that she would be burned, Joan asked:

> "How can they treat me so cruelly that my virgin body which has never been violated will be burned in the fire?" Turning to Bishop Cauchon, she said, "Bishop, I die by you." He responded, "Oh, Joan, you do not submit. This has happened because you did not keep your promise but relapsed." She fired back, "Alas, if you had put me in a church prison and confided me to guards of the church, as should have been done, this would not have happened. It is why I appeal from you to God."[50]

A young priest heard from one of those present that Joan asked, " 'Master, where will I be this evening?' " He responded: 'Do you not have great confidence in God?' She said yes, so with the aid of God she will be in paradise."[51] The priest said he had never heard such a beautiful confession. In his opinion, Joan walked the path of justice and holiness with God.[52]

About a half hour after confessing and receiving communion, Joan emerged from her prison cell in the Château de Bouvreuil wearing a long dress "that was the court's final expression of control over Joan."[53] On her head was a bonnet inscribed with the words "Relapsed, Heretic, Idolator, Schismatic." She mounted a cart pulled by four horses that was surrounded by as many as 120 English soldiers with pikes and swords to prevent any possibility of escape. For only the second time the people of Rouen, who packed the narrow streets, glimpsed Joan. The cortège wound its way through the narrow streets of Old Rouen, through the rue du Moulinet, rue du Sacre, rue Dinanderie, rue des Bons-Enfants, and finally the rue de la Prison to the Old Market.[54] The marketplace was packed with 700 to 800 people. Four platforms had been erected there for the judges, the assembled churchmen who chose to attend, the bailiff and his lieutenant, and a fourth for Joan and the preacher Nicolas Midi.[55]

Midi delivered a sermon based on I Corinthians 12:26: "Where one member suffer, all the members suffer with it." An execution sermon would normally take twenty to thirty minutes, but Midi's may have been hurried as a result of threats from English soldiers who at one point interjected: "Hurry up! Shall we dine here this day?"[56] At one point, when Midi maligned Charles VII, Joan interrupted as she had before, declaring, "What you say is not true, because I want you to know that there is no better Catholic than the king!" Bishop Cauchon then pronounced the final sentence:

> As often as the poisonous virus of heresy obstinately attaches itself to a member of the Church and transforms him into a limb of Satan, most diligent care must be taken to prevent the foul contagion of this pernicious leprosy from spreading to other parts of the mystic body of Christ. . . . Joan, commonly called The Maid, [has] fallen into diverse errors and crimes of schism, idolatry, invocation of demons and many other misdeeds. Nevertheless . . . the Church never closes her bosom to the wanderer who returns, esteeming that with a pure spirit and unfeigned faith you had cut yourself off from these errors and crimes because on a certain day you renounced them. . . . Since subsequently, after this abjuration of your errors the author of schism and heresy has

arisen in your heart, which he has seduced. Since you are fallen again – O, sorrow! – into these errors and crimes as the dog returns to his vomit . . . we declare that you are fallen again into your former errors and under the sentence of excommunication . . . and by this sentence which we deliver in writing and pronounce from this tribunal, we denounce you as a rotten member, which, so that you shall not infect other members of Christ, must be cast out of the unity of the Church, cut off from her body, and given over to the secular power.[57]

Throughout Joan listened and prayed.

At about ten o'clock in the morning, abandoned by the Church, Joan was seized by English soldiers and turned over to the executioner. The lieutenant bailiff, who should have taken part, recalled that without any delay or sentence of a lay judge, she was given to the executioner and led to the platform where the stake had been prepared for her to be burnt, even though lay judges were in attendance.[58] Not having a secular judgment pronounced was a direct violation of church law, but the English and their allies were determined to wait no longer.

Accompanied by Ladvenu and La Pierre, who had been with her since they left the castle, Joan was led up to a special scaffold and her body was bound to a wooden post. In most cases the condemned were simply tied to a stake and faggots lit under them, but in Joan's case a large plaster platform had been erected above the wood, so that the packed crowd could get a good view and have no doubts about Joan's death. Massieu was never able to forget her expressions of contrition, penitence, and the fervor of her faith. She cried out with piteous lamentations, invoking the Father, Son and Holy Spirit, the blessed Virgin Mary, and all the saints of paradise.[59] She asked people of all conditions, as much of her party as of the other, to pray for her. She then pardoned her judges and the executioner, continuing for about a half hour. The judges, assessors, and even several of the English were extremely moved. With great devotion, she asked for a cross. Hearing this, an Englishmen who was nearby made a small one of wood, which he gave to her. "She received it devoutly, kissing it, and making numerous piteous cries to God Our Redeemer who had suffered on the cross for our salvation." And she put the little cross on her breast between her flesh and her dress.[60]

Joan then asked that the crucifix be brought to her from the adjacent church of Saint-Sauveur. La Pierre retrieved it and held it up before her eyes so that she could see it without interruption until her death.[61] The fire was lit beneath her and the flames suddenly blazed up. Joan warned La Pierre and Ladvenu, who had mounted the scaffold with her: "Get down quickly!"[62] Before she was overcome she cried out "Jesus!" many times. She apparently died of smoke inhalation soon after the fire was lit.[63] Many of those present described seeing her engulfed in flames, as the height of the platform would have made it appear that she was being burned alive. In any case, the executioner told the Dominicans, whom he later accompanied in distress to their convent, that he was very upset at the level of cruelty and said that he had "burned a holy woman that day."[64] Executioners were normally paid to knock out or even strangle criminals in order to render them unconscious or alleviate their pain; because of the height of the platform he had been unable to reach Joan to strike her with his stave.

Many of Joan's enemies wept at the sight. Even Cauchon was said to have cried on this occasion. One English soldier had hated Joan vehemently and sworn many times that he would throw her into the flames with his own hands. Hearing Joan call out the name of Jesus until the moment of her death, he was overcome: "He lost his senses so completely that he had to be taken to a tavern in the Old Market to regain his strength."[65] Even Jean Tressart, secretary of the king of England, returning to the place of Joan's execution was sad and anguished, mournful at everything that had happened and what he had seen there. He then said: "We are all lost, because a saint has been burned."[66]

As Joan's body slumped from the post, the English, fearing that people would say she had escaped, told the executioner to tamp down the fire so that those in attendance could see she was dead.[67] The Bourgeois of Paris, who was not present but based his account on reliable sources, described the scene: "The fire was raked back. Everyone saw her completely naked with all that can and does characterize a woman, in order to remove any uncertainty they might have had." Why was it necessary to prove that Joan was female? Throughout her short career this had been a subject of some debate, especially from those who were far away. For many it seemed inconceivable that a girl could have accomplished as much as Joan had, especially in an arena reserved for men. The Bourgeois went on, describing the voyeuristic level of curiosity:

When they had looked upon her as long as they wanted, her dead body bound to the stake, the executioner got a large fire going again under her poor carcass, which was promptly engulfed, and her bones and her flesh were reduced to ashes. There were some there and elsewhere who said that she was a martyr, and that she had been a martyr for her true Lord. Others said that this was false, and that the French side had done badly to keep her with them for so long. That is what people were saying. But whether she died from cruelty or justice, she was burned that day.[68]

A few of the English laughed out loud, but this account demonstrates the uneasiness of many others.[69] When the spectators were satisfied that Joan was human, female, and dead, the executioner added oil and sulfur. The fire raged most of the day, for no trace of Joan could be allowed to remain.[70] It was finally over around four o'clock in the afternoon, eight hours after Joan had been summoned to appear that morning.[71]

The gruesome spectacle had finally come to an end but would not soon be forgotten by those in attendance. Even though he had served as a notary and not a partisan of the English, Manchon was so moved by her death that "he was terrified for a month, and ... with the salary he received from the trial bought a missal in memory of her."[72] The Old Market was filled with crying and moaning, with many saying they believed the English feared her more than all the rest of the army of the king of France.[73] The executioner confessed to the Dominicans his concern that he would be damned for what he had done that day. He said that all was burned save for Joan's heart,[74] but that is certainly fanciful. When the fire had fully consumed her, he gathered Joan's ashes in a sack and threw them from the Pont Mathilde into the Seine. Disposing of all her remains was essential, so that the people of Rouen would not try to gather bits and pieces of bone as relics. One of the trial notaries recalled that "the judges and those who participated in the trial had incurred the great reproaches of the people of Rouen, who regarded them with horror;"[75] many said that if the English had had such a woman, they would have showered her with honors and not treated her like this.[76]

Another Dominican of Saint-Jacques, Pierre Bosquier, who had taken no part in the trial, was present at the execution and unwisely spoke out at the time. He was forced to make a public confession:

I said that you and those who judged this woman Joan, commonly called The Maid, had done and did wrong; which words, seeing that this Joan had appeared before you in judgment and on trial of faith, are evil-sounding and appear to incline somewhat to heretical error; which words, so help me God, since it has been found that I uttered them, were said and uttered by me in thoughtlessness and inadvertence, and in drink. I confess that in this matter I have gravely sinned.

Even with Joan dead, Cauchon wanted to make an example, and who better than a Dominican from the local convent? Possibly it was intended to silence those who had tried to help Joan at the trial. Cauchon inserted his sentence into the trial record against a man "who seemed to favor this Joan and grievously sinned and erred" by claiming that all who judged her had done wrong. The Dominican was condemned to imprisonment on bread and water until the following Easter. Having made his point, Cauchon showed leniency by allowing him to serve his sentence in the convent headed by Le Maistre.[77]

The Grand Inquisitor of France, Jean Graverent, who had been "unable to attend" the trial, preached a sermon in Paris on July 4, 1431. He contended that Joan:

was the daughter of very poor people. From the age of thirteen, she wore the clothing of a man, and from that time her father and mother would have willingly had her killed had they been able to without going against their consciences. For this reason, she left them, possessed by the Enemy from Hell, and from that time lived murderously . . . breathing fire and blood up until the day she was burned. . . . The Enemy appeared to her in three forms, as Saint Michael, Saint Catherine, and Saint Margaret.[78]

Graverent was an avowed adherent of the English side, having taken an oath to them before the *parlement* of Paris in 1429. Presumably the Parisians could now rest easy, knowing that the girl who "breathed fire and blood" could never attack them again.

Some have suggested that Joan's execution was a way for the patriarchy in both Church and State to demonstrate their power.[79] While Joan's gender and clothing did become a major issue at the trial, such an idea fails to take into account the complex events and partisanship of the Hundred Years War. A specific church court *did* condemn Joan, but it was conducted in English-held Normandy with the knowledge that if Joan was not convicted she would be handed over to the English. Even as the trial proceeded under a cloud of threat and fear, some refused to participate, saying that the proceedings violated canon law in several respects. Full participation and regular attendance at the trial were for the most part limited to those of Cauchon's "inner circle" as well as to others who were forced to attend. But with the exception of some of the king's counselors who cared most about their own interests, those on the French side *had* supported Joan, even on the question of her clothing. Her military colleagues, soldiers, numerous French theologians, and many men throughout Europe who heard and wrote of her deeds, expressed awe and admiration.

A church court burned Joan of Arc, but they did so at the orchestration of the English leaders, not because Cauchon, the English-backed University of Paris theologians, and Bedford believed she was a witch or a heretic, but because she had shamed the English on the field of battle and they feared she would do so again. An English knight said that they feared her more than 100 soldiers,[80] which may explain why Joan's clothing provoked such strong reactions on the English side. Winning victories that broke the stranglehold the English had on France empowered Joan but emasculated the duke of Bedford, whose court in France was considered the equal of that of many European princes. His regency had permitted him to amass enormous wealth in the form of French property, royal collections, and ransoms. In 1427, he had planned a final series of conquests designed to add Anjou, Maine, and Poitou to the English holdings, joining them to English Gascony. All that began to change in 1429 with the appearance of a teenage peasant girl.

That Joan appropriated so many symbols of the chivalric knight would have incensed the English leadership. The honor of a knight and military commander depended upon his ability to inspire loyalty in his soldiers and win victories. Fear of Joan had deprived Bedford and his commanders of much-needed support. To be taunted and then defeated by a girl was an outrage that the duke could not tolerate. As he watched his French empire crumble, Bedford's troubles multiplied. Each defeat presented Bedford with challenges to his authority in England and limited his ability to recruit and keep men to fight in France. Joan *had* to be not only burned but annihilated, which is why the trial and execution were so carefully staged. As long as she lived, she inspired fear. Now that she was dead, the world had to know.

Throughout June, writing in the name of Henry VI, Bedford sent letters to the Holy Roman Emperor, kings, dukes, and other princes of all Christendom, announcing the death of that Limb of the Fiend, the "lying

prophetess" who had appeared in "our kingdom of France." His words
show the depth of his anger and loathing for Joan.

> A certain woman whom the vulgar called The Maid had in fact arisen,
> who with an astonishing presumption, and contrary to natural decency,
> had adopted man's dress, assumed military arms, dared to take part in
> the massacre of men in bloody encounters. . . . Her presumption grew
> until she boasted that she was sent from God to lead their martial strug-
> gles. . . . So for almost a whole year she gradually seduced the people
> until the greater part turned away from the truth, put their trust in fables
> about the accomplishments of this superstitious woman which common
> report spread through almost the whole world. At last, taking compas-
> sion on His people . . . the divine mercy delivered this woman into our
> hands and power. Although she had inflicted many defeats upon our
> men and had brought great harm to our kingdoms, and it would there-
> fore have been permissible for us to submit her forthwith to grave
> punishments, nevertheless not for one moment did we design to avenge
> our injury in that way.[81]

Since Joan had become known "to almost the whole world," the important
leaders of France also had to know. Hoping that with Joan's death he could
regain his conquests and reputation, Bedford wrote:

> She clad herself also in arms such as are worn by knights and squires, raised
> a standard, and, in excessive outrage, pride and presumption, asked to be
> given and allowed to bear the very noble and excellent arms of France,
> which she in fact obtained, and wore in many conflicts and assaults. . . . In
> such condition she went to the fields and led men of arms and passage in
> troops and great companies to commit and exercise inhuman cruelties by
> shedding human blood, causing popular seditions and tumults, inciting the
> people to perjury and pernicious rebellions, false and superstitious beliefs,
> by disturbing all peace and renewing mortal wars, permitting herself to be
> worshipped and revered by many as a holy woman.

He then described Joan's capture and recantation.

> But hardly had the fire of her pride seemed extinguished in her, when
> under the breath of the Enemy it burst out into poisonous flames, and

soon the wretched woman fell back into the errors and false madness which she had formerly professed. . . . She was again publicly admonished, and for her relapse into her wonted crimes and faults was abandoned to the secular justice which forthwith condemned her to be burned.[82]

Although he distorted the facts, Bedford wanted to leave no doubt: the witch was dead!

With the fire that had consumed Joan of Arc, Bedford envisaged a resurgent English presence in France. He was wrong. He died four years later, only a week before the Treaty of Arras (1435) ended hostilities been France and Burgundy. In 1437 King Charles VII regained his capital of Paris, which was followed by the capture of Normandy in 1450. The Hundred Years War ended three years later. The story that began in 1412 in the small village of Domremy with the birth of a girl everyone called Jehannette was largely forgotten, at least at the French court where she had become for Charles VII an uncomfortable detail in the history of his reign.

CHAPTER 10

Vindication

———— ⚜ ————

WHY DID CHARLES VII not have Joan rescued? Only two inconclusive bits of evidence suggest he made any effort on her behalf. The first is a receipt dated March 14, 1431 signed by the Bastard of Orléans acknowledging that he had received 3,000 *livres tournois* from the king for an expedition into Normandy.[1] One of Joan's most loyal comrades, La Hire, was also entrusted with various commissions in Normandy. On April 2, Charles enlisted his help for two secret undertakings against "our enemies for our good and that of our realm." Three and a half weeks later, the king sent La Hire 600 *l.t.* for "his good and agreeable service . . . that he takes on each and every day in our wars and for *certain other causes that move us*."[2] La Hire led a raid near Louviers, twenty miles south of Rouen. The move was significant because many later witnesses mentioned that the English feared Joan to the point that they did not dare besiege Louviers while she was still alive.[3] Both the Bastard and La Hire were probably paid only to continue fighting in Normandy, plans that Charles certainly would not have divulged in financial records. Even so, La Hire may have planned an attempted rescue on his own. Once Joan had won his respect as a soldier and leader, he had become one of her most devoted followers. They had a good deal in common. Like Joan, he had never followed orders to the letter but had wanted to move quickly at the Battle of the Herrings and the siege of Beaugency. If he had hoped to save Joan, his chance ended abruptly when he was captured and imprisoned as he slipped out of Louviers in late May. But even had he made it to Rouen, there was little likelihood he would have been able to free her. The English had taken extraordinary precautions after they had bought Joan from Jean of

Luxembourg. Since her arrival in Rouen she had been closely guarded at all times.

Charles did not mention Joan in any surviving document between 1431 and 1450. In a perfect world of chivalry or Arthurian romance, the king would have led a charge and rescued Joan from the stake. But Charles was not Lancelot and Joan was not Guinevere. Although as his reign continued his military prowess grew, the king at this time was still fearful and cautious. More importantly, his goals and those of Joan had diverged long before her capture in 1430. While Charles hoped to mend the fences that divided France and Burgundy, Joan had sought a military solution. Taking Burgundy out of the war, as happened in 1435, was the beginning of the king's grand plan to reclaim all of France for the crown. Joan had served her purpose. Besides, she remained a sore memory for Charles, a reminder that a girl had helped make him king and that the same girl had been executed for heresy.

The king of France had many more pressing concerns in the years after Joan's death. When in 1432 Charles was reconciled with the constable, Arthur de Richemont, it marked the beginning of the end for Georges de La Trémoïlle, who was charged with financial improprieties and banished from court. Both Richemont and the family of Yolande of Aragon now took center stage. In 1436, Richemont, who had been named lieutenant general for the Île-de-France, Normandy and Champagne, marched at the head of the French army into Paris, which capitulated on April 15. But factionalism still dominated Charles' court as many were disgruntled with Richemont's return to power. In the late 1430s a clique began to plot against the king and the constable. The conspiracy known as the "Praguerie" crystallized in 1440 around some leading nobles, including the duke of Alençon, supporters of La Trémoïlle, and the dauphin, the future Louis XI. The attempt at civil war failed, as the major cities of France rallied to Charles who, with Richemont, took decisive action to put down the rebellion.

The period from 1442 to 1449 began with the death of Yolande of Aragon, who had played such an important behind-the-scenes role in Joan of Arc's career. While continued factionalism, especially surrounding Prince Louis, demanded his attention, Charles now turned to England. In 1444 he concluded the Truce of Tours, sealed by a marriage between King Henry VI and Yolande's granddaughter Margaret of Anjou. Charles also began a successful reorganization of his military forces in 1445, creating a strong and disciplined standing army paid for by taxation and under the control of the monarchy.[4]

In mid-1449, English attacks in Brittany gave Charles the excuse he needed to break the truce. Supported by a strong Breton cohort at court, including Richemont and André de Laval, Charles's now superior army launched a strike into Normandy. Old enemies met once more, as the Bastard of Orléans, now count of Dunois, prepared to besiege Rouen, held by John Talbot, earl of Shrewsbury. Unlike Paris, Rouen and other Norman cities had never been content under English occupation, resorting to passive resistance or sullen acquiescence at best.[5] Its citizens now looked to Charles for relief. On October 9 the French army arrived before the city walls. When Talbot ordered the deaths of French supporters within the city, it was too much for the people of Rouen. On October 19, the Rouennais "seeing the English armed and marching through the city" pursued them so fiercely that it was only with great difficulty that they managed to make their way back to the palace and castle. The city opened its gates to the French army around noon: the English surrendered and Talbot was taken prisoner.

Less than a month later, Charles VII, wearing full armor, rode through the Beauvoisine Gate, the same gate by which Joan had entered Rouen eighteen years earlier. As trumpets began to ring out, huge crowds packed the narrow streets singing *Te Deum laudamus* to watch the king make his royal entry. The Bastard, now count of Dunois, led the way.[6] After Rouen opened its gates, Harfleur, Honfleur, and Caen fell quickly when the French besieged them in late 1449 and early 1450. The English began an attack in April of 1450 to try to protect their remaining holdings in France. At Formigny on April 15, considered the first battle in Western Europe when guns made a major difference to the outcome, an English army of nearly 3,800 men was attacked from the west and south by slightly larger French forces commanded by Richemont and Clermont. The English were routed, with most of their troops killed or seriously wounded. On July 6 Cherbourg fell, leaving all of Normandy in French hands. In southwest France, Gascony fell in 1451, followed by a decisive defeat of the English at the Battle of Castillon on the anniversary of Charles' coronation, July 17, 1453. The Hundred Years War was over.

Joan's goals had been achieved and her "noble king" had recovered his kingdom. But what about the role she had played to make that happen? What could or should be done about her judicial murder and the harm to

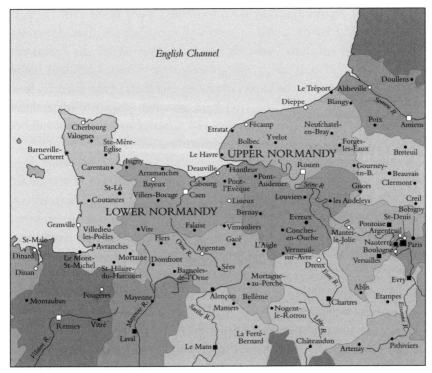

Map 11   Normandy in the Hundred Years War.

her reputation? Three conditions had to be met before an official inquiry could be launched into Joan's trial and execution. Both Paris and Rouen had to be in French hands. The University of Paris had supplied the majority of assessors who took part in the trial; most of the other assessors or people who had met Joan resided in Rouen. Finally, the pope had to authorize an investigation since the original trial had been an inquisition.

In February 1450 Charles appointed one of his counselors, Guillaume Bouillé, a doctor of the University of Paris and canon of Noyon, to make a preliminary inquiry into the way the original trial had been conducted. The impetus came from Bouillé rather than the king. In late 1449 he argued "it was wrong to remain silent about this iniquitous condemnation that harmed the king's honor, for it was as a soldier of the king that the Maid had been condemned as a heretic and sorceress. What a stain against the throne if later our enemies recount to the world that the king of France had such a woman in his army."[7] Bouillé, who over the next six years would prove to be among the most zealous of those fighting to restore Joan's reputation, may have touched a royal nerve. For his part, Charles would have preferred to leave well enough alone. Bouillé's investigation would open old wounds, reminding people of the ineffectual dauphin who had been disparagingly called the King of Bourges before Joan of Arc arrived on the scene. Involving members of the French clergy who had participated in the trial held potential risks.[8] With fighting continuing in parts of Normandy in 1450, Charles had a tenuous hold on his new subjects, especially the most important ones. He was understandably hesitant to dredge up memories that many would rather have forgotten. But as a result of Bouillé's recommendation, Charles felt compelled to take at least some action. He authorized Bouillé to look into the role the English had played in the 1431 trial with special attention being paid to mistakes and abuses they had committed, the hatred they inspired, and the cruelty of executing Joan.[9] By focusing on the English rather than Joan, the king could deflect some of the blame that would otherwise be imputed to the French churchmen who carried out the trial proceedings. Such an emphasis made the political nature of the trial evident. The initial inquiry was not so much about Joan as the wrongs that had been committed against the French king.

In Rouen on March 4 and 5, 1450, seven witnesses appeared: four Dominican friars from the Convent of Saint-Jacques and three priests. Then suddenly the proceedings ended. The king, or at least his loyal counselor Bouillé, had instigated the inquest but could make no rulings against the decision of a church court. It may also be that it was too soon and that Bouillé had ruffled some feathers. Why did Bouillé pursue the matter with such passion? Possibly he felt guilt by association, since so many members of the university had assumed prominent roles in Joan's trial. Yet it is equally likely that confronted with such a travesty of justice he hoped to correct it. But in his conclusions he added to the legend and diminished the actual girl.

In 1431, answering each one of the articles with which Joan had been charged, Bouillé pointed out that she had never sought honors for herself but only for France. She was in every way a good Catholic, rendering good for evil. Even her predictions had come true, although at the time no one would have believed it possible. He countered the charge that Joan had violated divine law through wearing men's clothing by insisting that she did not want to provoke "perverse desires" among soldiers and the men with whom she had to live. Quoting the famous theologian Jean Gerson,

Bouillé made the case that God had chosen her, a young virgin, as a standard-bearer to crush the enemies of the realm and save its poor and desperate people. Here he uses the favored medieval argument about the "power of the weak" to explain Joan's astounding deeds on the battlefield and at trial. Bouillé even claimed that Joan was raised among cowherds, a claim so similar to the English insults at Orléans that it would have enraged her. Ignoring the evidence of the trial record, he argued that she was powerless to respond to difficult questions because the simplicity and weakness of her sex rendered her incapable of understanding them. Bouillé failed to comprehend what so many who had been present at the trial did: that Joan handled difficult and subtle questions with stunning composure and considerable sophistication.

Despite Bouillé's good intentions, Joan was already being refashioned to suit the environment at the end of the Hundred Years War and beyond. Instead of a bold and charismatic leader, talented soldier, and quick-witted girl, she was recast symbolically as an agent of God, a simple peasant girl chosen to humble the great and powerful. In her own time, Joan had moved, fascinated, motivated, or inspired fear. With ample support from Yolande of Aragon and her party at Charles's court, Joan had been trained to fight and lead. She was aided in her mission by newly-spun prophecies about a young virgin warrior who would reclaim France for its divinely chosen king. That her innate talents and accomplishments were so dramatic was the one thing no one at the time could have predicted. But after her execution, Joan was mostly forgotten – except by the people of Orléans, who considered her their savior and began to make her into a mythological figure. From 1435 to this day, on May 8 the city commemorates its deliverance with a mystery play about the siege and other festivities.[10] But as the fifteenth century wore on and in the centuries to come, Joan was re-imagined as a poor shepherdess who wept constantly and swooned when saints spoke to her.

Bouillé would continue to play a leading part in the next two stages, in 1452 and 1455–6. In 1452, Cardinal d'Estouteville, the papal legate, reopened the dossier with the assistance of the Dominican Grand Inquisitor of France, Jean Bréhal. Most of the information about how the inquiry proceeded has been lost. Probably learning from what happened in 1450, it set out not to accuse or denounce, but as a special commission whose responsibility was to look into Joan's notoriety.[11] On May 4 a summons was sent out to the clergy of Rouen, requiring seventeen men to present themselves at the archbishop's palace, adding that those who did not appear would be suspended from their position or even excommunicated, this last suggesting Charles's hesitation had been justified and that many who had participated in the original trial were unwilling or afraid to testify.[12] Those called included clergymen, civil servants, and even workers who had had contact with Joan. Others who were not cited *did* appear. Among the important participants in the original trial, the notary Guillaume Manchon, the executor of writs Jean Massieu, Ysambard de La Pierre, Martin Ladvenu, and other Dominicans of the Convent of Saint-Jacques offered testimony. Yet some of the most important participants in the trial of condemnation were not called. Many were dead, including Bishop Cauchon, the promotor of the trial Jean d'Estivet, Nicolas Midi, and Nicholas Loyseleur, the man who pretended he was a priest from Lorraine to gain Joan's confidence. The Vice Inquisitor at the trial, Jean Le Maistre, had remained prior of Saint-Jacques in the late 1440s, but had probably died before the 1452 investigation, or was too ashamed to appear.[13] Many assessors from the university did testify in 1452 or 1455–6, but that number included only two of those who had been most hostile to Joan in 1431: Jean Beaupère and Thomas de Courcelles.

Between May 2 and 8, 1452, twenty-two witnesses were interviewed, including some who had already spoken to Bouillé in 1450. Joan was not the specific subject of the inquiry, but rather Cauchon's conduct of the trial.[14] Based on the results, Estouteville was more determined than ever to pursue the matter. Over the ensuing three years, along with Bréhal, he gathered what would be needed for a full and detailed inquiry into the 1431 proceedings. He wrote to the king:

My sovereign Lord,
    I recommend myself humbly to your grace.
    Let it please you to know that shortly the Inquisitor of the Faith and Master Guillaume Bouillé ... will come to you to make known what has been done regarding the trial of Joan the Maid. And because I know that this touches greatly on your honor and estate, I have used all my power and continue to do all that a good and loyal servant must do for his lord, as you will be more fully informed by those mentioned earlier.
    Your very humble and very obedient servant,
        Cardinal d'Estouteville.[15]

Estouteville's comment that the results of the trial touched on Charles' honor, along with Bouillé's challenge in 1450, were probably intended to secure greater involvement on the part of the king. Charles was not pleased and stalled. He informed the delegation that the mediocrity of his current lodgings prevented him from receiving them; they would have to wait until the king was ready to meet with them at Mehun-sur-Yèvre at the beginning of July.[16] To pursue the matter, Estouteville left for Rome to make his appeal to the pope. After all, the trial transcript, which Cauchon had had translated into French, German, and Italian and circulated to an international audience, recorded Joan's several appeals to the pope.[17] Estouteville, a major player in papal politics who would spend most of the rest of his life in Rome, may have hoped that he could win French support by championing Joan's cause and smoothing over some of the difficulties between France and the papacy over the appointment of bishops.[18]

It was now time to involve Joan's remaining family members in the trial. Jacques d'Arc had died in 1431 after his daughter's execution. But in 1440, finding herself in financial straits after the death of her eldest son Jacquemin, Isabelle Romée accepted an invitation from the city of Orléans to live there with her son Pierre and his family. Orléans paid her a monthly allowance as well as her medical expenses. As they began what would become the official nullification inquiry, the Cardinal Legate and Grand Inquisitor Bréhal contacted Joan's mother, for they needed a family member to make an appeal to Rome.

On the morning of November 7, 1455, in the sacristy of the church of Notre Dame in Paris, Isabelle, her sons Jean and Pierre, and several "serious" individuals from Orléans petitioned the archbishops of Reims and Paris, along with Bréhal, to open an inquiry to clear Joan's name. Isabelle dropped to her knees, weeping and moaning. In a scene that was dramatically staged, she read aloud a mandate from Pope Callixtus III that had been given to her by Estouteville:

> Joan's adversaries, without having been entrusted by any legitimate authority and after having eliminated all means for her to defend herself, condemned her mortally and iniquitously in a trial sullied by deception, violence and injustice. They showed contempt for the rule of law, untruthfully charging her with many crimes, falsifying many articles against her, and harassing and fatiguing her with their charges and insinuations in order to condemn her. After she received the eucharist

with great devotion, they had her burned, to the damnation of their souls, in a grisly fire that evoked tears from everyone and cast blame, infamy and irreparable damage on Isabelle and her family.[19]

The Grand Inquisitor proceeded carefully. On November 26, 1455, Isabelle and her son Jean appeared before a doctor of canon law and others, pleading with them to obey the will of the pope and call before them all who should testify. She asked them to nullify the original verdict and declare Joan and her family innocent.[20] After oaths were taken, appointments made, and articles drawn up, witnesses from Lorraine, Orléans, Paris, Rouen, and elsewhere in France were interviewed under oath between January 10 and May 28, 1456.

All who had any information were ordered to present themselves to the delegates of the inquisitor and archbishops. To secure maximum compliance, they reassured all who had knowledge or information about the original trial that they would be able to testify in complete peace and security.[21] In short, they offered an amnesty, almost certainly insisted upon by a king who did not want to alienate his subjects in Rouen.

The official nullification proceedings of 1455–6 focused on Joan's character and behavior, as well as those of her judges. One of the bases for proceeding was that:

Joan, frail and innocent, had all counsel or assistance denied her, even though she was asked subtle and difficult questions concerning the faith. Such a refusal was inhuman and contrary to justice. They added that an honest man,[22] attending one day at the trial, had wanted to guide Joan, but he was expelled with terrifying threats. . . . [They added] that Joan was a minor, and that she did not have the capacity to appear in court or to act without an advocate.[23]

On December 20, 1455, the promotor of the new inquiry issued a declaration calling on all named to testify under threat of being judged in contempt, although they were to be given a second opportunity if they did not come immediately. Some still did not appear, although no action was taken against them. The churchmen and notaries then compiled over a hundred articles that were to be investigated in several different locations. The results of the 1452 inquiry made by Cardinal d'Estouteville were inserted into the new dossier.

The proceedings began in Paris with the questioning of twenty witnesses from January 10 to May 11. Many of them had met Joan in Chinon, Poitiers, Orléans, Rouen, and even Beaurevoir Castle. Several of the king's officials testified, as did the duke of Alençon, Joan's page Louis de Coutes, and her confessor Jean Pasquerel.

Separately, authorities from Toul took depositions from men and women who had known Joan in her native region (see Appendix C, pp. 201–2). From January 28 to February 11, they interviewed thirty-four people, including former friends, neighbors, and godparents of Joan who lived in Domremy or Neufchâteau. They also questioned her second cousin, Durand Laxart, people who had come to know her in Vaucouleurs, local notables and churchmen, and the two men who accompanied her to Chinon, Jean de Metz and Bertrand de Poulengy.

A further part of the inquiry took place in Orléans, beginning on February 22 and lasting until late March. Among the thirty-five witnesses who testified were the Bastard, Raoul de Gaucourt, who had been governor of Orléans in 1429, some of the king's counselors and more than twenty-five men and women of bourgeois status. Most of the nineteen testimonies given at Rouen, aside from a few depositions taken late in 1455, were collected in mid-May. They included those of several of the trial assessors, all three notaries, Joan's usher Massieu, the Dominican Ladvenu, and the only person who had been present and able to give a full account of the Poitiers' inquiry, Guillaume Séguin. The head notary, Manchon, also presented a list of corrections that he had made at the time of the trial when he disagreed with the daily transcripts. Finally, on May 28, Jean d'Aulon, Joan's squire, presented himself to the Vice Inquisitor at Lyon to give his statement, which was transcribed and sent to Bréhal. Several other individuals, including Ysambard de La Pierre who had testified in both 1450 and 1452, were not questioned in 1456, but their earlier accounts were made part of the final document. When all the depositions had been taken, the results were compiled and Joan's new judges declared the original trial null and void.

We have no idea how many people were present on July 7, 1456, twenty-five years after Joan's death, when the Grand Inquisitor Bréhal publicly announced the nullification at the same palace of Rouen where Joan's fate had been decided in 1431. Isabelle Romée had been taken ill and had to return to Orléans, but her son Jean d'Arc and the family lawyer were present to listen to the statement of Joan's vindication. Bréhal stated that after mature deliberation among the judges, they had decided that Joan's actions were more worthy of admiration than condemnation. He went on, stating that Joan's trial had been conducted in a vicious, deceitful manner, fraudulently and with ill intent.

> The truth was passed over in silence and false assertions were introduced on several essential points and her responses had been altered, which changed everything. For this reason, we reject and nullify the charges as false. We pronounce that the trial and the sentences, full of slander, contradictions, and manifest error of law and practice, as well as the abjuration, execution and all that followed are declared null and void. . . . Joan and the plaintiffs, her relatives, will not incur or sustain any mark or stain of infamy in this matter.

Bréhal then demanded that their decision should immediately be read in the cemetery of Saint-Ouen, followed by a general procession and a sermon. The next day the judgment again would be read and a sermon delivered in the Old Market, where Joan had perished in the fire. There, Bréhal stated, a cross would be erected in her perpetual memory.[24] Joan had won her final battle, not a little due to her spirited and subversive performance at the trial.

Joan of Arc and her family had been exonerated in proceedings that were as openly political as her original trial. By 1456, Joan had become a symbol of France. As a result, churchmen – and the reluctant king – were able to create a narrative that presented the kingdom at the end of the Hundred Years War as a part of the prophesied salvation history. The nullification proceedings were, except for certain participants like Bouillé, much more about refashioning France and creating French unity than they were about Joan.[25] But even if the process was intended solely to alter the political landscape in which Charles VII now ruled, the testimonies of so many who had known Joan provide a rich and detailed portrait of the girl as well as her deeds.

"That Astonishing and Marvelous Maid"

❧

As Joan's legend grew in the centuries following her death, the girl she had been was forgotten, replaced by Shakespeare's clever witch, Voltaire's Maid whose chief accomplishment was resisting sexual temptation for a year, Schiller's romantic heroine, and Twain's wonderful, bonny child.[1] In the early nineteenth century, Joan's popularity was revived due in large part to Napoleon's interest in her and in the historical research of Jules Michelet and his student Jules Quicherat, who, from 1841–9, published five volumes of original sources relating to Joan.

In 1849, Félix Dupanloup, bishop of Orléans, began to collect documents to advance the cause of Joan's beatification; twenty years later he formally requested that Rome hold a preliminary inquiry. Great holiness of life, heroic levels of virtue and constancy, and miracles were required. Although some suggest that military and political events prompted the action in a desire to rouse nationalistic sentiments, the Franco-Prussian War delayed consideration of Joan's case. Because of conflict in Europe that included the papacy, it was only in 1894 that Pope Leo XIII authorized the case to be considered. Much like a trial, it involved Promotors of the Faith as well as Devil's Advocates who made the case for Joan. While recognizing Joan's actions as glorious and worthy of admiration, the Promotors argued spiritedly that she did not meet the criteria of sainthood. They claimed that she failed the test of heroic virtue because she had recanted when faced with the fire, she had relied too much on her own understanding of God's will, and that she had often acted with irreverence. Some even argued that she was hysterical. Finally, that she died not as a martyr to the faith but for a political cause. Even against such opposition, Joan's supporters in France and at the Vatican won their case.[2] Three miraculous cures of French nuns[3] were accepted and the pope issued a dispensation for the required fourth miracle, in view of the fact that she "had saved France." Joan was beatified in 1909, a recognition that she had led a holy life and was worthy of veneration. World War I interrupted the case for canonization, but after two more miracles[4] were attested she was declared a saint on May 16, 1920, nearly five hundred years after her death.

Marina Warner captures the image of Joan that remained pervasive from her canonization until the late 1990s:

> The Saint Joan of recent hagiography, and Saint Thérèse, the Little Flower, both give comfort. They provide for adults a simple image of perfection. They eliminate complications; by remaining childish, they do not present . . . moral dilemmas or ambiguities. Such a saint represents a reduction of conflict. Joan tending her sheep, the innocent country girl called by God, becomes simple. One of the most tantalizing puzzles of European history disappears under the cloak of primal innocence. This feels reassuring. Creating simplicity often makes the heart leap; order has been restored, the crooked made straight. But order is understanding that things cannot be made simple, that complexity reigns and must be accepted.[5]

The fictional popularizations of Joan, her sainthood, and symbolic use of her image for so many different and opposing causes over the past two centuries has obscured the girl who left her small village with a mission she said came from God. Who was the real Joan? Many who had known her, depending on their relationship to her, emphasized either her piety or her military talents. Some who got to know her best said that she resembled the most skillful captain in the world, in her conduct and disposition of troops, deeds of war, the organization of combat, and encouragement of troops. At the same time they emphasized her prayers and confessions, horror of swearing and contempt for camp followers. In her trial performance, Joan confounded her interrogators with her strength and the complexity and ingenuity of her responses. Although some said she was a simple girl in many ways, their further reflections suggest otherwise. Joan was guided by one principle – "Go boldly!" She said so at trial, and witnesses at the nullification proceedings and chroniclers constantly mentioned it as her unofficial motto.

Joan was first and foremost a soldier and a military leader. She yearned for action and scorned politics, except when she made her case for a unified France. Although her charisma had its basis in religion, Joan possessed a personal magnetism so unique that it inspired fifteenth-century men not only to admire her but also on many occasions to attempt the unthinkable and the impossible. She made them believe in her and in turn gave them faith in themselves. To some degree, she even made them believe in France.

Joan played a major role in the creation of France. It has often taken an outside force or enemy to forge a national consciousness and that began to happen between 1370 and 1430. Joan's conception of France did not appear to any great extent during her short lifetime; at that time dynastic politics and marital alliances still motivated most French dukes and counts, as did their desire for the "good old days" of a weak king when their power had been greater. But Joan had set an example by gathering men of divided loyalties under her standard. In Charles VII, she saw something few others recognized. The king who had used her – as she desired – and then left her to die, became a strong king, a "new monarch." Although his reign was marked by rebellions, including by his son Louis and Alençon, Charles died in 1461, ruler of a united and relatively prosperous France with a strong standing army. Although he never acknowledged Joan except by allowing the nullification process to happen, he owed a great deal of his success to a girl people called the Maid of Lorraine.

As for Joan's enemies, the stories of their ends became as legendary and even more fantastic than hers. According to the trial notary Boisguillaume, many of those who were responsible for her execution died lurid, sensational deaths. He claimed that Cauchon died suddenly while being shaved and Estivet was found dead in the muck of the gutters outside of Rouen. Midi was struck down with leprosy a few days after the trial. Loyseleur, he said, died suddenly at Basel, also of leprosy.[6] Perhaps more than anyone else the notary helped create the afterlife of Joan by portraying those who killed her as evil incarnate. Even though these stories are sometimes still related as historical fact, the truth was more mundane. They all died natural deaths.

The real story of Joan of Arc and the men in her life does not need to be exaggerated. Her own voice at trial and those of soldiers and peasants, too often silent in the historical record, along with nobles, royal coun-selors, theologians and judges – representing different sides – all flesh out the fifteenth-century girl. Joan was and remains one of the most astonishing figures in history, made all the more so because of her young age, sex, and class. Perhaps her best epitaph comes from Pope Pius II, the same pope who canonized another great woman, Catherine of Siena. The pope, who in 1429 had been a young humanist, had followed Joan's deeds with great interest. After hearing Cardinal Jean Jouffroy's account of the Maid in 1459, he admitted that "whether her career was a miracle of Heaven or a device of men I should find it hard to say. . . . Some think that when the English cause was prospering . . . one shrewder than the rest evolved the cunning scheme of declaring that the Maid had been sent by Heaven and of giving her the command she asked for." Yet the pope did not think it mattered very much. The results of her actions were enough for him. Writing in 1461, thirty years after Joan's execution and the same year Charles VII died, Pius describes Joan as impatient, storming towns and delivering aid to others, while the king dallied in his castles or concluded ineffective truces. Could the English, he asked, who had been vanquished by Joan in so many battles, ever feel really safe while she lived, even as a prisoner? No, for she might escape. So they had to find a pretext for her death. Pius does not give the details of the execution but captures in a few lines Joan's personality and her achievements:

> She bore the flames with wonderful and gallant courage. . . . Thus died [Joan], that astonishing and marvelous maid, who restored the kingdom of France when it was fallen and almost torn asunder; who inflicted so many heavy defeats upon the English; who being made general over men kept her purity unstained among companies of soldiers; of whom no breath of scandal was ever heard. . . . This at any rate is beyond question that it was the Maid under whose command the siege of Orléans was raised, by whose arms all the country between Bourges and Paris was subdued, by whose advice Reims was recovered and the coronation celebrated there, by whose charge Talbot was routed and his army cut to pieces, by whose daring the gate of Paris was fired, by whose quick wit and untiring effort the French cause was saved. It is a phenomenon that deserves to be recorded, although after-ages are likely to regard it with more wonder than credulity.[7]

In this short excerpt, the pope who had admired Joan's exploits captures the essence of how Joan was perceived by her contemporaries. He could not imagine that people in the future would possibly believe the amazing story of the Maid of Lorraine.

What of Joan the girl, the adolescent who claimed to hear voices and whose piety had evoked mockery among her childhood friends and admiration among those with whom she lived during her campaigns? Joan may not have fully envisioned her destiny in 1428, but she knew it would not be in Domremy as the wife of a peasant. If her earliest years had marked her as "different," in early 1429 she bid *adieu* once and for all to most of her friends and fellow villagers.

While Joan may have heard stories in her youth from wandering Franciscans about chivalrous battles and evil queens, how did she come to imagine herself as the Maid of Lorraine? Even at age sixteen, she had shown herself to be extraordinarily headstrong, which seems at odds with the simple devotional behaviors of her childhood. Against her parents' wishes, or unbeknownst to them, Joan had gone off to see the captain of Vaucouleurs and to fight a marriage contract. Daring to a fault, she sought out those who would support her evolving mission. Was she doing so at the behest of God? It is impossible to know. However, her statements at trial and her willingness to lie to achieve her goals suggest that she was setting off for a new frontier of her own volition. Life at home with her parents, who expected their daughter to lead an honorable peasant's life, had become too emotionally and physically constricted for the girl who had already shown that she had little regard for what was "normal" or community expectations.

Why did people believe in Joan, especially in the beginning when doing so might lay them open to ridicule? The answer is simple: the way had been paved for her. Some time in late 1428, Yolande of Aragon and her son René of Anjou, hearing of this determined girl, had the duke of Lorraine summon her to his court to assess her authenticity. Even in these early interviews, she showed no hesitation in speaking her mind or reproving her "betters." She also must have impressed the duke with her physical capabilities, since what she proposed required a long trip through enemy territory. Once she had proved her audacity, persistence, and native intelligence to the duke, the captain of Vaucouleurs sent her off to Chinon with an escort of trusted men. What followed was a series not only of tests but also of ruses, as the image of Joan the Maid was carefully constructed between February and April of 1429.

Cardinal Jouffroy, who served the duke of Burgundy, believed that the career of the Maid had been carefully crafted from the start.[8] He was right. Did Joan know she was being used? Probably not at first and maybe never, for it was in no one's interest to have a girl trying to play a part. Joan had to become convinced in her own mind that she and she alone could save France. Although she had the abilities necessary for such a role, it would not have worked had she been complicit. It was only after she endured endless questioning and examinations, responding with wit and bravado, that she could be convinced that trickery was an essential and acknowledged part of strategy. The first such trick occurred when she returned to Chinon, after the examination in Poitiers, when she was introduced to the whole court and "miraculously" picked out the dauphin Charles. By that time she had known him for nearly four weeks. Joan would have been a willing, albeit impatient, participant in the behind-the-scenes training, legend-making, and pageantry that preceded her entry into Orléans, even if she had been kept in the dark about the exact role she was expected to play. Joan fully believed that she would fight and win; those at court believed they could count on a contingent of trained knights and soldiers who would do the real fighting while the Maid of Lorraine sat on her white horse bearing her standard as God's soldier.

As Joan won the admiration and sometimes adulation of soldiers and townspeople, she grew into her role in a way that no one could have imagined only months earlier. She insisted, against the wishes of the captains, on being included in military preparations and soon gained their respect. The arrow wound at Orléans was a turning point. Joan was meant to be a figurehead but now showed herself to be an inspirational leader with a distinctive strategy for winning. Even though it was only a minor flesh wound, she now saw the degree to which people believed in her, Joan the Maid. The French saw God working in their midst while the English looked at her in fear and horror, wondering what she was. With the victories that followed, her boldness in war and intervention in politics revealed her increasing stubbornness and pride. The changes she had undergone since leaving Domremy were magnified by her youth and the reception accorded to her by the people of Orléans and elsewhere. The special knightly clothing sent to her by the duke of Orléans matched the identity she had now carved out for herself. With her conviction of the righteousness of her cause and personal infallibility, Joan took chances that seasoned commanders thought were rash or impolitic. She became a self-fulfilling prophecy.

Yet in her increasing audacity lay the seeds of Joan's destruction. By the time of the coronation she had come to believe that she was invincible, that her strategies and agenda for France were the only possible way to proceed. Her pride and self-confidence blinded Joan to the gathering forces that opposed her. With the failure at Paris, her opponents hoped to diminish her role so that they could pursue peace with Burgundy. While Joan would win a few more minor victories, her enforced stay at Sully in the winter of 1430 both bewildered and angered her for, as she told Catherine de La Rochelle, victory would only be won at the point of a lance. Joan's belligerence has often been downplayed, since it seems at odds with her piety, yet she was always the first to press for battle. Leaving Sully without permission must not have seemed so different to Joan to leaving Domremy for Vaucouleurs for the first time almost two years earlier. Even if her actions could be construed as treason, Joan believed that she was right and the court party was wrong. In her mind, she had to take action. Although her behavior seems rash, Joan had witnessed enough instances in which inertia had paralyzed or undermined French efforts. But by leaving, she lost the last vestige of support from anyone but her military comrades.

Joan's indomitable will and belief in herself remained strong during her captivity and at trial. Why did she not allow the ladies of Luxembourg to fit her out in women's clothing in their efforts to protect her? By this time Joan could not set aside her male clothing without giving up the person she had become, a knight and a soldier fighting the good fight. To do so would be like going back in time and place to Domremy, something she neither could nor would do. At her trial, Joan could not see that her satisfaction with her achievements and belief in the French cause would lead to her downfall, providing the material for the articles against her. She saw only that she must match her enemies, with sarcasm and mockery, a tactic that had worked well for her at Poitiers. Joan did not comprehend that her English foes and their French collaborators could not be silenced as others had been before them. In the end, she played her part too well by becoming in her own mind the maid of legend.

Joan of Arc is one of the most remarkable figures in history. Although she was brought to court to be a figurehead around whom the dispirited French could rally, Joan's actual abilities and achievements – far exceeding what she was taught – continue to astonish us today. To understand the fullness of her personality, with all her strengths and weaknesses, does not diminish her. It shows us that Joan was an all-too-human young woman of great conviction and belief in herself and in France. We can marvel, as did Pope Pius II, at the astonishing Maid.

Joan can be understood as much by who she was as by who she was not. She was not the shepherdess so often portrayed in paintings and drama, but a girl of extraordinary strength and character who followed a destiny that was only partly of her own creation. She succeeded at so much of what she attempted because of the conviction of youth. Her sense of invincibility, independence, fearlessness, and courage helped her accomplish so much and yet brought about her death at the stake. The girl who had been made fun of in her childhood reduced grown men to tears – many of them her inveterate foes – as she cried out to Jesus, Mary, and the saints amidst the flames of Rouen.

The Immediate Family of Joan of Arc

(Dates and family birth order are approximate)

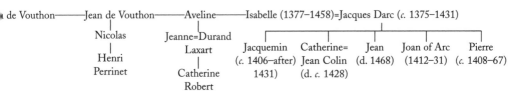

de Vouthon——Jean de Vouthon——Aveline——Isabelle (1377–1458)=Jacques Darc (*c.* 1375–1431)

Nicolas   Jeanne=Durand

Henri   Laxart   Jacquemin Catherine= Jean   Joan of Arc Pierre

Perrinet   Catherine   (*c.* 1406–after) Jean Colin (d. 1468) (1412–31) (*c.* 1408–67)

Robert   1431)   (d. *c.* 1428)

APPENDIX B

The Sources

Aɴʏ sᴛᴜᴅʏ ᴏғ Jᴏᴀɴ's life must deal with the extraordinary quantity, quality, and diversity of the primary sources. The first and most important source is the trial record, which provides extensive insight into the proceedings and deliberations, allowing us to "hear" Joan's voice.

Françoise Meltzer asserts:

> The trial is removed from us in countless ways: by five centuries of time elapsed; by the layers of language that muffle the original (out of the spoken, Middle French, it is transcribed into French, translated into Latin, and [in some cases] . . . rendered into English; by the fact that the voices we hear and read are long since dead . . .; by the rendering of voice into text in the first place; by the very syntax and protocol of fifteenth-century judicial proceedings; by the indirect discourse that characterizes most of the recorded aspects of questions and responses . . .; by the gaps and ellipses in the minutes. . . .[1]

She is right, yet even through all of the layers of filtering, Joan's voice remains striking in its authenticity and immediacy. Had her judges been trying to make her look bad, they failed miserably.

Despite the obvious desire of the English and their carefully managed church court to produce the desired result – Joan's execution – Cauchon, a prominent churchman and diplomat, for the most part followed the

[1] Françoise Meltzer, *For Fear of the Fire: Joan of Arc and the Limits of Subjectivity* (Chicago: University of Chicago Press, 2000), 121–2.

rules. As Daniel Hobbins, the translator and editor of the most recent edition of the trial record, notes:

> If anything Pierre Cauchon seems to have been obsessed with correct procedure. . . . The existence of a full record of the trial, unparalleled for length and detail among the inquisitorial collections of the Middle Ages, indicates that the judges took very seriously the task of recording their involvement. Beyond this, however, the fact that Cauchon ordered a translation of the trial into Latin, supplemented by numerous documents witnessing the development of the trial from beginning to end, testifies to a certain self-satisfaction on his part. This translation is powerful evidence that he believed his role in the trial would bear examination from even hostile observers. . . . Cauchon felt confident enough to circulate the text throughout Europe in the first place.[2]

Hobbins's translation is the most accessible version for contemporary readers and contains a superb introduction. However, the 1932 Barrett version, which I have used, is by far the most complete English translation of the Latin trial record.

All trial questions and proceedings in which Joan was directly involved were conducted in French, and at the end of each day the notaries would compare their accounts. This produced what is known as "the French minute." The main notary, Guillaume Manchon, later testified at the nullification proceedings that Cauchon sometimes pressured him to exclude or alter some of Joan's responses, but he refused and made notations where his notes did not agree with what Cauchon said. He also stated during the later nullification that the signatures on the Latin translations were indeed his own.

The existence of multiple copies of the trial text, in Latin and French, has led to some confusion. Thomas de Courcelles, one of the assessors most hostile to Joan, was responsible for compiling the Latin translation shortly after Joan's execution. Five copies were made, three of which were signed by the trial notaries, bearing the seals of the judges, Cauchon and Le Maistre, the reluctant inquisitor. Some writers continue to suggest that the Latin compilation was made in 1435, but that is impossible. When

---

[2] Daniel Hobbins, *The Trial of Joan of Arc* (Cambridge, Mass.: Harvard University Press, 2005), 18.

Manchon verified the authenticity of his signature, he also testified that the seals were those of the judges, Cauchon as bishop of Beauvais and Le Maistre. Since Cauchon was made bishop of Lisieux in August 1432, he would no longer have used the Beauvais seal after that. The Latin translation and compilation must have begun after Joan's execution on May 30, 1431 and before August 8, 1432,[3] so events would have been fresh in everyone's mind. However, parts of the final eight pages of the manuscript[4] were not signed by the notaries and must be used with caution. They include Joan's "confession," the revocation and sentence of a Dominican who spoke out against the proceedings on the day of Joan's execution, a letter from the king of England to leaders of the Church and nobility in France dated June 28, and undated letters of the University of Paris to the pope, cardinals, and emperor.

In addition to the trial records, we have letters dictated or signed by Joan. Of those still extant, three contain Joan's signature – a letter to the town of Riom from November 1429 and two to the city of Reims in March 1430. Six other letters dictated by Joan have survived, including her famous "Letter to the English." The majority of these letters flow freely and are less formal than what would be found in anything dictated by most nobles or military commanders. We also have letters from the king as well as from those who met her or who had heard of her, such as the Venetian noble Pancrazio Giustiniani and Gui and André de Laval.

Another very important set of original documents comes from the nullification proceedings of 1450, 1452, and 1455–6, often mistakenly referred to as the Rehabilitation Trial. Astonishingly, relatively few studies of Joan have taken these records seriously. On the one hand, the political goal was to undo the results of the earlier trial, so in many ways the questions mirrored those of Joan's interrogators in 1431 in an effort to produce the opposite result. On the other, the proceedings were split between the theologians evaluating the procedures and mistakes of the earlier trial and the witness depositions. For biographical purposes, the latter are far more important than the political and theological impetus. Jules Quicherat (1814–82), one of the first writers to gather sources related to Joan, viewed

---

[3] For a detailed explanation, see Jean Fraikin, "La date de la rédaction latine du procès de Jeanne d'Arc," *Quaerendo* 3 (1973), 45.

[4] *Bibliothèque de l'Assemblée Nationale*, no. 119.

the nullification testimonies as irrelevant, saying that they contained nothing historically important.[5] He was wrong.

The series of interviews conducted over a six-year period was neither a trial nor was it aimed at Joan's rehabilitation, although in the last phase restoring Joan's reputation was the pretext for calling witnesses. First solicited in 1450 and continued in 1452, the purpose of the testimonies taken under oath was to inquire into procedural irregularities of the condemnation trial of 1431 and declare it null and void. Just as the original trial was overtly political, even though it played out in an English-run church court, so too were the nullification proceedings biased toward the French side. That said, if used with care, these interviews provide an unprecedented amount of first-hand information about Joan, the people with whom she grew up, her military colleagues, priests, townspeople who came to know her, and assessors and judges at her trial.

The nullification proceedings provide information from those who are normally excluded from the historical record. However, we must bear in mind several concerns besides the political motivation. First is the problem of memory. The events about which questions were asked occurred from forty-four to twenty-five years earlier, from Joan's birth until her execution in Rouen. Especially in a small village such as Domremy, as well as among some witnesses in Orléans and Rouen, collective memory, understood "not as a collection of individual memories or some magically constructed reservoir of ideas and images, but rather as a socially articulated and socially maintained 'reality of the past,' "[6] would have played a significant role in recall. What psychologists refer to as "source pollution" as well as age, the emotion and importance of events, intellectual and educational development, and other personal variables, all contribute to the construction of memory. "We extract key elements from our experiences and store them. We then recreate or reconstruct our experiences rather than retrieve copies of them. Sometimes, in the process of reconstructing, we add on feelings, beliefs, or even knowledge we obtained after the experience."[7] In addition,

---

[5.] See Blair Deborah Newcomb, "Collective Authority and the Individual in the Rehabilitation of Jeanne d'Arc, 1450–1456" (Ph.D. diss. University of Michigan, 1999), 10–15.

[6.] Iwona Irwin-Zarecka, *Frames of Remembrance: The Dynamics of Collective Memory* (New Brunswick, N.J.: Transaction Books, 1994), 54.

[7.] Daniel Schachter, *The Seven Sins of Memory: How the Mind Forgets and Remembers* (Boston: Houghton Mifflin, 2001), 9.

especially with regard to the witnesses in Lorraine, many of those who had known Joan were dead by 1456.

A problem related to memory is suggestibility. In each of the inquiries, witnesses were asked specific questions. The way a question is framed influences the responses. With suggestibility, the respondents incorporate the words of the question, sometimes exactly, into the answer and usually limit their responses to the specifics of the question. In other cases the witness may give the answer he thinks the interrogator wants to hear and rarely elaborates. "Suggestibility's pernicious effects highlight the idea that remembering the past is not merely a matter of activating or awakening a dormant trace or picture in the mind, but instead involves a more complex interaction between the current environment, what one expects to remember, and what is retained from the past."[8] Suggestibility is compounded by "hindsight bias," in which witnesses "reconstruct the past to fit what they know in the present."[9] Especially in the case of someone as famous (or infamous) as Joan of Arc, it would have been difficult not to project the present onto the past.

While the nullification proceedings were not an inquiry meant to trap people into damning admissions, the prior investigation by Cauchon in 1431 probably led to a certain caution among the witnesses. After all,

> the inquisitors . . . have prepared a set of questions designed to prevent evasion. These questions serve as a filter [representing the] . . . inquisitor's working assumptions. . . . Rarely does the [witness] gain enough control of the process to answer questions the inquisitor has not thought to ask. Rarely does the [witness] state beliefs in any terms other than those assumed by the inquisitor's questions.[10]

This was especially true of the Domremy witnesses. By contrast Joan's noble comrades, her page, squire, confessor, and those present at her trial often gave detailed and seemingly spontaneous accounts.

Witnesses, especially those from the peasant classes, may have been wary when church officials came to interview them. When Joan's trial was getting under way, Bishop Pierre Cauchon had sent lawyer Nicolas Bailly, who

---

[8.] Schachter, *Seven Sins*, 129.

[9.] Schachter, *Seven Sins*, 147.

[10.] David Burr, "Inquisition: Introduction," http://www.fordham.edu/halsall/source/inquisition1.html.

testified in Toul on February 6, 1456, to find any incriminating information in the region where Joan grew up. Bailly testified:

> In his work as a lawyer making an inquiry [at the time Joan the Maid was imprisoned in the city of Rouen] . . . he had received letters of commission from the pretended king of France and England [Henry VI]. When he and Gérard Petit made their inquiry about Joan, they succeeded as a result of their diligence in getting depositions from twelve to fifteen witnesses. [When they heard and reported nothing but good things about Joan] they were suspected of having made this inquiry in bad faith.[11]

These inquiries, made while Joan was in captivity, would not only have helped reconstruct villagers' memories of Joan, but they might also have aroused fear and suspicion. Ever since inquisitors' manuals had made their début in southwestern France two centuries earlier, villagers had learned to be on their guard and evade questions. At the same time, many said no one interviewed them on that occasion, while a much larger number of witnesses was interviewed in 1456.

A related problem arises from questions *not* asked, an issue most challenging when the peasants from Domremy were interrogated over a short period of time. Few would have been expected to elaborate on issues not mentioned in the questions. To some degree the same might have applied to the assessors in Rouen if they felt their answers would be incriminating. On the other hand, Joan's military colleagues, especially those from the upper classes, *would* be expected to give less structured and more complete testimonies, which they did.

At the same time, especially important events from the past would be expected to trigger stronger memories, sometimes enhanced, in which some individuals might claim to have played a more important role than they actually did. We might assume that as a result of Joan's accomplishments, and the tax exemption she won for Domremy and Greux, witnesses there would have been inclined to say good things about her or inflate their role in her story. Surprisingly they did not, at least not in detail. Joan's fellow soldiers and commanders would also be expected to emphasize their heroic actions while downplaying those of Joan, whose name was almost

---

11. *Nullité 1456*, III: 290–1.

never uttered at Charles' court after her execution. We would expect this, especially in view of Charles' probable reluctance to have his kingship based on the accomplishments of a teenage girl who had been adjudged a heretic. For the most part, however, Joan's colleagues minimized their part in military events while vaunting her achievements or at the very least attributing them to divine inspiration. In some cases, intervening events might have skewed their views of the past. Joan's *beau duc*, Alençon, shared none of Joan's loyalty to Charles and began to negotiate with the English shortly after the Treaty of Arras. Almost immediately after he testified at the nullification proceedings in 1456, he was arrested by his former comrade, the Bastard of Orléans, and convicted of treason; he would spend most of the rest of his life in captivity. His testimony needs to be viewed within the context of his antagonism towards the king. Finally, the trial assessors would be most likely to minimize their role in Joan's conviction and stress efforts they might have made to help her or distance themselves from the English who controlled the trial. This is a problem, yet can be dealt with by cross-referencing testimonies among the witnesses and examining the motives of those involved.

Finally, the process of noting down and editing the testimonies is evident throughout, especially when peasants or workers were interviewed. The notary uses words that would not have been employed in spoken language. For example, several witnesses from Joan's childhood are recorded as saying Joan went to Vaucouleurs when she left the paternal household (*la maison paternelle*). Yet through all these layers and filters, an amazing story develops that gives us unprecedented access to those who played important roles in Joan's life and to Joan herself.

While the trial and nullification records in conjunction with one another are most valuable for our understanding of Joan and have been used to corroborate or challenge her version of events at trial, numerous chronicles and letters also speak of Joan. People as far away as Constantinople showed interest in the accomplishments of the Maid, so French, Burgundian, and English writers and correspondents kept people throughout Europe apprised of events. At the same time, the chronicles pose a unique problem – each individual has a different perspective, a different reason for writing, a different person to or for whom the chronicle was being kept. Accounts conflict, and we must judge the value of such sources based on eyewitness accounts, specific knowledge of the event(s), reports from others, date of composition, and bias. As with the nullification records, cross-referencing can be invaluable. In an excellent study, Olivier Bouzy highlights several "famous but incorrect events" in Joan's life that have become part of her legend simply because they have been repeated in books and films about Joan. Pointing out that each author writing about Joan begins with an apologia for "yet another book," he wisely adds:

> We will begin with an inverse postulate: that there remains much to do in order to know Joan of Arc more fully. First, because unedited texts continue to be found, even when they do not produce stunning new discoveries. The texts already known have not always been put to best use by authors, and many of these texts are not, even today, carefully edited. Finally, even the most well-known texts have not always been accurately read and interpreted.

Using as an example Joan's "famous" initial interview with Charles at Chinon, he continues: "That an episode so popular is in fact so inadequately understood shows the degree to which the history of Joan of Arc is ignored despite the fact that several authors seem persuaded to the contrary. . . . Some authors write without having taken into consideration the ensemble of sources."[12]

In supplementing the trial record and nullification proceedings, I have used numerous chronicles, letters, and account records. Since many give different versions, I have relied on a methodology that uses chronicles with the greatest knowledge of a particular situation (e.g., the *Journal du siège* for events in Orléans; Guillaume Gruel's first-hand account of the events at the Battle of Patay) or those who were in a position to know the most about Joan at a given time. I have also relied on negative evidence, for example when an Anglo-Burgundian chronicler writes positively about Joan.

Some of the most important chronicles include the *Journal du siège d'Orléans*, first published between 1467 and 1472, based on daily notations and oral memory. It provides critical and almost unique information for events pertaining to the siege. The account of Jean Chartier, who was the king's chronicler, was compiled between 1440–61, and gives insights into

---

12. Olivier Bouzy, *Jeanne d'Arc Mythes et Réalités* (Paris: Atelier de l'Archer, 1999), 7–8.

court life. Perceval de Cagny, master of the horse to the duke of Alençon, provides excellent information for the time when he was in the company of Joan and the duke, but is less informative and often wrong when he describes other events. The Bourgeois of Paris was singularly well informed about Paris, as well as about what was happening elsewhere, through his many clerical contacts. Georges Chastellain and Enguerrand de Monstrelet, although they represented the Burgundian side, provide invaluable information on how Joan was viewed as well as her capture and captivity after most other sources fall silent. Other important works include the notes kept by the notary of La Rochelle, the chronicle of Matthieu Thomassin, Thomas Basin's account, the *Chronique des Cordeliers*, Jean de Wavrin de Forestel's *Chronique d'Angleterre* and countless others.[13] As Bouzy makes clear, while many are more reliable than others, all must be used together to provide an accurate picture of Joan's life and deeds. While occasionally I have been able to use modern French editions, in most cases I have relied on the compilations in Ayroles and Quicherat.

Last but certainly not least, we have contemporary poems about Joan, military manuals, account books, and theological treatises about her actions in the context of divine inspiration and gender. Works by Christine de Pizan, Jacques Gélu, Jean Gerson, and Martin Le Franc all complement our knowledge of how Joan was understood in her lifetime, especially with regard to gender issues and her male clothing.

While no one set of sources can provide an unbiased and uncontested account of Joan's life, the plentiful sources mentioned here can be used critically to help understand who Joan of Arc really was after all the layers of legend and agendas have been stripped away.

[13.] For an excellent overview of the different chronicles and sources, see Charles Wayland Lightbody, *The Judgments of Joan of Arc: A Study in Cultural History* (Cambridge, Mass.: Harvard University Press, 1961).

Witnesses Interviewed

Name	Occupation, Location	Age in yrs	In 1429	Interview Date in 1456
Jean Morel	farmer, Domremy, godfather	70	44	28 Jan.
Jean Moen	wheelwright, Domremy	56	20	29 Jan.
Étienne de Syonne	priest, Neufchâteau	54	28	29 Jan.
Louis de Martigny	noble squire	56	30	29 Jan.
Jeannette de Vittel	widow, godmother, Domremy	60	34	29 Jan.
Jacquier de Saint-Amant	farmer, Domremy	60	34	29 Jan.
Perrin Drappier	church sacristan, Domremy	60	34	29 Jan.
Thévenin le Royer	carpenter, Domremy	69	43	29 Jan.
Jeannette [Roze]le Royer	godmother, Domremy	70	44	29 Jan.
Béatrice d'Estellin	godmother, widow, farmer of Domremy	80	54	29 Jan.
Bertrand Lacloppe	roofer of Domremy	90	64	29 Jan.
Dominique Jacob	priest, curé, Domremy	35	9	29 Jan.
Gérard Guillemette	farmer, Domremy	40	14	30 Jan.
Simonin Musnier	farmer, Domremy	44	18	30 Jan.
Hauviette de Syonne	wife of Gérard de Syonne, farmer of Domremy	45	19	30 Jan.
Jean Waterin	farmer, Domremy	45	19	30 Jan.
Mengette Joyart	wife of Jean, farmer of Domremy	46	20	30 Jan.
Colin fils	son of Jean Colin, farmer	50	24	30 Jan.
Isabelle d'Épinal	wife of Gérardin; Joan was godmother of their child	50+	24+	30 Jan.
Gérardin d'Épinal	farmer, Domremy (the "Burgundian")	60	34	30 Jan.
Jean Colin	widower of Joan's sister Catherine, mayor of Greux	66	40	30 Jan.
Michel le Buin	farmer, Domremy, Burey	44	18	31 Jan.
Geoffroy de Foug	noble, squire, Maxey	50	24	31 Jan.
Catherine Le Royer	wife of Henri, Vaucouleurs	54	28	31 Jan.
Jean de Metz	noble, comrade of Joan, of Vaucouleurs	57	31	31 Jan.
Durand Laxart	farmer, Joan's second cousin, Burey-le-Petit	60	34	31 Jan.
Henri Le Royer	wheelwright, Vaucouleurs	64	38	31 Jan.
Albert d'Ourches	noble, knight	60	34	1 Feb.

Guillot Jacquier	royal sergeant	36	10	6 Feb.
Nicolas Bailly	notary, substitute provost of Domremy	60	34	6 Feb.
Bertrand de Poulengy	noble, squire, comrade	63	37	6 Feb.
Henri Arnolin	priest, Domremy	64	38	6 Feb.
Jean le Fumeux	canon and curé, Vaucouleurs	39	13	7 Feb.
Jean Jaquard	farmer, Greux	47	21	11 Feb.

Principal Characters

French Court

King Charles VI (1368–1422) was crowned on the death of his father, Charles V, who had regained much of the momentum during the second stage of the Hundred Years War, in 1380. Charles VI suffered from schizophrenic episodes beginning in the 1390s that worsened with time. He died in 1422, only two years after his seal was appended to the Treaty of Troyes.

Queen Isabeau of Bavaria (1371–1435), wife of Charles VI. With her husband incapacitated, she served as regent. Extremely unpopular, Isabeau allied with Duke Louis of Orléans, leading to rumors of an affair and other misconduct. In 1420, she signed the Treaty of Troyes with Henry V, that included a marriage alliance between her daughter Catherine and the English king. The treaty made Henry V and his successors heirs to the French kingdom.

Louis, Duke of Orléans (1372–1407). Brother of Charles VI, his association with Queen Isabeau and his meddling in the government made him as unpopular as the queen. His interference with John the Fearless's control over the royal children led to his murder by John's supporters in Paris in 1407.

Charles, Duke of Orléans (1394–1465) became duke upon the murder of his father Louis in 1407. He also held territories in Italy thanks to his mother Valentina Visconti, the daughter of the duke of Milan. His wife, the widow of King Richard II, gave birth to a daughter, Jeanne, who would marry the duke of Alençon. Allied with Bernard, count of Armagnac, he fought at the Battle of Agincourt in 1415. He was captured and spent the next twenty-five years in England. Famed for his poetry, he followed Joan of Arc's progress in France and paid for her knightly clothing after her victories in the Loire. He was freed in 1440 through the efforts of Philip the Good and his wife Isabelle of Portugal.

King Charles VII (1403–61), fifth son of Charles VI and Isabeau of Bavaria. His four elder brothers died childless, leaving him heir to the throne (dauphin). In 1419 his supporters assassinated John the Fearless, leading to the split with Burgundy. Disinherited by the Treaty of Troyes, he was mockingly referred to as the "King of Bourges" after he retreated to his castles in the Loire Valley. Surrounded by factions, ineffectual and penniless, he was unable to mount a challenge to the English and Burgundians until the armies of Joan of Arc began to win victories. He was crowned king at Reims in July of 1429. Signing the Treaty of Arras in 1435, he ended Burgundy's involvement in the Hundred Years War. By 1449 he had recaptured Normandy and in 1453 the Hundred Years War came to a close. Although faced with numerous rebellions by his nobles, he proved himself a capable "new monarch," creating a standing army and bringing relative prosperity to France. Jean Chartier was made his official chronicler in 1437.

Queen Yolande of Aragon (1384–1443), was known as Queen of Four Kingdoms, Aragon, which she briefly inherited, and Sicily, Jerusalem, and Cyprus through her husband Louis II of Anjou. Her actual possessions lay in Anjou, Provence, and the duchy of Bar. While Isabeau largely ignored her youngest son Charles, Yolande served as a surrogate, mentoring the dauphin. She played a crucial part in supporting Charles VII as rightful heir to the French throne, first marrying her daughter Marie to him and then playing an important role in policy-making. In 1429, she promoted Joan of Arc against the wishes of Charles's other advisors.

Queen Marie of Anjou (1404–63), daughter of Yolande of Aragon. She married Charles in Bourges in 1422. Although they had twelve children, in later years most of Charles's affections were reserved for his mistress Agnès Sorel.

René of Anjou (1409–80), son of Yolande of Aragon and brother of Queen Marie. Raised with Charles VII, his loyalties were split because of allegiance owed to Burgundy for his lands. Joan met him at the time she was sent to the duke of Lorraine. He supported the French side and attended the coronation at Reims. He was named duke of Bar in 1430 and four years later duke of Lorraine. As king of Sicily, he was famed for his poetry, painting, and patronage of the arts.

Georges de La Trémoïlle (1382–1446) had served John the Fearless as Grand Chamberlain for several years. He fought and was captured at the Battle of Agincourt, but was soon released. In 1427, he became Lieutenant General for Burgundy and Grand Chamberlain of France under Charles VII, over whom he exerted great influence. He opposed Joan of Arc and the constable Richemont, seeking reconciliation with Burgundy. He fell from power in 1433 and joined the Praguerie against Charles in 1440.

Regnault de Chartres, archbishop of Reims (1380–1444), Chancellor of France and counselor under Charles VII. He later became archbishop of Embrun and Agde and bishop of Orléans. His half-brother was Guillaume Flavy, captain of Compiègne, where Joan was captured.

Charles d'Albret, count of Dreux (1407–71), half-brother of Georges de La Trémoïlle. He fought in the Loire campaign and became Lieutenant General for the king in Berry in 1430. He fought alongside Joan at La Charité.

Raoul de Gaucourt (1371–1462) had sided with Burgundy in the late fourteenth century. He fought at Agincourt and was taken prisoner, remaining in captivity until 1425. He served as captain of Chinon, bailiff of Orléans and counselor to the king and was one of those sent to Rome to request that the pope begin the nullification proceedings.

Simon Charles (c. 1396–?), president of Charles's Wardrobe Accounts at the time of the nullification, he had served as a diplomat for Charles to Italy. He related many of the earliest events in Joan's career after she arrived at Chinon.

Courts of Burgundy and Luxembourg

John the Fearless, duke of Burgundy (1371–1419) had Duke Louis of Orléans assassinated in the streets of Paris in 1407. He took no part in Agincourt, nor did he stop the English siege of Rouen. In 1418, he captured Paris but the dauphin Charles escaped. Seeking revenge for his brother's assassination, Charles gathered allies, including Bernard, count of Armagnac, whose name would become attached to the dauphin's "party." Purportedly working toward a reconciliation, Charles and his men agreed to meet John at the bridge of Montereau, where one of the dauphin's men assassinated the duke.

Philip the Good, duke of Burgundy (1396–1467) became duke upon his father's assassination in 1419. The following year he aligned himself with King Henry V of England, sealed by his sister Anne's marriage to Henry's brother, John, duke of Bedford. His main objectives were to protect, join, and extend his territories in the northeastern corner of France and down beyond Dijon. His vassal, Jean of Luxembourg, took Joan into captivity in 1430. In 1435 Philip signed the Treaty of Arras, ending Burgundian involvement in the Hundred Years War. Besides his role in Joan of Arc's life, Philip was known primarily as a great patron of the arts. His court was considered the most magnificent in Europe.

Jean of Luxembourg, count of Ligny and lord of Beaurevoir (1392–1440), a supporter of Philip the Good whose men captured Joan. He held her for several months before selling her for 10,000 *l.t.* to the English.

Jeanne of Luxembourg, countess of Ligny and St.-Pol (d. 1430), aunt of Jean of Luxembourg. She made Joan's captivity tolerable and tried to prevent her nephew from selling Joan to the English, but she died in the fall of 1430.

English Court and Military Leaders

King Henry V (1387–1422), considered one of the greatest military leaders in history. On his accession to the throne in 1413, he pursued an aggressive foreign policy in France. In 1415 he landed and captured Harfleur. His victory at the Battle of Agincourt over superior French numbers was decisive, with much of the French nobility killed or captured. Rouen fell after a dreadful siege in 1419. In 1420 he signed the Treaty of Troyes, by which he married the dauphin Charles's sister Catherine and was able to claim the French throne for himself and his heirs. After a short return to England, he returned for another campaign in 1421. He died in August 1422 of dysentery, after a siege near Paris, leaving his eight-month-old son as king of England and France.

King Henry VI (1421–71), the child king in whose name Bedford issued many edicts and letters regarding Joan of Arc. He was crowned in Westminster Abbey in 1429 and Notre Dame Cathedral in Paris in 1431. Because of his age, his role in Joan's story is small. But through his father's marriage to Catherine of Valois, he became not only titular king of France but also inherited his grandfather's madness.

John, duke of Bedford (1389–1435), younger brother of Henry V, was made regent of France in 1422. The next year he married the duke of Burgundy's sister Anne. Known as an accomplished general and leader, he amassed enormous wealth and property during his regency and became known as a patron of the arts, especially illuminated manuscripts. When Anne of Burgundy died in 1432, he quickly remarried, straining relations with Philip the Good. He was forced to return to England in 1433 to defend his actions in France. He came back to France when representatives began to gather at Arras, but died in Rouen in 1435.

Richard Beauchamp, earl of Warwick (1382–1439), counselor of Henry V. He took part in the French campaigns and arranged the Treaty of Troyes. He was officially made tutor to the young Henry VI in 1428. In 1430 he went to France and was responsible for the supervision of Joan's trial.

Henry Beaufort, cardinal of Winchester (1375–1447), part of the regency council in England after the death of Henry V. He was made a cardinal in 1426 and papal legate to the Holy Roman Empire a year later. As a result of dissension within the council, he left for France in 1430 and was in Rouen during Joan's trial.

Thomas Montague, earl of Salisbury (1388–1428), served with distinction in English battles including Agincourt and the siege of Rouen. Bedford appointed him Chief Lieutenant for the war after Henry V's death in 1422. As a result of his military successes, he was granted important lands and titles. In 1428 he was once again sent to France to begin the siege of Orléans. He was killed after a freak accident in Les Tourelles shortly after his arrival.

Thomas, Lord Scales (1399–1460), Bedford's lieutenant who shared authority with Suffolk and Talbot after the death of Salisbury. Captured at Patay, he was ransomed and later fought against Alençon and La Hire. He was murdered because of his Lancastrian activities during the Wars of the Roses.

John Talbot, earl of Shrewsbury (c. 1390–1453), considered one of the boldest and most aggressive soldiers of his time, served in France and Ireland in the 1420s. He was captured at Patay and held for four years before being exchanged for Joan's comrade Poton de Xantrailles. Bedford then named him Lieutenant General for the King. He helped delay the French reconquest of Normandy and was respected by both sides for his "honorable behavior."

Joan's Family (see Chapter 1)

Joan's father died the same year as his daughter was executed. Jacquemin, her eldest brother, died some time after that. Her brothers Jean and Pierre, who fought alongside her – but whom no one mentions in the nullification testimonies – were ennobled along with the rest of the family as "du Lys" by Charles VII in December 1429. In 1436, both brothers claimed their sister was alive in the form of a pretender at Metz, Claude des Armoises. Jean served as provost of Vaucouleurs and captain of Chartres. He died after 1468. Pierre, who was captured with Joan, was ransomed and received important gifts and property from the duke of Orléans. He died around 1467. Isabelle, Joan's mother, who had been given a pension and medical care by the city of Orléans, died in 1458, two years after the sentence of nullification was pronounced.

Joan's military entourage

Jean, Bastard of Orléans, count of Dunois (1402–68), illegitimate son of Duke Louis of Orléans and half brother of the captive Duke Charles. Captured by the Burgundians in 1418, he was released in 1420 and joined up with the future Charles VII. He fought against the English at Verneuil and Montargis and was in charge of Orléans when Joan arrived in 1429. Although initially skeptical, he became one of her leading supporters. In 1439 he was made count of Dunois. In 1458 he was sent by Charles VII to arrest his former comrade the duke of Alençon for treason. Demonstrating the continuation of factionalism at court, he too plotted against Charles's son Louis XI and briefly lost some of his estates.

Jean II, duke of Alençon (1409–76) became duke after his father's death at the Battle of Agincourt. In 1424 he married Jeanne, the daughter of the duke of Orléans. He was captured at the Battle of Verneuil in 1424 and held by the English until he paid an enormous ransom in 1429. Joan's favorite, he proved less loyal to Charles VII, taking part in the Praguerie of 1439–40. Two years after his nullification testimony in 1456, he was convicted of treason and arrested by his former comrade the Bastard. Sentenced to death, he gained a reprieve with the death of Charles VII but was again arrested and died in the Louvre. Perceval de Cagny was one of his leading servants and chronicled the events of his life, with considerable attention to Joan.

Étienne de Vignolles (La Hire) (1380–1443), a Gascon mercenary captain who first joined Charles's side in 1418. He participated in all of the Loire campaigns. The king made him Captain General of Normandy in 1438. He was one of Joan's most loyal supporters, and the one closest to her in military temperament.

Jean de Novillomport (de Metz) (1398–after 1456) first met Joan when she went to Vaucouleurs in 1428, where he served as squire to Robert de Baudricourt. He was appointed to accompany her part of the way to the meeting with the duke of Lorraine, and later accompanied her to Chinon. The king ennobled him in 1444.

Bertrand de Poulengy (1392–after 1456), knight of Robert de Baudricourt and one of Joan's first companions. He later became lord of Gondrecourt and squire to the king.

Arthur de Richemont, earl of Richmond and duke of Brittany (1393–1458). He fought against the English at the Battle of Agincourt, where he was wounded and captured. Released in 1420, he helped persuade his brother, then duke of Brittany, to sign the Treaty of Troyes. At the behest of Yolande of Aragon he was made Constable of France in 1425 but was banished in 1427 by Georges de la Trémoïlle and his allies. His arrival with troops at Beaugency in 1429 helped turn the tide against the English, although it aroused the antagonism of his enemies at court. After La Trémoïlle's fall from grace in 1432–3, he regained some power and helped negotiate the Treaty of Arras. He headed the French army at Formigny, leading to the reconquest of Normandy. Guillaume Gruel, who accompanied Richemont on the campaigns, wrote a chronicle of the events.

Jean d'Aulon (1390–1458), appointed squire to Joan in 1429. He was captured with Joan at Compiègne and was later appointed chamberlain to the king.

Louis de Coutes (1414–83), Joan of Arc's first page. He had earlier served in the same position to Raoul de Gaucourt. He was appointed Master of the King's Bakery in 1436. Joan was later given a second page named Raymond.

Jean Pasquerel (n.d.), an Augustinian friar from Tours, served as Joan's main chaplain.

Note: Joan had many other important comrades-at-arms who fought in the Loire campaigns, such as Poton de Xantrailles, Gilles de Rais, and Florent d'Illiers, but they are not mentioned as often as the others in most chronicles and testimonies.

Judges and Assessors at Rouen

For the English participants, see above.

Pierre Cauchon, Bishop of Beauvais (1371–1442), a University of Paris canon lawyer. He played an important role in university administration and politics throughout his life, serving as a diplomat and envoy. As a partisan of Burgundy, he helped instigate a major uprising in Paris. In 1415 he took part in the Council of Constance. In 1418 he was named

Master of Requests for King Henry V and two years later was appointed bishop of Beauvais. A confidante of Bedford, he served as a "counselor" to the young King Henry VI. As a result of Joan's military activities in May 1429, Beauvais joined the French side and Cauchon could no longer serve as bishop there. He went to Rouen, from which Bedford sent him on missions and gave him numerous appointments. Because of his loyalty, rhetorical skills, and strong University of Paris connections, Bedford appointed him as judge in Joan's case, using the technicality that she had been captured in his jurisdiction of Beauvais. With the trial concluded, Cauchon was appointed bishop of Lisieux in 1432. He continued to serve the English until his death, probably from heart failure, in 1442.

Jean Le Maistre, Vice Inquisitor and prior of the Convent of Saint-Jacques (d. *c.* 1452), Dominican bachelor of theology from a university other than Paris. He was prior of the convent and preacher in Rouen from the 1420s until his death.

Jean de La Fontaine, Examiner (n.d.), a native of Bayeux and University of Paris lawyer who questioned Joan most often when Cauchon did not. In 1422 he was sent by the university on a mission to Bedford to confirm the university's privileges. He left Rouen in March 1429.

Jean d'Estivet, promotor of the Trial (d. 1438), a canon of Beauvais cathedral and close friend of Cauchon. According to the trial notaries, he was despicable in his conduct toward Joan and others.

Jean Massieu, Executor of Writs and Usher (*c.* 1405–after 1456) testified numerous times about Joan and the trial from 1450–6, emphasizing his sympathy for Joan.

Jean Beaupère (1397–*c.* 1462), theologian and chancellor of the University of Paris. He received numerous appointments from the papacy and in 1430 was made a canon of Rouen by Henry VI. A strong opponent of Joan, he was one of the few who voluntarily appeared in 1450 before Guillaume Bouillé to testify at the preliminary inquiry.

Nicolas Loyseleur (1390–after 1442), a university friend of Cauchon, his job at the trial was to gain Joan's confidence by pretending he was a priest from her home region. Cauchon and others listened in the adjoining cell as she made her confessions.

Thomas de Courcelles (1393–1469), professor of theology and rector of the University of Paris, he served on numerous missions and at the Council of Basel. One of Joan's strongest antagonists, he edited the Latin trial transcript in the summer of 1431. Later he served the pope and in 1461 he gave the funeral sermon for Charles VII.

The Notaries: **Guillaume Manchon, Boisguillaume, Nicolas Taquel**

Dominicans of Saint-Jacques of Rouen. Le Maistre (see above). **Ysambard de La Pierre, Martin Ladvenu, Jean Toutmouillé** all served as electors in convent decisions. Ladvenu heard Joan's confession early on the morning of her death in the presence of Toutmouillé. Both Ladvenu and La Pierre accompanied Joan to her execution. **Raoul Le Sauvage**, the convent's main counselor and spokesman at the trial, was a bachelor and later master of theology and renowned preacher. **Guillaume Duval** was present at one session on March 27 at the castle and commented on Ysambard's efforts to assist Joan. **Pierre Bosquier**, who had not attended the trial but spoke ill of the execution, was condemned to recant his words and be imprisoned for several months on bread and water. Others from the convent attended once or twice, but played no role.

The Nulllification Proceedings

Guillaume Bouillé (n.d.), king's counselor, doctor of theology, professor and rector at the University of Paris, he was often sent on missions to Rome. He convened the first inquiry into Joan's trial of condemnation in 1449–50 and followed up in the later proceedings.

Guillaume d'Estouteville (1403–83), cardinal, archbishop of Rouen and papal legate. In 1451 he was charged by the pope with efforts to make peace between France and England. Although a candidate for the papacy, he lost out to Pius II, who spoke so glowingly of Joan's prowess (see Epilogue). He instituted the 1455–6 proceedings, although he was not personally present for most of the nullification.

Jean Bréhal (d. *c.* 1479), Grand Inquisitor of France at the time of the nullification. He was a Dominican master of theology and prior of the Convent of Saint-Jacques in Paris in 1445. In 1452 Estouteville instructed him to initiate further inquiries. In July 1456 he condemned Joan's trial and execution as iniquitous and unjust.

Others

Charles II, duke of Lorraine (1364–1431), was a friend of the duke of Burgundy and antagonist of Louis of Orléans. He went on crusade twice in the 1390s. Despite his Burgundian connections, his tutor was Bernard VII, count of Armagnac. He was appointed constable in 1418, a position he resigned from in 1425. With the growing power of Burgundy and the duke's desire to connect their holdings in the Low Countries and the area around Dijon, the duke of Lorraine decided to protect his territories by allying with the French court. He married his daughter to Yolande of Aragon's son, René. Although his meeting with Joan could not have been satisfactory in view of her responses to his questions, it was enough to convince Baudricourt to send her, Jean de Metz, Bertrand de Poulengy and others along with a letter of introduction to Charles in Chinon.

Robert de Baudricourt (*c.* 1400–54), captain of Vaucouleurs. He was a close friend of René of Anjou, whom he later served as Chamberlain and counselor.

Brother Richard (n.d.), a Franciscan known for his preaching who claimed to have come from the Holy Land to warn people of the imminent end of the world. He preached for some time in Paris but was banished from the city in April 1429. He met Joan in July at Troyes, alleging he supported her, but she was not deceived. In March 1431 he was incarcerated at the convent in Poitiers as a possible heretic and not permitted to preach.

Catherine de La Rochelle (n.d.), disciple of Brother Richard, she tried to convince Joan of the authenticity of her own visions of the Virgin. Joan sat with her two nights waiting for the White Lady to appear, but said she never saw anything and told her to go home to her husband.

Abbreviations

Astell	Ann W. Astell and Bonnie Wheeler, eds. *Joan of Arc and Spirituality*. New York: Palgrave Macmillan, 2003.
Ayroles	Jean-Baptiste-Joséph Ayroles. *La Vraie Jeanne d'Arc*, 6 vols. Paris: Gaume et Cie, 1890, repr. Éditions Saint-Remi, 2005.
Barrett	W. H. Barrett. *The Trial of Jeanne d'Arc*. New York: Gotham House, 1932
L'Enquête 1450	P. Doncoeur and Y. Lanhers, eds. *La Réhabilitation de Jeanne la Pucelle: L'Enquête ordonnée par Charles VII en 1450 et le codicille de Guillaume Bouillé*. Paris: Librairie d'Argences, 1956.
L'Enquête 1452	P. Doncoeur and Y. Lanhers, eds. *L'Enquête du Cardinal d'Estouteville en 1452*. Paris: Librairie d'Argences, 1958.
Journal	P. Charpentier and C. Cuissard, eds. *Journal du siège d'Orléans, 1428–29, augmenté de plusieurs documents, notamment les comptes de ville*. Orléans: Cuissard, 1896.
Luce	Siméon Luce. *Jeanne d'Arc à Domremy: Recherches critiques sur les origines de la mission de la Pucelle accompagnés de pièces justificatives*. Paris: H. Champion, 1886.
NRSV	*The Holy Bible: New Revised Standard Version*. New York: Oxford University Press, 1989.
Nullité 1456	Pierre Duparc. *Procès en nullité de la condamnation de Jeanne d'Arc*, 5 vols. Paris: C. Klincksieck, 1986.
Pernoud	Régine Pernoud and Marie-Véronique Clin. *Joan of Arc: Her Story*, trans. Jeremy DuQuesnay Adams. New York: Saint Martin's Press, 1998.
Quicherat	Jules Quicherat, ed. *Procès de condemnation et de rehabilitation de Jeanne d'Arc dite la Pucelle*, 5 vols. Paris: Jules Renouard, 1841–9.
Warner	Marina Warner. *Joan of Arc: The Image of Female Heroism*. Berkeley: University of California Press, 1981.
Wheeler	Bonnie Wheeler and Charles T. Wood. *Fresh Verdicts on Joan of Arc*. New York and London: Garland Publishing, 1996.

Notes

Preface

1. Justin Kaplan, "Introduction," in Mark Twain, *Personal Recollections of Joan of Arc* (New York: Oxford University Press, 1996), xxxviii.
2. Susan K. Harris, in Twain, *Recollections*, 1.
3. As Harris notes, "both as a testament to the cult of Joan of Arc and as a document of *fin-de-siècle* loss and alienation, Twain's novel points to some of the major currents, and contradictions, of turn-of-the-century life and thought." Twain, *Recollections*, 11.
4. Ann W. Astell, *Joan of Arc and Sacrificial Authorship* (Notre Dame, Ind.: Notre Dame University Press, 2003), 11, 185.
5. Mary Gordon, *Joan of Arc: A Life* (Penguin Lives) (New York: Viking, 2000), xxiii–xxv.
6. Daniel Hobbins, *The Trial of Joan of Arc* (Cambridge, Mass.: Harvard University Press, 2005), 241.
7. See, e.g., Aviad Kleinberg, *Prophets in their Own Country: Living Saints and the Making of Sainthood in the Later Middle Ages* (Chicago, Ill.: University of Chicago Press, 1997); Donald Weinstein and Rudolph M. Bell, *Saints and Society: The Two Worlds of Western Christendom, 1000–1700* (Chicago, Ill.: University of Chicago Press, 1986); Catherine M. Mooney, *Gendered Voices: Medieval Saints and their Interpreters* (Philadelphia, Pa.: University of Pennsylvania Press, 1999).

Prologue: The Hundred Years War

1. Kelly DeVries argues that in the Hundred Years War, both sides understood the "far-reaching implications of the technology, [and they] surpassed any others in Europe at the time [to] ensure the continual, rapid technological evolution of gunpowder weaponry. The period from 1382 to 1436 saw the greatest increase in the number of guns and in the production of different sizes and types of weapons. It was also the period in which the first hand-held guns were invented." "The Use of Gunpowder Weaponry By and Against Joan of Arc During the Hundred Years War," *War and Society* 14 (1996), 5.

2   Miri Rubin, *The Hollow Crown: A History of Britain in the Late Middle Ages* (London: Penguin, 2005), 121.

3.   Jeanne, the daughter of Isabelle and Duke Charles, married Joan of Arc's favorite military comrade, Jean, duke of Alençon, in 1424.

4.   For example, Henry VI was Charles VII's nephew; John the Fearless was uncle to Charles VII; the sister of John's son, Philip the Good, was married to John, duke of Bedford. René of Anjou was raised together with the future Charles VII, yet had to swear fealty to Henry VI for his duchy. He was also frequently in conflict with his father-in-law, Duke Charles of Lorraine.

5.   Although probably not true, enough people hated the queen that the rumors were widely believed. Richard C. Famiglietti, "Royal Intrigue: Crisis at the Court of Charles VI, 1392–1420" (Ph.D. diss., CUNY, 1982), 41–5.

6.   Christine de Pizan, *The Epistle of the Prison of Human Life with An Epistle to the Queen of France and Lament on the Evils of the Civil War*, ed. and trans. Josette A. Wisman (New York and London: Garland, 1984), 85, 87.

7.   Anne Curry, *Agincourt: A New History* (Stroud, Glos.: Tempus, 2005), 192, 246.

Chapter 1: Jehannette

1.   Ayroles, II: 242.

2.   Luce, lv–lvii.

3.   Ayroles, II: 92.

4.   Luce, li–lii.

5.   François Rigolot, ed., *Journal de Voyage de Michel de Montaigne* (Paris: Presses Universitaires de France, 1992), 8.

6.   Pierre Marot, *Joan of Arc's Birthplace*, trans. Stan and Rita Morton (Colmar: Imprimérie S. A. E. P. Colmar-Ingersheim, 1979), n.p.

7.   E. de Bouteiller and G. de Braux, *La famille de Jeanne d'Arc* (Paris and Orléans: A. Claudin, 1878), 183.

8.   Jacques's native village of Ceffonds was not very far from the town of d'Arc, from whence his family may have migrated. Surnames in the Middle Ages were based on circumstances – a proper noun, often based on occupation – or geographical origin. Athanase Renard, *Du nom de Jeanne d'Arc: Examen d'une opinion de M. Vallet de Viriville* (Paris: J. Claye, 1855), 15. Apostrophes were not typically used in medieval spelling.

9.   Luce, 97.

10.   Luce, xlix, l, li.

11.   Bouteiller and Braux, *Famille*, 91. The authors, specialists in genealogy, state that Jacques died in 1431.

12.   E. de Bouteiller and G. de Braux, *Nouvelles recherches sur la famille de Jeanne d'Arc: Enquêtes inédites* (Paris and Orléans, 1879), 8–9.

13.   Quicherat, IV: 252.

14.   Bouteiller and Braux, *Nouvelles recherches*, 8–10.

15.   Luce, II: 262–6.

16.   Bouteiller and Braux, *Nouvelles recherches*, xviii.

17.   Bouteiller and Braux, *Nouvelles recherches*, xvi.

18.   Barrett, 38, 135.

19. Bouteiller and Braux, *Famille*, 185–6.
20. Barrett, 39.
21. Barrett, 43.
22. Barrett, 54.
23. Barrett, 53–4.
24. Barrett, 54–5.
25. Barrett, 74.
26. Barrett, 127.
27. Barrett, 55.
28. *Nullité 1456*, III: 142.
29. *Nullité 1456*, III: 247.
30. *Nullité 1456*, III: 300, 240.
31. *Nullité 1456*, III: 238–9.
32. Nicholas Wright, *Knights and Peasants: The Hundred Years War in the French Countryside* (Woodbridge, Suffolk: Boydell & Brewer, 1998), 127, 115, 117.
33. Barrett, 53.
34. *Nullité 1456*, III: 283.
35. *Nullité 1456*, III: 250, 253, 281, 292, 299.
36. *Nullité 1456*, III: 245, 250.
37. *Nullité 1456*, III: 252.
38. *Nullité 1456*, III: 259.
39. *Nullité 1456*, III: 246, 248, 272.
40. *Nullité 1456*, III: 270.
41. *Nullité 1456*, III: 275.
42. *Nullité 1456*, III: 251.
43. *Nullité 1456*, III: 259.
44. *Nullité 1456*, III: 268, 265, 241.
45. *Nullité 1456*, III: 241, 288.
46. *Nullité 1456*, III: 282.
47. *Nullité 1456*, III: 275.
48. *Nullité 1456*, III: 265.
49. *Nullité 1456*, III: 252.
50. *Nullité 1456*, III: 270.
51. *Nullité 1456*, III: 263.
52. *Nullité 1456*, III: 279–80.
53. *Nullité 1456*, III: 252.
54. *Nullité 1456*, III: 252, 265, 275, 280, 292. The statue of the Virgin, to which Joan showed special devotion at Notre Dame de Bermont, has been relocated to the small chapel in the lower chapel of the twentieth-century basilica.
55. *Nullité 1456*, III: 241.
56. *Nullité 1456*, III: 268.
57. *Nullité 1456*, III: 270.
58. *Nullité 1456*, III: 248.
59. *Nullité 1456*, III: 267.
60. *Nullité 1456*, III: 244.
61. *Nullité 1456*, III: 269.
62. Pernoud, 162.
63. Wright, *Knights and Peasants*, 5.

Chapter 2: The Mission

1.   Deborah Fraioli, "The Literary Image of Joan of Arc: Prior Influences," *Speculum* 56 (1981), 811.
2.   *NRSV* Judges 5:1–3, 7.
3.   Deborah A. Fraioli, *Joan of Arc: The Early Debate* (Woodbridge, Suffolk: Boydell Press, 2000), 60.
4.   Renate Blumenfeld-Kosinski, *Poets, Saints and Visionaries of the Great Schism, 1378–1417* (University Park, Pa.: Pennsylvania State University Press, 2006), 92.
5.   Matthew Tobin, "Le 'Livre des Révélations' de Marie Robine (1399)," in *Mélanges de l'École française de Rome, Moyen Age, Temps modernes* 98 (1986), 246.
6.   *Nullité 1456*, IV:59. This version was part of the final nullification, but in fact goes beyond the visions of Marie, which can be found in Ms. 520 of the Bibliothèque de Tours. Several aspects of Marie's life and visions seem to match those of Joan, including contacting the king and even suggesting that if Charles did not listen to her voices, he would "be abandoned by God." But if he did, much as Joan hoped for an attack against the Hussites, Marie predicted he could win victories not only over warring Christian factions but even over a good part of the "Saracens." Although the manuscript that contains Robine's prophecies does not include this passage, her *Book of Revelations* is incomplete. It is likely that the theologian Érault had either heard the other revelations or read them. Noël Valois, *Jeanne d'Arc et la prophétie de Marie Robine, Mélanges Paul Fabre. Études d'histoire du Moyen Age* (Paris: Picard, 1902), 457, 462–3. If Valois is correct, the prophecy may have helped convince Érault and the other examiners at Poitiers to approve Joan's mission. Matthew Tobin argues that this version unquestionably comes from the prophecies of Robine. Tobin, "Livre," 231.
7.   Fraioli, "Literary Image," 819.
8.   R. Jacquin, "Un précurseur de Jeanne d'Arc," *Revue des deux mondes* (1967), 222, 224.
9.   Deborah Fraioli, "Gerson Judging Women of Spirit: From Female Mystics to Joan of Arc," in Astell, ch. 7.
10. Luce, 124.
11. Luce, cxli, cxlv.
12. See Ayroles, II: ch. 6.
13. *Nullité 1456*, III: 246.
14. Warner, 22–3.
15. See Preston Russell, M. D., *Lights of Madness: In Search of Joan of Arc* (Savannah, Ga.: Frederic C. Beil, 2005), 159, 165, 173, 178, 189. He asks: "Were [Joan's voices] from God or only from her imagination? Or today would they be considered from neither, the product of a psychotic mind? [The writer] Anatole France confided to his secretary, 'Do you know what the fate of Jeanne d'Arc would be today? Prison or the madhouse'. . . . Could [Joan] have had a split personality? . . . Sensations of voices are the most common hallucination among psychotics. A few who initially hear their own thoughts spoken aloud may progress to a state in which the voices come from without, conducting a running commentary on the person. Visual hallucinations may accompany the voices."
16. Fasting was an obligation for Christians on many days of the year. Female saints often fasted excessively, perhaps as a means of controlling their religious lives. Some

were described as surviving only on the eucharistic host. See, e.g., Caroline Walker Bynum, *Holy Feast and Holy Fast: The Religious Significance of Food to Medieval Women* (Berkeley, Calif.: University of California Press, 1997). While some scholars label this "holy anorexia," the notion projects too much of the modern mentality onto medieval people. See Rudolph M. Bell, *Holy Anorexia* (Chicago, Ill.: University of Chicago Press, 1985). From a medical standpoint, excessive fasting can produce hallucinations and euphoria. Joan's statement must be taken in this context.

17. *NRSV* Luke 1:12, 29–30.

18. In *Joan of Arc: Heretic, Mystic, Shaman* (Lewiston, N.Y.: Edwin Mellen, 1986), 10, 45, Anne Llewellyn Barstow describes a shaman as someone who "both envisions *and enacts* the role of a salvific leader. . . . In the 'good' myth, the shaman presides over the victory sacrifice; in the tragic myth, the shaman herself is the sacrifice, the propitiation for the failure of her group." She contends that Joan "did regard herself as a Chosen One. . . . She became for her compatriots a shaman, one, that is, who crossed the barrier between this world and the realm of the spirits to become a source of healing strength and saving knowledge."

19. Barrett, 43–4.

20. Barrett, 47.

21. Barrett, 52.

22. *Nullité 1456*, III: 296.

23. The examination at Poitiers will be discussed in Chapter 3. Except for a short excerpt and one testimony at the nullification proceedings, no record is extant. (It was probably destroyed by the king's council after Joan was executed.) Her references to the report from Poitiers, which were favorable to her mission, should not be taken at face value. The trial leaders in Normandy would have been unable to obtain a copy of the examination report in French-controlled Poitiers.

24. Barrett, 59–60.

25. Jacobus de Voragine, *The Golden Legend*, trans. William Granger Ryan (Princeton, N.J.: Princeton University Press, 1993), I: 368–70.

26. Voragine, *Golden Legend*, II: 336.

27. Colette Beaune, *The Birth of an Ideology: Myths and Symbols of Nation in Late Medieval France*, trans. Susan Ross Huston, ed. Fredric L. Cheyette (Berkeley, Calif.: University of California Press, 1991), 131.

28. E. de Bouteiller and G. de Braux, *Nouvelles recherches sur la famille de Jeanne d'Arc: Enquêtes inédites* (Paris and Orléans, 1879), xxxv–xxxvi. When he knew Joan, Jean de Metz was described as "of free condition." Although he inherited the lordship of Novillompont from his father, he was not ennobled by Charles VII until 1448.

29. *Nullité 1456*, III: 278. The term "brothers in paradise" (*ses frères du paradis*) is problematic, but probably referred to celestial beings. Who did she mean by brothers? Saints are the obvious answer, and perhaps she was grouping Saint Michael with God in the masculine. But if she were speaking of Michael, Catherine, and Margaret she would, according to French usage, have said *frères et soeurs* (brothers and sisters) or *les saints et les saintes* (male and female saints).

30. *Nullité 1456*, IV:4.

31. Beaune, *Ideology*, 159.

32. Karen Sullivan, " 'I Do Not Name to You the Voice of St. Michael': The Identification of Joan of Arc's Voices," in Wheeler, 101.

33. Barrett, 60.

34.   Sullivan, "I Do Not Name," 102, 104.
35.   Barstow, *Joan of Arc*, 73.
36.   Barrett, 72.
37.   Barrett, 75.
38.   Sullivan, "I Do Not Name," 104–5.
39.   Barrett, 49, 53.
40.   *NRSV* Luke 1:26–8.
41.   Larissa Taylor, *Soldiers of Christ: Preaching in Late Medieval and Reformation France* (New York: Oxford University Press, 1992), 107.
42.   Barrett, 78.
43.   This was a critical time for Joan. The attempt to besiege Paris failed and a week later the French army was dissolved.
44.   Barrett, 304.
45.   *Nullité 1456*, III: 283.
46.   Durand Laxart was her second cousin, but was commonly referred to as her uncle.
47.   Barrett, 44.
48.   *Nullité 1456*, III: 283.
49.   *Nullité 1456*, III: 273.
50.   *Nullité 1456*, III: 271, 273.
51.   *Nullité 1456*, III: 264.
52.   *Nullité 1456*, III: 265.
53.   *Nullité 1456*, III: 286.
54.   Bouteiller and Braux, *Nouvelles recherches*, 10.
55.   *Nullité 1456*, III: 296.
56.   Camp followers often numbered in the hundreds or thousands in medieval armies, depending on the latters' size. They were often prostitutes or women of "loose morals," so Jacques d'Arc's worries might have been warranted if Joan had mentioned going off to war.
57.   Ayroles, II: 292.
58.   Barrett, 100–1.
59.   Barrett, 98.
60.   This is how Joan would have addressed him since she was godmother to his son; there is no exact English translation.
61.   *Nullité 1456*, III: 267. Gérardin d'Épinal, despite being the only "Burgundian" in the village, knew Joan well. Godmother to his son, she told him things, which he subsequently reported during the nullification proceedings, that other witnesses did not mention. Although this response is recorded at the end of his answer to question twelve about whether Joan was always in her parents' company when at Neufchâteau, he seems here to be adding different and supplemental information about Joan's state of mind at home. The change from talking about Joan and family members to talking of Joan alone in the last couple of sentences is notable. The key French word, *pénible*, does not accurately describe the villagers' position regarding the flight to Neufchâteau. A number of French specialists have agreed that while fatiguing, difficult, or tiresome can be correct definitions, in context it almost certainly means painful or "*qui cause une peine morale*," an emotional difficulty. Combined with what d'Épinal says elsewhere about Joan's leavetaking, it suggests tensions were palpable in the d'Arc household before Joan left for Vaucouleurs the second time.

62. The "daughter of the King of the Scots" was Margaret, born to James I of Scotland and Joan Beaufort. England and Scotland had signed a seven-year truce in 1424, although the Scots continued to aid the French fighting in the Loire Valley. Between 1425 and 1428, the dauphin raised the issue of a marriage between his child Louis and James's daughter. The best known aspect of Scottish involvement was at the Battle of the Herrings on February 12, 1429, which ended in disaster and death for the Scots and their leader, John Stewart, lord of Darnley and constable of Scotland, and his brother William. In order to extend the truce, especially after news of the Maid had reached the English, the council in England approached James I several times in the hope of brokering an alliance between the young King Henry VI and Margaret of Scotland. The dauphin Charles then offered a match with his son, the future Louis XI (born in 1423). James played both sides off against each other before finally agreeing to an alliance with France in 1435; his daughter Margaret was sent to France in 1436 and she and Louis were married that year. France had signed the Treaty of Arras with Burgundy in 1435, ending that stage of the Hundred Years War. With the marriage of Louis and Margaret, hostilities between England and Scotland worsened and the original treaty, which had been extended for five years in May 1431, expired in 1436. See C. Macrae, "The English Council and Scotland in 1430," *English Historical Review* 54 (1939).

63. *Nullité 1456*, III: 277.

64. *Nullité 1456*, III: 292–3.

65. *Nullité 1456*, III: 278.

66. Ayroles, II: 295.

67. Quicherat, IV: 331.

68. Barrett, 45.

69. *Nullité 1456*, IV: 61.

70. There can be little doubt that Yolande had a role in Joan's acceptance at court and in the construction of Joan's image before the battle of Orléans. See Gérard de Senneville, *Yolande d'Aragon: La reine qui a gagné la Guerre de Cent Ans* (Paris: Librairie Académique Perrin, 2008).

71. *Nullité 1456*, III: 287.

72. *Nullité 1456*, III: 294.

73. *Nullité 1456*, III: 285.

74. Donald Weinstein and Rudolph M. Bell, *Saints and Society* (Chicago, Ill.: University of Chicago Press, 1998), 30–1, 44.

75. *Adieu* means farewell; *À Dieu* means "To God!"

76. Women could wield significant power in the religious sphere. Besides female prophets, famous abbesses and writers included Hildegard of Bingen and Clare of Assisi. Catherine of Siena, a Dominican third order nun, wrote hundreds of letters of advice and reproach to leaders of Church and State during the Avignon papacy. Famous mystics included Elisabeth of Schönau, Mechtild of Magdeburg, and Hadewich of Brabant. See, e.g., Jeffrey F. Hamburger and Susan Marti, eds., *Crown and Veil: Female Monasticism from the Fifth to the Fifteenth Centuries* (New York: Columbia University Press, 2008); Penelope D. Johnson, *Equal in Monastic Profession: Religious Women in Medieval France* (Chicago, Ill.: University of Chicago Press, 1991); Monica Furlong, *Women Mystics in Medieval Europe* (New York: Paragon Press, 1989).

Chapter 3: The Making of the Maid

1. Barrett, 45.
2. Many writers have dated the departure to February 22 or 23, but Jean de Metz said they left on the 13th. (*Nullité 1456*, III: 278.) Furthermore, the disastrous "Day of the Herrings," in which a French supply convoy was ambushed and many Scottish allies killed, occurred on February 12. It was said that Joan told Robert de Baudricourt of what had happened there immediately before she left for Chinon. (Ayroles, III: 68, 202.)
3. *Nullité 1456*, III: 293–4.
4. *Nullité 1456*, IV: 61.
5. *Nullité 1456*, III: 278.
6. Barrett, 81.
7. Ayroles, III: 202.
8. Quicherat, V: 108.
9. Ayroles, III: 258.
10. Adrien Harmand, *Jeanne d'Arc: Ses costumes, son armure: Essai de reconstitution* (Paris: Librairie Ernest Leroux, 1929), 35.
11. *Nullité 1456*, IV: 70.
12. *Nullité 1456*, I: 486.
13. *Nullité 1456*, I: 475–6.
14. *Nullité 1456*, IV: 81–2.
15. Barrett, 46.
16. Barrett, 44–5.
17. Olivier Bouzy, *Jeanne d'Arc: Mythes et Réalités* (Paris: Atelier de l'Archer, 1999), 7.
18. Gérard de Senneville, *Yolande d'Aragon: La reine qui a gagné la Guerre de Cent Ans* (Paris: Librairie Académique Perrin, 2008), 212.
19. *Nullité 1456*, IV: 60.
20. Marcellin Fornier, *Histoire générale des Alpes-Maritimes ou Cottiènes* (Paris: H. Champion, 1890–2), II: 314.
21. Deborah A. Fraioli, *Joan of Arc: The Early Debate* (Woodbridge, Suffolk: Boydell Press, 2000), 23.
22. Ayroles, III: 584.
23. Quoted in Fraioli, *Early Debate*, 18.
24. Fraioli, *Early Debate*, 8.
25. P. Boissonade, "Une étape capitale de la mission de Jeanne d'Arc," *Revue des questions historiques*, 3rd sér. XVII (1930): 50. It is impossible to know what standards were used to determine virginity in the Middle Ages, especially since horseback riding often breaks the hymen.
26. *Nullité 1456*, IV: 48.
27. Boissonade, *Étape*, 30, 41–2.
28. *Nullité 1456*, IV: 52–3.
29. *Nullité 1456*, IV: 58.
30. *Nullité 1456*, IV: 150–1.
31. Fraioli, *Early Debate*, 41, 93.
32. Ayroles, I: 42–3.
33. Ayroles, I: 42–3.
34. Ayroles, I: 46.

35. Charles Wood, "Joan of Arc's Mission and the Lost Interrogation at Poitiers," in Wheeler, 23.
36. In some works, he is called Seguin Seguin or Seguin de Seguin.
37. The Limousin dialect was an Occitan language from the region of the Limousin that was considered different from the *langue d'öil* that dominated northern France and became the basis for modern French.
38. *Nullité 1456*, IV: 150-1.
39. *Nullité 1456*, IV: 13-4.
40. *Nullité 1456*, IV: 52-3.
41. *Nullité 1456*, IV: 151-2.
42. Ayroles, I: 685-6.
43. Wood, in Wheeler, 20-1.
44. Ayroles, III: 203.
45. *Nullité 1456*, IV: 72.
46. Scholars still debate the authorship of *De quadam puella*, but it was probably written by the famous theologian Jean Gerson.
47. Fraioli, *Early Debate*, 30, 57. See Chapter 4 for a thorough discussion of the treatise.
48. Fraioli, *Early Debate*, 66.
49. Fraioli, *Early Debate*, 65.
50. Marie-Joseph and François Belon, eds., *Jean Bréhal Grand Inquisiteur de France et la rehabilitation de Jeanne d'Arc* (Paris: P. Lethielleux, 1893), 72-3.
51. Fraioli, *Early Debate*, 62.
52. Quoted in Craig Taylor, ed., *Joan of Arc: La Pucelle* (Manchester and New York: Manchester University Press, 2006), 77-8.
53. *Nullité 1456*, III: 285; Laxart, 282.
54. *Nullité 1456*, IV: 64-5.
55. *Nullité 1456*, IV: 70.
56. *Nullité 1456*, IV: 86.
57. Florence A. Gragg, trans., *Secret Memoirs of a Renaissance Pope: The Commentaries of Aeneas Sylvius Piccolomini Pius II* (London: Folio Society, 1988), 196.

Chapter 4: The Siege of Orléans

1. Barrett, 63.
2. Olivier Bouzy, *Jeanne d'Arc: Mythes et Réalités* (Paris: Atelier de l'Archer, 1999), 74.
3. Paul Charpentier and Charles Cuissard, eds., *Journal du siège d'Orléans 1428-1429, augmenté de plusieurs documents, notamment des comptes de ville 1429-31* (Orléans: H. Herluison, 1896), 49-50.
4. Bonnie Wheeler, "Joan of Arc's Sword in the Stone," in Wheeler, xi-xv.
5. Barrett, 64.
6. The official currency of France in the Middle Ages, *livres tournois* could be divided into 20 *sols* or *sous*, each of which was made up of 12 *deniers*. *Livres tournois* largely displaced the earlier *livres parisis*, but the latter were still used. 4 *l.p.* equaled 5 *l.t.* Other units of currency introduced by Louis IX in 1266 were the gold *écu d'or* and the silver *gros d'argent*, which were about the same weight as a *livre tournois*.
7. Quicherat, V: 257-8.

224 NOTES to pp. 52–57

Adrien Harmand, *Jeanne d'Arc: Ses costumes, son armure, Essai de reconstitution* (Paris: Librairie Ernest Leroux, 1929), 244.
9. *Nullité 1456*, IV: 72–3.
10. Barrett, 64.
11. A type of fine buckram or linen.
12. Barrett, 80.
13. Jean-Claude Colrat, "A Study of Jeanne d'Arc's Standard," http://stjoan-center. com/j-cc, 13–16.
14. Most biographies suggest that Joan's mother met Pasquerel along with de Metz and Poulengy at the famous pilgrimage site of Le Puy-en-Vélay during the feast of the Annunciation on March 25th. As Bouzy has shown, this was physically impossible, Le Puy being 360 miles from Tours. Joan's traveling companions were not apart from her long enough. The transcript of Pasquerel's testimony does state that Joan's mother was at Puy with the companions from Joan's journey, but if she had been at Puy-Notre-Dame, why did she not come and see Joan, who had just returned to Chinon? Bouzy suggests that this is a transcription error and that instead one of her brothers was there and met with the others. Bouzy, *Jeanne d'Arc*, 65–7.
15. *Nullité 1456*, IV: 71.
16. *Nullité 1456*, IV: 47.
17. *Nullité 1456*, IV: 47.
18. Joan stated at trial that "where in this copy it read *Surrender to the Maid* it should read *Surrender to the King*. There are also these words, *body for body* and *chieftain of war*, which were not in the original letters." Barrett, 46, 71. Despite her disclaimer, almost all references to the letter include these words.
19. Several copies of the letter were reproduced in the *Journal du siege d'Orléans*, the *Chronique de la Pucelle*, the register of Mathieu Thomassin, and the trial. Quicherat produced this translation based on a copy that was in his time preserved in the Bibliothèque Royale. Quicherat, V: 95–8.
20. Barrett, 71.
21. *Nullité 1456*, IV: 57, 90.
22. Jacques Debale, "La topographie de l'enceinte fortifée d'Orléans au temps de Jeanne d'Arc," in *Jeanne d'Arc: Une époque, un rayonnement. Colloque d'histoire médiévale, Orléans, Octobre 1972* (Paris: Éditions, Centre Nationale de la Recherche Scientifique, 1982), 24–7.
23. Françoise Michaud-Fréjaville, *Une ville, une destinée: recherches sur Orléans et Jeanne d'Arc en l'honneur de Françoise Michaud-Fréjaville* (Paris: H. Champion, 2005), 91; Régine Pernoud, "Orléans dans la guerre de cent ans," in Jacques Débale, ed., *Histoire d'Orléans et de son terroir* (Roanne: Horvath, 1983), 378; C.T. Allmand, *Society at War* (Edinburgh: Harper & Row, 1973), 9.
24. The best English-language account of the siege of Orléans and its aftermath can be found in David Nicolle, *Orléans 1429: France Turns the Tide* (Westport, Conn.: Praeger, 2005). Régine Pernoud's *La libération d'Orléans* (Paris: Gallimard, 2006) provides more detail along with appendices containing original sources. The best primary source, aside from the nullification testimonies, is the *Journal du siège d'Orléans*. Although copied down around 1467 by a clerical notary named Soudan, it is based on notations from earlier chroniclers and notaries and oral accounts.

25. L. Douët-Darcq, ed., *La chronique d'Enguerrand de Monstrelet en deux livres avec pieces justificatives 1400–1444* (Paris: Jules Renouard, 1860), IV: 298–9.; cf. *Journal*, 14–6.

26. *Journal*, 7.

27. Auguste Vallet de Viriville, *Chronique de la Pucelle* (Paris: A. Delahays, 1859), 261; Adam S. Boss, "A City at War: Daily Life and Society in Orléans during the Siege of 1428–1429" (unpublished thesis, Colby College, 2008), 47–8.

28. *Journal*, 18–9.

29. Monstrelet, in Ayroles, III: 396.

30. Douët-Darcq, ed., *Monstrelet*, IV: 299–300.

31. *Journal*, 22.

32. *Journal*, 23.

33. *Journal*, 43.

34. *Journal*, 46–7.

35. *Journal*, 52.

36. Ayroles, III: 400.

37. *Journal*, 70.

38. A tun was a vat that contained 252 gallons of wine.

39. *Journal*, 66.

40. *Nullité 1456*, IV: 48.

41. *Nullité 1456*, IV: 73.

42. Katherine Allen Smith, "Saints in Shining Armor: Martial Asceticism and Masculine Models of Sanctity, ca. 1050–1250," *Speculum* 83 (2008), 572–602.

43. The Bastard was made count of Dunois in 1439. Some of the references in books refer to him as Dunois in this earlier period because they base their accounts on his status in 1456.

44. *Nullité 1456*, IV: 55.

45. *Nullité 1456*, IV: 3–5.

46. Ayroles, III: 151.

47. Estimates of numbers of those militia already in Orléans and those brought by different commanders vary greatly and are unreliable. What is known is that as news of Joan's impending arrival spread, more and more troops who had earlier held back now joined the French army.

48. *Journal*, 75.

49. *Journal*, 76.

50. *Nullité 1456*, I: 477.

51. *Journal*, 76–8.

52. *Nullité 1456*, IV: 5.

53. *Journal*, 79.

54. *Nullité 1456*, IV: 48.

55. *Nullité 1456*, IV: 76.

56. *Journal*, 80.

57. *Nullité 1456*, IV: 16.

58. Ayroles, III: 158.

59. *Nullité 1456*, IV: 11.

60. *Nullité 1456*, IV: 88–90.

61. *Nullité 1456*, IV: 25.

62. *Nullité 1456*, IV: 57.

63.   *Nullité 1456*, I: 479.
64.   *Nullité 1456*, IV: 50.
65.   *Nullité 1456*, IV: 48–9.
66.   "The same day in the evening, Joan being at her lodging, told him that the next day was the feast of the Ascension of the Lord, that there would not be combat, that she would not arm out of respect for the day, but that she wanted that day to confess and receive the sacrament of the eucharist, which she did. She ordered that no one would have the audacity the next day to leave the city and to go on the attack." *Nullité 1456*, IV: 75.
67.   *Nullité 1456*, IV: 49.
68.   *Nullité 1456*, IV: 83.
69.   *Nullité 1456*, I: 481–2.
70.   *Nullité 1456*, IV: 76–7.
71.   *Nullité 1456*, I: 482–4.
72.   "Et entre les autres y fut blecée la Pucelle et frappée d'un traict entre l'espaule et la gorge, si avant qu'il passoit oultre . . ." *Journal*, 85. I owe special thanks to my colleagues in the French department at Colby College, Valérie Dionne, Jane Moss, Jon Weiss and Marina Davies, for their help in translating the last part of this phrase.
73.   *Nullité 1456*, IV: 77.
74.   *Nullité 1456*, IV: 6.
75.   *Nullité 1456*, IV: 77.
76.   *Journal*, 86–7.
77.   *Nullité 1456*, IV: 6.
78.   Barrett, 65.
79.   Stephen W. Richey, *Joan of Arc: The Warrior Saint* (Westport, Conn.: Praeger, 2003), 64, 97, 99.
80.   Kelly DeVries, *Joan of Arc: A Military Leader* (Stroud, Glos.: Sutton Publishing, 1999), 187.
81.   N. H. Nicolas, ed., *Proceedings and Ordinances of the Privy Council of England from the Year 1386 to 1542* (London, 1834–7), V: 223.

Chapter 5: "She Would Only Last a Year"

1.   *Nullité 1456*, IV: 69.
2.   *Journal*, 89.
3.   *Nullité 1456*, IV: 6–7, 56.
4.   *Journal*, 90; *Nullité 1456*, I: 484.
5.   Douet-Darcq, ed., *Monstrelet*, 322; Ayroles, III: 126; *Nullité 1456*, IV: 22, 24.
6.   *Nullité 1456*, IV: 21–2.
7.   *Nullité 1456*, IV: 59.
8.   Barrett, 82.
9.   Kelly DeVries, *Joan of Arc: A Military Leader* (Stroud, Glos.: Sutton Publishing, 1999), 99–100.
10.   *Nullité 1456*, IV: 17.
11.   His capture at Verneuil in 1424 had resulted in an exorbitant ransom and a prohibition against fighting at Orléans.
12.   *Nullité 1456*, IV: 67.

13. Quicherat, V: 107–9.
14. Warner, 159.
15. *Nullité 1456*, IV: 57.
16. *Nullité 1456*, IV: 66.
17. *Nullité 1456*, IV: 22.
18. Ayroles, III: 181.
19. Barrett, 65.
20. Ayroles, III: 181.
21. *Nullité 1456*, IV: 67.
22. *Nullité 1456*, IV: 67–8.
23. Ayroles, III: 86.
24. *Nullité 1456*, IV: 10.
25. An ell was a unit of length equivalent to 45 inches. Crimson and dark green were the colors of the duke of Orléans' livery in this period.
26. Quicherat, V: 112–13.
27. Ayroles, III: 442.
28. For a thorough discussion of the intricate relationships of Arthur de Richemont with all parties, see Pernoud, 198–200.
29. *Nullité 1456*, IV: 68.
30. Quicherat, IV: 317.
31. Ayroles, III: 495.
32. Ayroles, III: 495, 497.
33. Ayroles, III: 407.
34. *Journal*, 102–3.
35. *Nullité 1456*, IV: 69.
36. Ayroles, III: 91.
37. *Nullité 1456*, IV: 7–8.
38. *Nullité 1456*, IV: 85.
39. Ayroles, III: 499.
40. Bedford reacted to Fastolf's cowardice by stripping him of the Order of the Garter, although it would later be reinstated. Ayroles, III: 411.
41. Ayroles, III: 501–3.
42. Ayroles, III: 91, 157.
43. Ayroles, III: 183–4.
44. *Nullité 1456*, IV: 9; Ayroles, III: 86.
45. Ayroles, III: 94.
46. Ayroles, III: 158.
47. *Nullité 1456*, IV: 9.
48. She was incorrect, since Fastolf had not been captured.
49. Quicherat, V: 125–6.
50. Ayroles, III: 185.
51. Ayroles, III: 355.
52. Ayroles, III: 356.
53. *Nullité 1456*, IV: 83.
54. *Nullité 1456*, IV: 9.
55. *Nullité 1456*, IV: 83.
56. DeVries, *Military Leader*, 123–4.
57. Barrett, 82.

58. Pierre Champion, *Splendeurs et Misères de Paris (XIVe–XVe siècles)* (Paris: Calmann-Lévy, 1934), 142.
59. Barrett, 81.
60. Ayroles, III: 185.
61. Ayroles, III: 84.
62. *Nullité 1456*, IV: 69.
63. Warner, 68–9.
64. Christine de Pizan, *The Book of the Body Politic*, ed. and trans. Kate Langdon Forhan (New York: Cambridge University Press, 1994), 63–4.
65. Ayroles, III: 166.
66. Pizan, *Body Politic*, 66.
67. Pizan, *Body Politic*, 73–4.
68. DeVries makes the important point that "all of the late nineteenth-/early twentieth-century French sculptors knew this, but most late twentieth-century historians seem to have forgotten it." DeVries, *Military Leader*, xiii.
69. DeVries contends otherwise: "although Joan may have been adept in the military arts, she refused to use her sword in battle or to shed blood, preferring to carry her standard instead." DeVries, "A Woman as Leader of Men: Joan of Arc's Military Career," in Wheeler, 9.
70. Stephen W. Richey, *Joan of Arc: The Warrior Saint* (Westport, Conn.: Praeger, 2003), 97, 99–100.

Chapter 6: The King and the Maid

1. Ayroles, III: 99.
2. *Nullité 1456*, III: 243, 267.
3. *Nullité 1456*, III: 267.
4. Ayroles, III: 440.
5. Ayroles, III: 211.
6. Ayroles, III: 333.
7. Abbé Jean Goy, ed., *Ordre pour oindre et couronner le roi de France* (Reims: Atélier Graphique, 2002), lines 567–87.
8. Ayroles, III: 365–6.
9. Ayroles, III: 101.
10. Scrofula, known as the "king's evil," was a group of skin diseases associated with infection of the lymph nodes in the neck or tuberculosis. Kings of both France and England ceremonially touched for the "king's evil" after their coronation.
11. Quicherat, V: 126–7.
12. Quicherat, IV: 4, 5, 7, 9, 11, 12, 14.
13. *Nullité 1456*, IV: 78.
14. Ayroles, III: 227.
15. Quicherat, V: 138.
16. *Nullité 1456*, IV: 10.
17. Chris Snidow's *Joan of Arc and the God of the Bible* (New York: iUniverse, 2006) juxtaposes passages of Joan's statements with biblical quotations.
18. *NRSV* Matthew 26:39.
19. Quicherat, V: 139–40.

20. Ayroles, III: 190.
21. Guy Llewellyn Thompson, *Paris and its People under English Rule: The Anglo-Burgundian Regime 1420–1436* (Oxford: Clarendon Press, 1991), 76–83 offers the best description of Paris' defenses, the alliances within the city, and the organization of the people.
22. There is a good discussion of the "Bourgeois" in Janet Shirley, ed., *A Parisian Journal 1405–1449* (Oxford: Clarendon Press, 1968), 12–30. For his discussion of the different factions, see pp. 132–4, 147, 168, 250, 255–7.
23. Quicherat, IV: 457.
24. Ayroles, III: 520–1.
25. Ayroles, III: 191–2.
26. Ayroles, III: 192–3.
27. Ayroles, III: 521–2.
28. Barrett mistranslates (p. 225) the passage as "that it was a whole black suit of armor for a man-at-arms, with a sword, which she had *worn* at Paris." The correct translation of what Joan said at trial when interrogated is: "that it was a full suit of armor belonging to a soldier, with a sword, that she had *won* at Paris. Asked why she offered them, she responded that it was out of devotion, as is normally done by soldiers when they have been wounded; and since she was wounded at Paris, she offered them at Saint-Denis." Pierre Tisset and Yvonne Lanhers, *Procès de condamnation de Jeanne d'Arc* (Paris: Klincksieck, 1960), 170–1.
29. Jean Pierre Reverseau, "L'armement défensive à l'époque de Jeanne d'Arc: L'armure de l'Héroine," in *Jeanne d'Arc: Une époque, un rayonnement* (Paris: Centre Régional de Publication de Paris, 1982), 69.
30. Barrett, 64.
31. *Nullité 1456*, IV: 70.
32. *Nullité 1456*, IV: 51.
33. Ayroles, III: 159.
34. Ayroles, III: 527.
35. Ayroles, III: 193.
36. Barrett, 110.
37. Barrett, 111.
38. Thompson, 110.
39. Ayroles, III: 479.
40. Ayroles, III: 194.
41. Along with several other leading nobles, the duke of Alençon fought a domestic rebellion against Charles in 1440, known as the Praguerie, but was forgiven. He also entered into negotiations with the English after 1440. After testifying about Joan at the nullification proceedings in 1456, he was arrested by his former comrade the Bastard of Orléans, by then count of Dunois. He was convicted by his peers in 1458 and imprisoned at Loches. Upon Charles's death in 1461 he was pardoned by the new king, Louis XI. He ignored the terms of his release and was arrested and condemned. Although he was imprisoned in the Louvre the sentence was not carried out and he died there in 1476.
42. *Nullité 1456*, IV: 61.
43. *Nullité 1456*, IV: 61.
44. Barrett, 84–5.

45. Barrett, 92.
46. Barrett, 85.
47. *Nullité 1456*, I: 484–5.
48. *Nullité 1456*, IV: 15.
49. *Nullité 1456*, IV: 78.
50. Quicherat, V: 146.
51. Quicherat, V: 147–8.
52. Barrett, 85, 110, 122.
53. Ayroles, III: 164.
54. Ayroles, III: 252, 195.
55. Ayroles, III: 344.
56. Quicherat, V: 154–6.
57. The letter was first found in a German history book in 1834 without mention of its provenance. But the German Dominican Johannes Nider mentioned in his *Formicarium* of 1439 that Joan had shown so much presumption that she had even written to the Bohemians. Quicherat, IV: 503.
58. Quicherat, V: 156–9.
59. Ayroles, III: 451.
60. Quicherat, V: 160.
61. Quicherat, V: 161–2.
62. Ayroles, III: 195.
63. Ayroles, III: 164–5.
64. Ayroles, III: 462–3.
65. Ayroles, III: 429–30.
66. Nothing is known about this person. Presumably one of her troops knew the man, who might have served as a source of intelligence for the French at the time of their siege.
67. Barrett, 116–17.
68. Barrett, 83–4.
69. Ayroles, III: 195.
70. Ayroles, III: 551.
71. Ayroles, III: 524.
72. Richard Vaughan, *Philip the Good* (Woodbridge, Suffolk: Boydell Press, 2002), 63.
73. Vaughan, *Philip*, 63–4.
74. Barrett, 90.

Chapter 7: Captivity

1. Pernoud has an excellent section on Joan's capture at Compiègne. Pernoud, 231–3; see also Kelly DeVries, *Joan of Arc: A Military Leader* (Stroud, Glos.: Sutton Publishing, 1999), 171–3.
2. Ayroles, III: 253.
3. Barrett, 86.
4. Leslie Stephen and Sidney Lee, eds., *Dictionary of National Biography* (London: Smith, Elder, 1908).
5. Ayroles, III: 196.
6. Ayroles, III: 464–5.
7. Ayroles, III: 196.

8.   Barrett, 90.
9.   Ayroles, III: 465.
10. Ayroles, III: 466.
11. Ayroles, III: 431.
12. Quicherat, V: 166–7.
13. Ayroles, I: 81–2.
14. Quoted in Richard Vaughan, *Philip the Good* (Woodbridge, Suffolk: Boydell Press, 2002), 24–5.
15. Barrett, 120.
16. Barrett, 12.
17. Barrett, 79–80.
18. *Nullité 1456*, IV: 86.
19. Ayroles, III: 453.
20. Barrett, 113.
21. Barrett, 85–6.
22. Barrett, 118.
23. Barrett, 120.
24. Ayroles, III: 283.
25. Barrett, 7.
26. Barrett, 9.
27. Quicherat, V: 179.
28. Ayroles, III: 379.
29. Ayroles, III: 379.
30. Germain Lefevre-Pontalis and Léon Dorez, trans. and comm., *Chronique d'Antonio Morosini: Extraits relatifs à l'histoire de France* (Paris: Renouard, 1941), 333, 335.
31. Barrett, 13–14.
32. "Once the dauphin learned [that she had been sold to the English], he sent an embassy to the Duke of Burgundy to tell him not to hand her over for anything in the world, or he would take revenge on those of his men whom he had in captivity." December 15 from Bruges. Ayroles, III: 608.
33. Lucien René Delsalle, *Rouen et les Rouennais au temps de Jeanne d'Arc 1400–1470* (Rouen: Éditions PTC, 2006), 117.
34. Pierre Cochon, *Chronique normande de Pierre Cochon notaire apostolique à Rouen publiée pour la première fois en entier par Ch. de Robillard de Beaurepaire* (Rouen: A. le Brument, 1870), 342.
35. Jean-Louis Eloy, *Cinq siècles d'histoire religieuse normande, le couvent de Saint-Jacques de Rouen 1224–1790* (Rouen: Lecuire, Le Cornec et fils, 1965), 120–1.
36. Delsalle, *Rouen*, 84.
37. Eloy, *Saint-Jacques*, 131.
38. Léon François Puiseux, *Siège et prise de Rouen par les Anglais (1418–1419) principalement d'après un poème anglais contemporain* (Caen: E. le Gost-Clérisse, 1867), 270.
39. Delsalle, *Rouen*, 100.
40. Delsalle, *Rouen*, 119.
41. Barrett, 16–17.
42. Delsalle, *Rouen*, 119.
43. Barrett, 18–19.
44. Henry Ansgar Kelly, *Inquisitions and Other Trial Procedures in the Medieval West* (Aldershot, Hampshire: Ashgate, 2001), ix, xii.

45.   Barrett, 21.
46.   Delsalle, *Rouen*, 120.
47.   *L'Enquête 1450*, 52.
48.   Barrett, 22.
49.   *Nullité 1456*, IV: 105.
50.   Barrett, 27.

Chapter 8: Judging the Maid

1.   *Nullité 1456*, IV: 112.
2.   *Nullité 1456*, IV: 45.
3.   *Nullité 1456*, IV: 63.
4.   Barrett, 28.
5.   Barrett, 29.
6.   Barrett, 94–5.
7.   Barrett, 103.
8.   See Daniel Hobbins, *The Trial of Joan of Arc* (Cambridge, Mass.: Harvard University Press, 2005), 15–23.
9.   Jean Guiraud, *The Mediaeval Inquisition*, trans. E. C. Messenger (London: Burns, Oates & Washbourne, 1929), 206–7.
10.   Jean-Louis Eloy, *Cinq siècles d'histoire religieuse normande, le couvent de Saint-Jacques de Rouen 1224–1790* (Rouen: Lecuire, Le Cornec et fils, 1965), 140.
11.   Barrett, 37.
12.   Henry Ansgar Kelly, *Inquisitions and Other Trial Procedures in the Medieval West* (Aldershot Hampshire: Ashgate, 2001), xii.
13.   François Neveux, *L'Évêque Pierre Cauchon* (Paris: DeNoël, 1987), 101, 122, 193.
14.   "In spite of all her implicit and explicit protests, no specific charges were leveled, no witnesses were produced to establish *fama publica*, and no proofs of any crimes were brought forward. She was convicted solely on responses that she made to enforced questioning." Henry Ansgar Kelly, "Saint Joan and Confession: Internal and External Forum," in Astell, 62.
15.   Barrett, 38.
16.   *Nullité 1456*, IV: 112.
17.   *L'Enquête 1450*, 54.
18.   *Nullité 1456*, IV: 101–2.
19.   *Nullité 1456*, IV: 117.
20.   Barrett, 42–3.
21.   Kelly, "Saint Joan," 65.
22.   Henry Ansgar Kelly, "Joan of Arc's Last Trial: The Attack of the Devil's Advocates," in Wheeler, 212.
23.   Barrett, 78.
24.   Barrett, 49.
25.   Barrett, 70.
26.   Barrett, 45.
27.   Barrett, 51.
28.   Barrett, 51–2.

29.   Rather then it being a form of witty repartee, Joan was quoting a common prayer. L. Carolus-Barré, " 'Jeanne, êtes-vous en état de grace?' et les prières du prône aux XVe siècle," in *Bulletin de la Sociéte des Antiquaires de France* (1958), 204–8.

30.   *Nullité 1456*, IV: 118.

31.   *L'Enquête 1452*, 144.

32.   *Nullité 1456*, IV: 102.

33.   *L'Enquête 1452*, 130.

34.   *L'Enquête 1452*, 148.

35.   *Nullité 1456*, IV: 63.

36.   *L'Enquête 1452*, 96.

37.   Barrett, 61.

38.   Barrett, 114.

39.   Barrett, 68.

40.   Eugenius' pontificate would soon be challenged by those who gathered at Basel after he unsuccessfully attempted to dissolve the council and reassert papal authority. Although he was forced into exile for ten years and an antipope elected, Eugenius was restored in 1443.

41.   See Chapter 2 pp. 28–9 for full transcriptions of Joan's words.

42.   Barrett, 62.

43.   Barrett, 109.

44.   Barrett, 63–4.

45.   Barrett, 98, 100.

46.   Barrett, 120–1.

47.   Barrett, 97.

48.   Barrett, 75.

49.   Barrett, 93.

50.   Barrett, 49.

51.   Barrett, 71.

52.   Barrett, 127–8.

53.   Barrett, 107.

54.   Barrett, 128.

55.   Quicherat, V: 6–7, 9, 11–13, 17.

56.   Barrett, 130.

57.   Barrett, 53–4.

58.   *L'Enquête 1450*, 48.

59.   *L'Enquête 1450*, 49.

60.   *Nullité 1456*, IV: 99–100.

61.   Barrett, 125.

62.   Barrett, 130–1.

63.   *Nullité 1456*, IV: 35.

64.   *Nullité 1456*, IV: 121, 124–6.

65.   *Nullité 1456*, IV: 111.

66.   *L'Enquête 1450*, 46.

67.   Barrett, 147.

68.   Barrett, 154.

69.   Barrett, 159.

70.   Barrett, 167.

71.   Barrett, 240.

234 NOTES to pp. 147–154

72. Barrett, 254.

73. Barrett, 248.

74. An excellent discussion of this subject, along with analysis of how Joan's trial changed the theological understanding of personal experience of revelations, can be found in Jane Marie Pinzino, "Joan of Arc and *Lex Privata*: A Spirit of Freedom in the Law," in Astell, 85–109; also in Jane Marie Pinzino: "Speaking of Angels: A Fifteenth-Century Bishop in Defense of Joan of Arc's Mystical Voices," in Wheeler, 161–76.

75. *L'Enquête 1452*, 54.

76. Barrett, 281–4.

77. Eloy, *Cinq siècles*, 143.

78. Barrett, 285.

79. Barrett, 286.

80. *Nullité 1456*, IV: 34.

81. *Nullité 1456*, IV: 36.

82. Barrett, 293.

83. Barrett, 294.

84. Barrett, 297.

85. Barrett, 301.

86. James Given, *Inquisition in Medieval Society: Power, Discipline and Resistance in Medieval Languedoc* (Ithaca, N.Y.: Cornell University Press, 1997), 93–6.

87. Kelly, *Inquisitions*, 1017.

88. Dominicans from the convent of Saint-Jacques present at the trial were: Jean Le Maistre, prior of the convent and Vice Inquisitor (almost always present after his initial reluctance); Ysambard de la Pierre (present fifteen times, beginning after Le Maistre was forced to attend); Raoul le Sauvage (eight times); Martin Ladvenu (twice); Guillaume Duval (once, the occasion on which La Pierre nudged Joan); Jean Toutmouillé never participated in the trial, but was present at Joan's confession the morning of her execution. Pierre Bosquier (see Chapter 10) did not attend the trial but was punished for words he spoke against the proceedings on the day of Joan's execution. The only other Dominican who actually took part in the trial and was not a member of the local convent was Guillaume Adélie, a bachelor of theology at the University of Paris.

89. *L'Enquête 1450*, 40.

90. *L'Enquête 1452*, 51.

91. Edward Peters, *Inquisition* (Berkeley, Calif.: University of California Press, 1988), 129; Malcolm Lambert, *Medieval Heresy: Popular Movements from the Gregorian Reform to the Reformation* (Oxford: Basil Blackwell, 1979), 101.

92. Chartier, in Ayroles, III: 168.

93. Dylan Thomas (1914–53).

Chapter 9: From Fear of the Fire

1. Barrett, 300–1.

2. Barrett, 304.

3. *Nullité 1456*, IV: 136.

4. Barrett, 304.

5. Barrett, 305–6.

6. Barrett, 309, 311.
7. Barrett, 321.
8. Barrett, 327.
9. Barrett, 332–3.
10. *NRSV*, Deuteronomy 22:5.
11. *L'Enquête 1452*, 54.
12. *L'Enquête 1450*, 34–5.
13. *L'Enquête 1450*, 50. Many others, including Ladvenu, Taquel, and Grouchet, stated that Joan had submitted to the Church. *L'Enquête 1452*, 58, 82, 130.
14. Ayroles, III: 240.
15. *L'Enquête 1450*, 36.
16. Susan Crane, "Clothing and Gender Definition: Joan of Arc," *Journal of Medieval and Early Modern Studies* 26 (1996), 304.
17. Barrett, 340.
18. *Nullité 1456*, IV:130.
19. *Nullité 1456*, IV:142.
20. *L'Enquête 1450*, 53.
21. Barrett, 343.
22. The version in the trial transcript is over forty lines long, compared to the six to eight lines mentioned by Massieu and others. Part of it reads as follows:

> Therefore, I, Joan, commonly called The Maid, a miserable sinner, recognizing the snares of error in which I was held, and being by God's grace returned to Our Holy Mother Church, in order to show that my return is made not feignedly but with a good heart and will, I confess that I have most grievously sinned in falsely pretending to have had revelations and apparitions from God, His angels, St. Catherine and St. Margaret; in seducing others; in believing foolishly and lightly; in making superstitious divinations; in blaspheming God and His Saints; in breaking the divine law, Holy Scripture, and the canon laws; in wearing a dissolute, ill-shaped and immodest dress against the decency of nature, and hair cropped round like a man's, against all modesty of womankind; also in bearing arms most presumptuously; in cruelly desiring the shedding of human blood; in declaring that I did all these things by the command of God, His angels and the said saints, and that to do so was good and not to err; in being seditious and idolatrous, adoring and calling up evil spirits. I confess also that I have been schismatic and in many ways erred from the path. These crimes and errors, I, being by God's grace returned to the way of truth through the holy doctrine and good counsel of yourself and the doctors and masters whom you sent me, unfeignedly and with a good heart abjure and recant, renouncing and cutting myself off from them all. Upon all the aforesaid things I submit to the correction, disposition, amendment and entire decision of Our Holy Mother Church and of your good justice. (Barrett, 343–4)

23. *L'Enquête 1452*, 104.
24. *L'Enquête 1452*, 84.
25. *L'Enquête 1452*, 124.
26. *Nullité 1456*, IV:113–14.
27. *Nullité 1456*, IV: 88.
28. *L'Enquête 1452*, 104.
29. *Nullité 1456*, IV: 38.

30. Barrett, 347–8.
31. *Nullité 1456*, IV: 37. Guillaume La Chambre added that he was close enough to see the form [*cedula*] and that it contained only six or seven lines.
32. *L'Enquête 1452*, 154.
33. Barrett, 348.
34. *L'Enquête 1452*, 80, 148.
35. *L'Enquête 1450*, 44.
36. *L'Enquête 1450*, 36.
37. *L'Enquête 1450*, 54; see also *Nullité 1456*, IV:37, 39, 80.
38. Ayroles, III: 608.
39. *L'Enquête 1450*, 57.
40. *L'Enquête 1450*, 55.
41. *Nullité 1456*, IV: 107.
42. *L'Enquête 1452*, 54.
43. Barrett, 349–50.
44. Barrett, 351.
45. Barrett, 354.
46. Barrett, 357.
47. *L'Enquête 1450*, 36.
48. *Nullité 1456*, IV: 114, 108.
49. *Nullité 1456*, IV: 122–3.
50. *L'Enquête 1450*, 41–2.
51. *Nullité 1456*, IV: 140.
52. *Nullité 1456*, IV: 35. Additions to the trial transcript were made on June 7 but *not* signed by the trial notaries, including a falsified confession.
53. Crane, "Clothing," 314.
54. Jean-Louis Eloy, *Cinq siècles d'histoire religieuse normande, le couvent de Saint-Jacques de Rouen 1224–1790* (Rouen: Lecuire, Le Cornec et fils, 1965), 157.
55. René Herval, *Histoire de Rouen I: Des origines à la fin du XVe siècle* (Rouen, 1947), 198–200.
56. Herval, *Rouen*, 199.
57. Barrett, 362.
58. *Nullité 1456*, IV: 147.
59. The description of her words closely matches the prayer known as the Confiteor: "I confess to Almighty God, and to you my brothers and sisters, that I have sinned through my own fault, in my thoughts and in my words, in what I have done, and what I have failed to do; and I ask blessed Mary, ever virgin, all the angels and saints, and you, my brothers and sisters, to pray for me to the Lord our God."
60. *L'Enquête 1450*, 56.
61. *L'Enquête 1450*, 38.
62. Herval, *Rouen*, 200.
63. See Norman Boutin, http://www.stjoancenter.com/topics/Death_by_Heat_Stroke .html.
64. *L'Enquête 1452*, 121.
65. *L'Enquête 1452*, 122.
66. *Nullité 1456*, IV: 133.
67. *Nullité 1456*, IV: 141.
68. Ayroles, III: 528.

69. *Nullité 1456*, IV: 37.

70. Modern crematoria reach a temperature of 1600–1800° F to consume a body, and while such temperatures may not have been possible in the Middle Ages, the fire would have had to burn for some time in order to reduce Joan's body to ashes. In 1498, Savonarola was executed in the Piazza della Signoria in Florence. When he was dead, "the executioner set fire to the great mound of straw and firewood, setting off 'sharp sounds of rockets and cracking.' Gunpowder had been added to the combustibles. . . . The fire was fueled for an hour or two" until the hangman took down the body and tried to reduce it to ashes. (Lauro Martines, *Fire in the City* (New York: Oxford University Press, 2006), 276.) The executioner in Rouen did not – and could not – use gunpowder in view of the crowds and the confined area of the marketplace, so the process must have taken much longer.

71. *L'Enquête 1450*, 44.

72. *Nullité 1456*, IV: 108.

73. *L'Enquête 1452*, 86.

74. *L'Enquête 1452*, 122; *L'Enquête 1450*, 38.

75. *Nullité 1456*, IV: 120.

76. *L'Enquête 1452*, 148.

77. Barrett, 381–3.

78. Ayroles, III: 529.

79. Françoise Meltzer, *For Fear of the Fire: Joan of Arc and the Limits of Subjectivity* (Chicago, Ill.: University of Chicago Press, 2000), 7, 117–18.

80. *Nullité 1456*, IV: 92.

81. Barrett, 374.

82. Barrett, 377–8, 380.

Chapter 10: Vindication

1. Robert Garnier, *Dunois: Le Bâtard d'Orléans (1403–1468)* (Paris: Éditions Fernand Lanore, 1999), 193.

2. Francis Rousseau, *La Hire de Gascogne: Étiennes de Vignolles (1380–1443)* (Mont-de-Marsan: Lacoste, 1969), 206.

3. *L'Enquête 1452*: 112, 150.

4. Paul D. Solon, "Popular Response to Standing Military Forces in Fifteenth-Century France," *Studies in the Renaissance* 19 (1972), 78–111.

5. See C. T. Allmand, *Lancastrian Normandy, 1415–1450: The History of a Medieval Occupation* (New York: Clarendon Press, 1983).

6. Lucien René Delsalle, *Rouen et les Rouennais au temps de Jeanne D'Arc 1400–1470* (Rouen: Lecuire, Le Cornec et fils, 1965), 131–41. Monstrelet's chronicle also provides a detailed account of the royal entry.

7. *L'Enquête 1450*: 66, 68.

8. Malcolm Vale, *Charles VII* (Berkeley, Calif.: University of California Press, 1974), 61.

9. *L'Enquête 1450*, 13–14.

10. Gérard Gros, ed., *Mystère du siège d'Orléans* (Paris: Poche, 2002).

11. *L'Enquête 1452*, 14.

12. *L'Enquête 1452*, 17.

13. Jean-Louis Eloy, *Cinq siècles d'histoire religieuse normande, le couvent de Saint-Jacques de Rouen 1224–1790* (Rouen: Lecuire, Le Cornec et fils, 1965), 125.

14. *L'Enquête 1452*, 23.

15. *L'Enquête 1452*, 28.

16. *L'Enquête 1452*, 28–30.

17. Daniel Hobbins, *The Trial of Joan of Arc* (Cambridge, Mass.: Harvard University Press, 2005), 241.

18. Charles had issued the Pragmatic Sanction of Bourges in 1438. It stated that general councils of the Church must be called every ten years; that the authority of a council was superior to that of the pope; that the king could make recommendations for appointments to ecclesiastical offices without papal approval; that the pope could not collect annates (the revenues of the first year of a church appointment); and that no appeal could be made to Rome until all other jurisdictions had been exhausted. Needless to say, popes were anxious to have the Pragmatic Sanction overturned, since it was for all intents and purposes a declaration of independence from Rome. See http://www.fordham.edu/halsall/source/1438pragmatic.html.

19. *Nullité 1456*, III: 7–10.

20. *Nullité 1456*, III: 15–16.

21. *Nullité 1456*, III: 57.

22. This is almost certainly a reference to Ysambard de La Pierre.

23. *Nullité 1456*, III: 74.

24. *Nullité 1456*, V: 227–9.

25. Jane Marie Pinzino, "Heretic or Holy Woman? Cultural Representation and Gender in the Trial to Rehabilitate Joan of Arc" (Ph.D. diss., University of Pennsylvania, 1996), 4–5, 115–16. See also Blair Deborah Newcomb, "Collective Authority and the Individual in the Rehabilitation of Jeanne d'Arc, 1450–1456" (Ph.D. diss., University of Michigan, 1999), 224. She argues that "political features are not entirely lost from her image, but a 'new' [Joan] was emerging. The war in which her mission was embedded was now over. The rehabilitation is a product of the time after the war, and her image is re-fashioned in keeping with that reality. At the opening of the nullification trial at Notre Dame in Paris, [Joan's] family said that the recovery of Normandy marked the completion of [Joan's] mission. This would turn out to be the second in a long series of images that continues to be generated even until the present day."

Epilogue: "That Astonishing and Marvelous Maid"

1. An excellent account of how Joan's image was transformed over the centuries can be found in Ellen Ecker Dolgin, *Modernizing Joan of Arc: Conceptions, Constumes and Canonization* (London: McFarland, 2008).

2. For an extensive discussion of the arguments and counter-arguments, see Kelly, "Devil's Advocates," in Wheeler, 205–36.

3. The miracles were not of the highest order. Sr. Thérèse of Saint Augustine of Orléans was cured of leg ulcers; Sr. Julie Gauthier of Faverolles and Sr. Marie Sagnier of Frages were cured of cancer of the breast and stomach, respectively.

4. One woman was cured of tuberculosis when Joan's name was invoked in a prayer; the other woman was cured of a hole in her foot.

5.   Warner, 267.

6.   *Nullité 1456*, IV: 117, 118, 120.

7.   Florence A. Gragg, *Secret Memoirs of a Renaissance Pope: The Commentaries of Aeneas Sylvius Piccolomini Pius II* (London: Folio Society, 1988), 199–201.

8.   In 1459, Cardinal Jean Jouffroy, bishop of Arras, appeared at the Congress of Mantua representing the duke of Burgundy's interests. Jouffroy's words may have led to the pope's caution about the source of Joan's mission. While there, Jouffroy spoke of a:

> supposed miracle, skillfully disclosed, recklessly believed in – the young girl the French named the Maid. We must believe a noble skillfully exploited the stratagem of this young girl to uplift hearts beaten down and without strength. Had the courage of this little peasant girl been inflamed by the desire to lead a life of indigence and delights? Did the desire of glory push the girl who had served in an inn and carried wood and stones to a métier in arms? One who pushed the plow and watched the herds in Lorraine? There is nothing miraculous in this. . . . Now, Philip, who would not be terrified of phantoms, stopped the progress of the Maid at La Charité-sur-Loire; first he had repulsed her before Paris and he alone took her. . . . At Compiègne, attacked on the flank by archers, the young girl was rendered according to her nature as a woman and could find nothing better than flight. But as it is said that Charles VII, now king of the French, vaunted the Maid to the skies and that in the time of Alexander, as Cicero wrote, one could only write that which was agreeable to Alexander, I will cease, according to the advice of Plautus, to press the abscess. (Ayroles, III: 537–8)

Further Reading

Sources

Although the Barrett translation has been used for the trial because of its accessibility and completeness, Daniel Hobbins has produced the best abridged English version of the trial transcript with a superb introduction, *The Trial of Joan of Arc* (Cambridge, Mass.: Harvard University Press, 2005).

There is no comprehensive translation of the nullification records, so I have translated the original French and Latin throughout. Excerpts are available at http://www.stjoan-center.com/Trials/#nullification. A wonderful new selection of sources, including the trial and nullification proceedings as well as chronicles, treatises, and letters is available in Craig Taylor, *Joan of Arc: La Pucelle* (Manchester: Manchester University Press, 2006). Most chronicles have not been translated, except for *The Journal d'un Bourgeois de Paris: A Parisian Journal 1405–1449*, trans. Janet Shirley (Oxford: Clarendon Press, 1968) and *The Chronicle of Enguerrand de Monstrelet*, trans. Thomas Johnes (London: W. Smith, 1840). Many works of Christine de Pizan are available in English, including the "Ditié de Jeanne d'Arc." See Charity Willard, *The Writings of Christine de Pizan* (New York: Persea Books, 1994); *Epistles: English Selections*, trans. Josette A. Wisman (New York: Garland, 1984); *The Book of the Body Politic*, ed. and trans. Kate Langdon Forhan (Cambridge: Cambridge University Press, 1994).

Biographies

As Daniel Hobbins points out, there is no standard critical biography of Joan, the lack of which inspired this book. For other figures prominent in

Joan's life, only a few studies are available in English. Malcolm Vale's *Charles VII* (Berkeley, Calif.: University of California Press, 1974) devotes only one chapter to Joan and is dismissive of her importance. E. Carleton Williams's *My Lord of Bedford 1389–1435* (London: Longmans, 1963) is the only real biography of the duke. Richard Vaughan, *Philip the Good*, is excellent for the duke of Burgundy's life, but contains little information on Joan. Bertram Wolffe's biography of *Henry VI* (New Haven and London: Yale University Press, 1981) is the best available, although because of Henry's age during Joan's lifetime only the parts on the duke of Bedford are particularly useful.

Military

The best discussion of Joan of Arc's military role can be found in Kelly DeVries, *Joan of Arc: A Military Leader* (Stroud, Glos.: Sutton Publishing, 1999). Stephen W. Richey's *Joan of Arc: The Warrior Saint* (Westport, Conn.: Praeger, 2003) examines modern views on military tactics and strategic planning in great depth to determine how and why Joan succeeded. The simplest explanation of the siege of Orléans and its deliverance is David Nicolle's *Orléans 1429* (Westport, Conn.: Praeger, 2005). Deborah Fraioli offers the larger perspective in *Joan of Arc and the Hundred Years War* (Westport, Conn.: Greenwood Press, 2005). Anne Curry's *Agincourt: A New History* (Stroud, Glos.: Tempus, 2005) offers a gripping and fresh understanding of the battle that changed French history. Matthew Bennett, Jim Bradbury, Kelly DeVries, Iain Dickie, and Phyllis Jestice's *Fighting Techniques of the Medieval World AD 500–AD 1500: Equipment, Combat Skills, and Tactics* (New York: Thomas Dunne Books, 2006) provides specifics on siege warfare and analyses of the different components of a medieval army.

Religion and Theology

Deborah Fraioli's *Joan of Arc: The Early Debate* (Woodbridge: Boydell Press, 2000) is an in-depth study of Joan's assertion that she was sent by God, a discussion of discernment of spirits in the late Middle Ages, and the examination at Poitiers. Karen Sullivan's original insights into Joan's relationship with her clerical interrogators as well as "her saints" in *The Interrogation of Joan of Arc* (Minneapolis: University of Minnesota Press, 1999) helped inspire my own understanding of Joan. An expert on canon law, Henry Ansgar Kelly published his articles on Joan of Arc and other aspects of inquisitorial procedure in *Inquisitions and Other Trial Procedures in the Medieval West* (Burlington, Vt.: Ashgate, 2001). George Tavard's *The Spiritual Way of Joan of Arc* (Collegeville, Minn.: The Liturgical Press, 1998) is a scholarly analysis of Joan's spirituality. Jane Marie Pinzino has conducted most of the research on the nullification proceedings. Parts I–III of Astell and Wheeler deal with all aspects of religion and spirituality during Joan's lifetime.

Gender

In addition to the books of Warner and Meltzer, the best articles on the subject can be found in the collections by Wheeler and Wood, and Astell and Wheeler. They include articles by Susan Schibanoff, Deborah Fraioli, Nadia Margolis, Anne Lutkus, and Julia Walker. Studies of theological and popular treatises that dealt with the gender issues at the time, including the works of Jean Gerson, Jacques Gélu, and Martin Le Franc, can also be found in these collections. Susan Crane's "Clothing and Gender Definition: Joan of Arc," *Journal of Medieval and Early Modern Studies* 26 (1996), 297–320 is an excellent study of how Joan's cross dressing provided authorization for her mission.

Index